# Contextual Safeguarding and Child Protection

This book offers a complete account of Contextual Safeguarding theory, policy, and practice frameworks for the first time. It highlights the particular challenge of extra-familial routes through which young people experience significant harm, such as child sexual exploitation, criminal exploitation, serious youth violence, domestic abuse in teenage relationships, bullying, gang-association, and radicalisation.

Through analysing case reviews, observing professionals, and co-creating practices with them, Firmin provides a personal, philosophical, strategic, and practical account of the design, implementation and future of Contextual Safeguarding. Drawing together a wealth of practice examples, case studies, policy references, and practitioner insights for the first time, this book articulates a new safeguarding framework and provides a detailed account of its translation across an entire child protection system and its relevant component parts.

It will be of interest to all scholars, students, and professionals working within social work, youth justice and youth work, policing and law enforcement, community safety, council services, forensic and clinical psychology, counselling, health, and education.

**Carlene Firmin** MBE is a Principal Research Fellow at the University of Bedfordshire, where she leads their Contextual Safeguarding programme. Carlene has researched young people's experiences of community and group-based violence since 2005, advocating for comprehensive approaches that keep young people safe in public places, schools, and peer groups.

*I heard Dr Firmin outline the principles of Contextual Safeguarding at the end of 2019 and I commented then that her ideas were among the most innovative I had encountered during some 30 years working in UK universities. Now that I've read this book I am even more convinced of its originality and importance.*

**David Shemmings OBE PHD is emeritus professor of child protection research at the University of Kent, UK and visiting professor at Royal Holloway, University of London, UK**

*In my opinion, Contextual Safeguarding is one of the most significant developments for the safeguarding sector in many years. This book makes a vital contribution to the knowledge base, providing challenge and provoking thought in every chapter. Most impressively, it does so whilst also offering hope. It is essential reading for anyone interested in protecting young people and promoting safe communities.*

**Dez Holmes, Director, Research in Practice and Research in Practice for Adults, UK**

*If you want to know what the 'Contextual Safeguarding' buzz is about, the new kid on the Child Protection block, you've arrived. This is a corker. In her inimitable style, Dr Carlene Firmin effortlessly unpacks this compelling, ground-breaking concept with a potency that leaves you wondering how we've ever done without it. An absolute game-changer for mis-labelled children and families needing protection from extra-familial harm – hope now on the horizon.*

**Founder, SPACE (Stop & Prevent Adolescent Criminal Exploitation), UK**

# Contextual Safeguarding and Child Protection

Rewriting the Rules

**Carlene Firmin**

Routledge
Taylor & Francis Group

LONDON AND NEW YORK

First published 2020
by Routledge
2 Park Square, Milton Park, Abingdon, Oxon OX14 4RN

and by Routledge
52 Vanderbilt Avenue, New York, NY 10017

*Routledge is an imprint of the Taylor & Francis Group, an informa business*

*British Library Cataloguing-in-Publication Data*
A catalogue record for this book is available from the British Library

*Library of Congress Cataloging-in-Publication Data*
A catalogue record has been requested for this book

ISBN: 978-0-367-24585-6 (hbk)
ISBN: 978-0-429-28331-4 (ebk)

Typeset in Times
by Integra Software Services Pvt. Ltd.

Printed and bound by CPI Group (UK) Ltd, Croydon, CR0 4YY

For Obinna and Ziora-Blue, with whom I am home; my most important context

# Contents

# Illustrations

# Acknowledgements

I start by acknowledging all of the young people, parents, and practitioners who have joined us on the road to Contextual Safeguarding. We have only reached this level of understanding due to your insight, engagement, and challenge. This truly has been a co-produced effort – and long may this partnership continue. In particular I want to thank the young people whose cases form the basis of this work, the practice leads in our test sites, voluntary organisations that attend our implementation meetings and each one of our 6,000+ practice members who are championing the approach in their own teams and local areas.

Secondly, I want to acknowledge the efforts of the Contextual Safeguarding team at the University of Bedfordshire – all of you have contributed to the ideas shared throughout this book. The values that underpin the approach, the systematic learning from practice, and the suite of practice resources that have come to the fore are due to your efforts. You inspire me every day. We have grown rapidly as a team since 2018 and with this in mind I want to give particular thanks for Dr Jenny Lloyd who has been by my side in developing the approach since 2016 and who was the first embedded researcher to attempt implementation in Hackney. I see you now more as a member of my family, and am privileged to call you a friend as well as a colleague. Your hard work knows no bounds and your commitment to excellence is evident in all that you do.

I also want to thank my line managers and mentors who continue to guide and support me. Dr Helen Beckett, Professor Jenny Pearce, Professor John Pitts, Dez Holmes, and Derek Bardowell have all played a critical role in keeping me on track, and mopping up tears when the pressure has got a bit much.

I am grateful for the support of many established scholars who over the past 18 months have reached out to encourage my efforts. I reference many of you in this text, and want to acknowledge the camaraderie you have shown in a sector which isn't always seen as collegiate.

And finally, but certainly not least, I want to thank my family for always being by my side; despite the late nights, dinner table debates and many work trips away. My mum for her lifelong support and inspiration – and for being such a wonderful grandmother to my son; the work-life juggle is made immeasurably easier with you along for the ride. My husband Obinna – for everything you do, big and small, to encourage me to fulfil my goals and be there at the end of the day to talk them all through (over and over again); for making sure I have plenty to smile about and to be thankful for when times are tough; and for supplying copious tea and wine. And not forgetting my ray of sunshine – Ziora-Blue – my biggest motivation and my greatest achievement.

# Part 1

# The challenge we face and the lens through which we view it

# 1    Opening

My husband is weary about my preferences for television shows. For him evenings are about settling into the sofa for some laughs courtesy of a witty stand-up comic masterfully critiquing the politics of the day. I on the other hand wax and wane between two extremes: the whimsy and heartbreak of so-called reality television or the raw and challenging content featured in documentaries – or films that document real life events – where young people have come to harm. The reasons for this are not, thankfully, the subject of this book; and hopefully the upfront confession hasn't sent potential readers running in the opposite direction.

My TV choices have, however, provided all manner of material for his book – and none more so than this poignant quote from the film *Spotlight*:

> Mark my words Mr. Rezendes, if it takes the village to raise the child, it takes the village to abuse one.
>
> *(Spotlight*, 2015)

It was 2018 and I was getting ready for bed in friend Lucie's spare room – she often kindly put me up for the night when I needed to spend a few days at my university in Luton, rather than travelling to and from London. The film had been out some years before, and I hadn't watched it then, but (given the aforementioned questionable preferences) I was pleased to see it had been made available on a streaming service that evening – the perfect thing to watch before settling down for the night. The film documented how journalists at the *Boston Globe* newspaper had investigated the abuse of children in the city's Catholic churches. In one scene journalist Mike Rezendes played by Mark Ruffalo is interviewing the lawyer, Mitchell Garabedian, who is representing the then adult men who had been sexually abused by clergy members as children. He is clear: many figures in the church, in the media, in politics and local residents had been aware of the allegations for years. Their inaction, and in some cases complicity, meant that priests were able to access and abuse children for decades; without this wider contextual scaffold the abuse may never have occurred – particularly on the scale that it did.

Nearly two years on from when I first heard the phrase from *Spotlight* and I still remember the rasping sensation I felt as my sharp intake of break clipped the back of my throat the moment I heard it. It was uncomfortable, anger-inducing even, but also very true. I heard it at a time where *Contextual Safeguarding*, the subject of this book, was already in progress. I was developing it because, like Mitchell Garabedian, I had become all too aware of the bus drivers, security guards, teachers, shop keepers, residents, paramedics, councillors, park wardens and youth workers, who oversaw, managed or could reach into the contexts in which young people had been exploited. I was also aware of how our societies and statutory systems were responding to the abuse of children by looking almost exclusively at the parents who had raised those children (as both the source of potential harm and protection) and not that wider village who often managed the place in which they were abused.

I know why my husband rolls his eyes every time I take hold of the remote control. My choice of 'light' entertainment is, to him, 'heavy' – and in short depressing. This book, however, is not. As unlike Garabedian's quote, this book will focus on how a village, in 2019, can protect a child. We also have to recognise the truth in what he said, however, to get to that hopeful place. I will use the first part of this book to do that: summarising the abuse that young people experience; outlining the ways child protection systems have developed to respond;[1] and detailing the theories and concepts that have given me a lens through which to see and understand our challenge. The three parts that follow it will take you on the same journey that I've been on for the past five years, reaching a destination in which we have a clear framework for how to safeguard young people from the abuse they experience beyond their family homes.

Much of what this book will suggest isn't novel. It borrows from a range of research and practice traditions in which we have learnt how to create safe and protective communities, institutions, friendships and families. From community and social justice, social work, youth work and community development, and public health approaches to violence through to safer-by-design approaches to crime reduction, situational crime prevention and problem-solving policing agendas, I will pull the established contextual wisdom of many to build a novel child protection framework – a Contextual Safeguarding framework. And in doing so I pull the intention behind the idea of a village raising a child into political, social and practical system in which the extra-familial forms of harm that children experience has been framed as a child protection issue.

This process is important. In April 2019 the Sky News anchor Jayne Secker challenged musician and practitioner Guvna B when he called upon communities to play a role in safeguarding young people from knife crime:

GUVNA B:   My mum's from Ghana, and she used to say this Ghanaian saying that 'it takes a village to raise a child'.

JAYNE SECKER: But we're not in a village in Ghana; and people don't necessarily feel there is much of a community in some parts of London at least.

In many respects Secker seemed to have purposefully misunderstood the point that Guvna B was trying to make with an undercurrent of racism that was infuriating at best. Despite this attempt to undermine him, however, Guvna B's point is clear. We have to identify 'the village' that is raising our children and provide a framework and approach that will maximise its safeguarding potential. Contextual Safeguarding is one approach to doing that, and having been co-created between researchers and practitioners since 2013, this book is my first attempt to compile this iterative evidence-base into one publication.

## The abuse

This is a book about Sara. And it is a book about Malik – both of whom you will meet in chapter 2. It's also book about countless other young people who are abused by peers or adults unconnected to their families. As they enter adolescence, the heady mix of physical, emotional and social changes that colour this time in human development, they begin stepping out on their own. In shopping centres, parks and libraries, on social media platforms, waiting in transport hubs and navigating much bigger schools and colleges; and for the most part they are fine when they do. But for the young people who are approached at their local take-away shop, groomed and trafficked to distribute drugs around the country, the journey through adolescence is a darker shade of gloom. As it is for young people who are sexually harassed and abused by peers at school; or exploited via organised crime networks who see them as sexual commodities for their own financial gain. Or young people who are emotionally and physically abused by their first, same-age, romantic partner. Young people who experience robbery, are threatened with weapons, or even stabbed on their way home from school. Or those who are bullied to a point where they can't see a future beyond the blurred vision of their tears. There are many things about each of these experiences that will be particular to the harm in question, and unique to the young person who experiences them. And yet, the extra-familial dynamics of these experiences, the community and peer relationships in which they occur, and the school and neighbourhood settings where they play out, are often shared. The villages in which our young people are abused are all around us – they are merely broader than the family homes which have been the traditional target of systems in place to tackle abuse.

## The system response

And so this is also a book about how the state and wider societies have responded to Sara and Malik. It is about a child protection system, designed to protect children from abuse within their families, and the difficulties that have arisen in England (and could arise elsewhere) when people have tried to use that system to deal with abuse in peer groups, schools and community settings. In England all manner of harms experienced by young people like Sara and Malik have been classified as abuse. A series of public inquiries and campaigns have called on the state to respond accordingly. A spotlight has been shone on the efficacy of statutory services, and individual children's social care departments and police forces have been found wanting.

This is the place from where my team and I sought to understand, and respond to, the realities of Sara and Malik's lives: and the struggles that professionals and their parents had in trying to keep them safe. What were child protection systems, specifically, doing in response to extra-familial abuse – and what would it take for those systems to act differently? In particular how could child protection systems, and the social work workforce, engage with the peer groups, school environments and public places where young people were coming to significant harm – and thereby broaden their field of vision beyond the children and families with whom they had traditionally worked? Our endeavour to answer this question has involved coining, theorising and then applying the idea of Contextual Safeguarding – creating child protection systems and wider safeguarding partnerships that can: target the extra-familial contexts and social conditions in which abuse occurs; do this through the lens of child welfare and child protection (not solely through policing and community safety); leverage the extensive partnerships that can reach into extra-familial contexts; and measure the impact of such systems contextually.

As such it is important to emphasise that our primary concern has been child protection responses to extra-familial harm – rather than all possible responses to the issue. In this book I will make reference to a range of partners who are involved in mounting a response to extra-familial abuse, and whose expertise has informed the development of Contextual Safeguarding. But it is important to emphasise the parameters of the work to date, and the intention behind its inception.

Contextual Safeguarding has been six years in the making – and so in many respects is a very young idea. But in that time we have already learnt a substantial amount about what it takes to extend the remit of a child protection system so that it can engage with the extra-familial dynamics (and contexts) of abuse. In this book I will outline three critical stages of learning so far. The first involving attempts to implement small contextual tweaks to child protection systems that otherwise remained solely focused on the assessment of, and intervention with, children and families in response to abuse. The second being focused on implementing whole system change to embed a Contextual Safeguarding approach throughout child protection systems. And the third considering the conceptual, policy and practical implications of learning so far, and signalling immediate and more long-term questions to be explored in the years ahead. Understanding each stage of development is important for ensuring that those interested in Contextual Safeguarding understand where it has come from – and where it could go: maximising opportunities for further co-creation of the approach in the future.

## The evidence base

In writing this book I bring together findings from five key projects that have been used to build Contextual Safeguarding since 2011.

The first study (2011–2015) involved a review of nine cases of peer-on-peer abuse, involving 145 young people (detailed in chapter 2). This study provided a contextual analysis of extra-familial harm, and in doing pointed towards a need to contextualise safeguarding responses.

In response to the case reviews I led an action research project from 2013 to 2016 (The MsUnderstood Project) in which 11 local areas in England contextualised elements of their response to peer-on-peer forms of extra-familial abuse. This work evidenced the value of contextual approaches; the challenges of sustaining contextual approaches without system wide change; and was the evidence base that underpinned the Contextual Safeguarding framework – first published in 2016.

The need for system-wide change was explored through two projects that ran from 2016 and 2017 respectively. The first was the 2016 launch of a Contextual Safeguarding practice network – through which practitioners could test, and provide feedback on, contextual approaches – engage in learning events, produce case studies to support practice development and continue the development of practices initiated from 2013 to 2016 in the original 11 sites. Then, in 2017, we embarked on our first whole system application of the Contextual Safeguarding Framework – working with children's services colleagues in the London Borough of Hackney to create a root-and-branch children's social care response to the extra-familial contexts in which young people were being abused.

In 2018, we built on the learning emerging from Hackney to the launch the Contextual Safeguarding Scale-Up project – a bid to test the framework in additional localities. We had funding to work with three areas but 50 applied to take part; so in the end we selected nine (and secured additional funding to support this) – five outside of London and a further four within the capital. This project will run until 2022, but learning has already emerged from system review activities in all sites to track progress to date, and identify priorities for the year ahead.

Across these five projects we have used a series of largely qualitative research methods to build, understand, document, disseminate and enable contextual practices. Core techniques have included: embedded research methods – sitting alongside practitioners to capture, and inform, the system-change process; content analysis of policy documents; meeting and practice observations; focus groups with young people and practitioners; surveys; reflective workshops; and system mapping. The methods employed in these different studies are detailed in the respective parts of this book where they most feature – in particular chapters 2, 4, 5 and 8.

All of the data collected within, and across the projects, have been analysed through a two-tier conceptual lens. The principal approach to analysis has been to use the Contextual Safeguarding framework (chapter 6) to document and assess the contextual capabilities of local safeguarding systems. My research team and I have regularly organised our data against this framework – as you will see in various parts of the book – to both understand whether Contextual Safeguarding is being realised in a local area, and to articulate what we are learning about the operational reality of such an approach. Underpinning the Contextual Safeguarding Framework is a series of larger theoretical ideas that are detailed in chapter 4 of this book: the central ones being the concepts of social field, capital and habitus offered by Pierre Bourdieu to explain the social world. As our work has developed, theories of critical social work, ecologies of human development, public health approaches to violence reduction and situational crime prevention have all provided a home to Contextual Safeguarding, and have been drawn upon to advance and explain the idea. As such, all are also referenced in this book, providing an overarching framework in which to explain the positions we have reached, and also to anchor my recommendations for where we should go next.

## The path to change

Most importantly this is a book about what child protection systems could be; how the state could act; and what we as a society could be doing to re-write the social rules of extra-familial contexts in which Sara, Malik and other young people are abused. To create a system capable of achieving this we not only need to tackle the norms of schools, neighbourhood and peer contexts in which abuse has occurred, but we need to tackle the rules of child protection systems that themselves have focused on intervention with families as the primary route for protection in the face of abuse. To tell this tale of challenges, opportunities and reforms I have structured the book into four parts.

The first details the challenge that we face by outlining: the contextual nature of extra-familial harms in adolescence (chapter 2); the difficulties that arise when such harm interacts with child protection systems designed to respond to harm within families (chapter 3); and the various spectacles we have drawn upon to view, make sense of, and try to resolve, this dilemma (chapter 4). The case review study, as well as our observations of practice across all the studies that followed, and our wider work on the use of relocations and school sanctions to manage extra-familial harm are drawn upon over these chapters.

The second part presents how we laid the groundwork for testing a Contextual Safeguarding system. In chapter 5, I detail the methodology used in the 11 sites that participated in the MsUnderstood project, the contextual activities we trialled during this time, and the thematic learning that materialised from the work. I use chapter 6 to present the four domains of the Contextual Safeguarding Framework – how they emerged from our work and the vision they offered us all for the system change we needed to achieve. In chapter 7, I detail how policy frameworks in England adapted from 2016 to 2018 to create an authorising environment for testing the Contextual Safeguarding Framework.

I use the third part the book to share test results – from our first site in London, our nine new test sites and via our online practice network. In chapter 8, I detail the data collection activities we used to run tests, and the key stakeholders (local area practitioners and members of our online practice network) who were involved in developing and reviewing the approach alongside my research team. I also use this chapter to explain how we came to understand that testing needed to occur on two levels – one in regards to work with children and families and the other in regards to work with extra-familial contexts. The following two (chapters 9 and 10) detail the work that occurred at each level respectively; and what testing told us about the system changes required to bring Contextual Safeguarding to life. In chapter 11, I examine the policy implications of the test work; in particular the learning gleaned about the differences between integrated and holistic approaches to extra-familial harm, and how the latter is required for a contextual approach to thrive. Finally in chapter 12, I explain what testing told us about the Contextual Safeguarding Framework itself, and the changes we have made as a result to articulate the values that underpin it and the lens through which its ambitions should be viewed. Throughout this Part I will reaffirm that Contextual Safeguarding is an approach and not a model, hence much variation in its application seen around England. And yet, parameters have still been required to ensure the intention of the framework is honoured in practice: without such parameters we risk the framework being warped by the system challenges it seeks to resolve.

In the final part of the book I signal the direction of travel for Contextual Safeguarding: the questions it asks of individuals, organisations and states, and the assumptions it pulls apart in the process. To begin I interrogate the idea of 'thresholds' for state intervention in cases of abuse (chapter 13); how this has been interpreted for extra-familial harm, and why this requires attention in any endeavour to deliver a child protection response to the issue. I then explore what Contextual Safeguarding means for the role of social work; demonstrating how tests have applied key social work activities to contemporary concerns, and in doing so both extended and maintained the ethics and values of the profession (chapter 14). In chapter 15, I reflect on our methods for achieving change to date: identifying how these may need to bear different weight in the future to ensure Contextual Safeguarding reframes, rather than reaffirms, child protection responses to extra-familial harm, and are owned by the practitioners, young people and families who will ultimately put it to use. In the penultimate chapter (16) I highlight the key legal and ethical questions that emerge when testing Contextual Safeguarding and the need to hold these in mind and practice as work continues. The fact that they have grown from tests has been our biggest indication that Contextual Safeguarding does rewrite what we have assumed about child protection systems – and until they can be answered the future of the approach will be in question. I use chapter 17 to close the book, summarising the essential directions of travel for states, communities, families and child protection organisations as we continue to build contextual approaches to safeguarding the welfare of young people.

By the end of this book I will have laid bare all I know, in 2019, about a Contextual Safeguarding approach. By documenting both the superficial and fundamental adaptations we have made to child protection systems in England to better respond to extra-familial harm – I will arrive at a pit stop, and a series of practical, legal and ethical questions that require resolve, before we take our next steps. In raising these questions I will demonstrate how our test work has required a rewrite of many rules of child protection which either formally, or informally, have coloured social work responses to young people in need of support. And yet in doing so the work has simultaneously reaffirmed, or reinvigorated, the rules of social work and child protection that social justice advocates have long promoted. The harms in question may have a contemporary flavour, and my magpie approach to system design may bring together many disparate ideas and schools of thought: but the output is, in many ways, a reaffirmation of children's rights to safety and protection – and our collective duty to honour them. So welcome to the journey towards Contextual Safeguarding – a road of twists, turns and bumps, often in the absence of a map: with a destination in sight, albeit not yet reached.

## Note

1  Throughout this book I use England's child protection system as a case study drawing parallels and identifying multi-country implications where relevant.

# 2 Extra-familial abuse in context

Cos [sic] I know what these boys are like if they don't get what they want they'll beat you up or get girls to beat you up and they'll switch for no apparent reason ... if you say no they consider it as being rude and they don't like getting talked to like that, and if you're rude to them then they'll beat you up and I've seen how they beat up people, how everyone's scared of them. ... I said no for something very little I've been beaten up and bottled and I realised if I did say no what would happen ... I was pressurised and scared, I knew deep down I didn't want it cos I was still young but I didn't have a choice.

(Sara's (age 13) Witness Testimony,
Case File 4, Review 2011–2014)

These are the words of 'Sara' – spoken aged 13 during an interview with the police. This is what happened to Sara in her local park. It is the park, and the group of boys who hang out there, through Sara's eyes and in Sara's shoes. Sara's account of her local park and what had happened in the days and weeks before she was raped there depict the social world – or sets of contexts – that were her reality. Sara was navigating contexts where violence had been normalised, male entitlement to sex soaked the fabric of her social relationships, and consent did not exist.

The road to Contextual Safeguarding started with Sara – and so does this book. To understand what is required from child protection systems – the issues they are trying to address, and their contextual impacts, require attention. Stepping into Sara's world is a helpful introduction to an international evidence base that has uncovered the contextual nature of extra-familial forms of harm. It was where I started in 2011 when I began reviewing nine cases in which young people had been sexually, physically and/or emotionally abused by their peers: three of these young people were killed, and the cases in total resulted in six police investigations into rape and three into murder. I sat with these cases for three years, documenting the recorded dynamics of every family home ($n$=160), peer or friendship network ($n$=21), school environment ($n$=30) and local authorities spaces ($n$=9), featured within them (Firmin, 2017a, 2017b). The files were held in local police stations, and

featured social care assessments, school reports, police investigation documents (including social media data, witness statements, location maps) and
a range of other multi-agency documents that had informed the response
leveraged in each case from 2007 to 2010. Box file after box file unearthed
what felt like endless examples of the how risks permeated peer relationships,
school cultures and community locations – and how these dynamics were
excluded from safeguarding responses.

By stepping into Sara's world, along with another young man Malik whose
case I reviewed years after the original nine, this chapter brings to the fore
the contexts associated to abuse as it is experienced during adolescence and
lays bare the dynamics of abuse which confront professionals and parents
who are trying to keep our young people safe. By considering the intricate
dynamics of two cases and the international evidence base that they illustrate,
this chapter will evidence the significance of extra-familial contexts to adolescent welfare; the rules at play in those contexts; the influence that the rules of
extra-familial contexts have on individual decision-making; and the significance of peer, as well as familial, relationships in creating the conditions in
which protection or abuse can flourish.

## Stepping into the social fields of abuse

Sara's account with which this chapter opens, describes not only the actions
that occurred in the park that day, or the peer group she was with when she
was there, but the social rules – or sets of expectations – that permeated this
context, and many others, where she spent her time. These contexts weren't
just brick buildings, muddy paths, blossoming trees or non-descript encounters with peers. They were social fields (Bourdieu, 1992 – explored further in
chapter 3): spaces seeping with codes of conduct that she learnt through time
spent navigating them. Echoing the messages from studies of abuse in the
United Kingdom, United States and Australia (Anderson, 1999; Brayley,
et al., 2011; Harding, 2014; Powell, 2008; Rogowoski, 2012), Sara gradually
embodied these rules and demonstrated her implicit understanding of them
in the way that she talked, walked and fell silent. She was compliant when
faced with a sexual assault; she knew there were little point in resisting the
demands of the boys that surrounded her, and; she was afraid of the consequences that she would endure on a path of defiance.

Seeing Sara's interactions within the (constraining, violent and oppressive)
social fields in which she was abused provides a necessary context to understanding her 'decisions'. As the quote which opened this chapter clearly and
concisely makes clear – at the age of 13, Sara articulated the interplay
between the social realities or her life and the decisions that she made.
Through this interplay Sara experienced a sequence of events in which she
was sexually exploited by a group of 14–15-year-old boys for 18 months.

One day Sara stood at a bus stop waiting to travel home. Two boys she knew
approached her and asked her how she was – and how her day was going. She

had already been sexually assaulted by some of their friends. These boys had been present in the houses or parks where these events unfolded, but they had never been directly involved: not until this day. During the conversation one boy showed Sara a knife and gave it to her to hold. Sara described the interactions that followed as being so quick that before she knew it a knife was in her hands – placed there with a casual instruction of 'hold this for me for a minute would you'. The boys then started to joke – her fingerprints were on the knife; wasn't she worried about that; but she didn't need to worry really as they had her back; or did they; hahaha – ha. During this brief but loaded conversation a bus arrived. The bus went. And Sara still stood at the bus stop – rapidly losing any morsel of control she may have initially felt in that situation and being all too aware of this fact.

When I was reading Sara's account I could picture the bus stop, the bus coming and going, and Sara's feet rooted to the concrete below her. She could see what was about to happen – the days and months before, and all the conversations that had taken place during them, swirled around her head like a heavy plume of acrid smoke gradually shutting out any air of freedom and locking her in a mental fog of dead ends. To many people looking at Sara she would have just been a girl, stood at a bus stop talking to two boys. She could have walked away. She could have boarded a bus at any point. The superglue of fear that fixed her trainers to the pavement and rendered her paralysed was only visible to her and the two boys in front of her. They all knew the social rules of this interaction – the code of conduct in this social field.

According to the boxes of paperwork I read through when reviewing Sara's case I came to understand she was a slight child, a whisker over five foot tall. She wore her hair pulled up in a bun on top of her head, wisps of afro hair stubbornly sticking out of her hair scrunchie and framing her face. Through the words in her social care files, police interviews and school reports, her face became etched in the fibres of my mind – along with the hundreds of other young people whose words I have read, or lives I have heard about, over a decade. And that face – full of fear, resignation to the worst possible outcome and a complete loss of any belief that the adults around her could keep her safe – was at the forefront of my mind when I thought about her at that bus stop.

Having given her the knife, and then taken it away again, the boys told Sara to come with them. Walking away from the bus stop they commented that if Sara was their friend she would walk alongside them. The term 'friend' being important. After all it was because she was their 'friend' that they wouldn't possibly hurt her with the knife they had shown her or get her in trouble by using the fact that her fingerprints were all over that same knife. Sara followed them as they jumped over a small wall and in a grassy area off the back of some houses.

And it was there that they sexually assaulted Sara. According to them it was their 'turn now'.

This was just another one of many days that Sara was abused her community.

Sara's route to survival was to rarely wash, gain weight and keep her head down – actions she thought would ward off anyone with sexual intentions. The relentless abuse she endured however suggested that these repellent techniques failed to provide a pathway to safety in the social fields of Sara's world. Sara was angry, lost and resigned to a life, and world, of abuse. Her reaction to this world was initially to shut down. She was in a world in which adults were often present but seemingly without power or an ability to protect. After all, adults were in the park, in the school, at the bus stops and take away shops, where Sara was assaulted. But their presence had little effect on her safety – perceived and real.

It was, therefore, she, and she alone, who needed to work out how to make do, and play the rules of the world in which she found herself. She learnt those rules over time and sought options that would result in the least 'painful' outcome. That meant compliance with the sexual demands of her male peers and pushing adults away, particularly those from statutory services like social care or the police, whose intervention was, she felt, likely to increase rather than reduce the risks she faced. After all, her experiences suggested to Sara that the adults around her (a) didn't understand the social fields she navigated and (b) had minimal influence over, or status in, these social fields. Sara on the other hand did understand these social fields and spent time maximising the capital she had access to in order to achieve some form of status in them. For Sara this led to gradually understanding the cultural cues and norms of those fields – like 'not snitching' – to achieve the 'least harmful' outcome in any particular circumstance. Sara also tried to align herself with a network of peers who might in time see her as an equal rather than someone who they could abuse. In Sara's mind it was safer to try and stand alongside those who posed a risk to her safety than come up against them.

Sara's decisions made sense to me. Her experiences, and her embodied understanding of the social fields she was in, implied that she had a better handle on her situation and how to survive it then the adults around her. And furthermore, that adult interference in her life could compromise her current routes to 'safety', and potentially decimate the minimal status that she had acquired in her social world (Allnock, 2019; Beckett, et al., 2013; Cossar, et al., 2013).

In their notes professionals interpreted Sara's behaviour as evidence of who Sara was, rather than indicative of the world that Sara was in. According to professionals, Sara was 'anti-police', 'aggressive' and had 'no interest in exiting the gang culture of which she was a part'. The oppressive, constrained and in many respects dystopian gauntlet of streets, school corridors and peer relationships she managed to get through each day seemed somehow invisible to them. They were visible in Sara's accounts but not in their own. Instead, they took what Sara said, and interpreted her actions, to focus solely on her – abstracted from all social contexts that informed her actions. This singular focus on Sara resulted in professional assessments and conversations that were dominated by frustrations with Sara's decisions and the problems 'she had caused for herself'.

The absence of social context from professional accounts created an impression that Sara was making decisions while walking down safe and community-filled streets where everyone looked out for each other – streets where if she ever felt threatened there were places she could go to get help, evaporating risks in the process. Or that when she was at school all of her peers were kind and supportive, and any disagreements were settled amicably and with the support of teachers who understood the challenges of being a teenager and worked with the opportunities that this time in life presents. Of course they didn't actually present this rose-soaked account of Sara's life in their files – but the lack of recognition of what these contexts were actually like for Sara, combined with their fixation on the decisions that Sara made as if there was all manner of other options available to her, gave room for such a conclusion to be reached. Sara's life, in their notes, appeared full of endless choices and it was in her gift to choose well and flourish. There were no constraints, influences, pressures or dead-ends that limited safety – only Sara's poor thinking.

These social fields, and the professional response to a child navigating them, were not unique to Sara.

In 2016, I once again sat at a desk reviewing case file material. This time I was examining the notes of school pastoral worker 'Joe'. Joe had written an account of a conversation he'd had with Malik. Malik was 15 years old. He had arrived into school clearly injured and Joe had stopped him as he walked through a school corridor to ask him what had happened. Malik initially stated he had tripped and hurt himself – an account Joe queried. Joe expressed how concerned he was about the injuries he could see and in response Malik slowly opened up and explained how he was being bullied at school.

Some months later my research team and I combed through police, school and social care records associated to this case. Once again these pages illustrated how the nature of social contexts and the abuse that occurred within them were inextricably tied. And these social fields were, once again, largely absent from how adults had interpreted Malik's behaviour.

Malik's school were aware of bullying between some of their students; they were not aware that this involved Malik. What they did know was that Malik had started to arrive late to school in the mornings, was regularly late to lessons and would then ask to be excused from classes to use the toilets. School professionals had initially used sanctions including detentions to deter Malik from skipping classes. There was a belief that Malik could be punished into changing his behaviour. This belief was misguided.

When Malik's behaviour failed to change school professionals picked up the phone to children's services to ask for some advice. These conversations – between professionals rather than with Malik – resulted in a false 'light bulb' moment. It was identified that Malik had a family member with disabilities, and it was believed that this might have created some support needs for Malik's family. Professionals thought that if they worked with Malik's family, then Malik's behaviour would change at school.

This made sense to the professional network around Malik. For them family difficulties commonly featured in the lives of young people who were struggling with their behaviour in school. This position is closely aligned to the mantras of 'I blame the parents' or 'you have to ask yourself what the parents were doing' – common within the public discourse that can emerge when things go wrong in the lives of young people. More importantly, however, there is also substantial research evidence that identifies a relationship between familial experiences of abuse and neglect, and difficulties in extra-familial settings (Ellis & Dietz, 2017; Ewell Foster, et al., 2017; Hallett, et al., 2019; Hanson, 2016; Scott & Skidmore, 2006). Young people's experiences of abuse in early childhood, living with domestic violence between parents or carers, and living with a parent who is addicted to alcohol, drugs or struggling with their mental health have all been identified in the backgrounds of *some* young people who experience difficulties during adolescence.

However, Malik was not one of these young people – and intervention with his family failed to impact his behaviour at school. On top of this, Malik's parents felt judged and scrutinised by the actions taken by the school and children's services staff. They were equally perplexed and struggling to understand why Malik's behaviour was difficult at school. They were increasingly stressed by it, and felt further anxiety when their ability to explain their son's behaviour was interpreted as a deficit in them as parents. As Malik continued to skip classes, and relationships between the school and his parents became strained, a threat was made to fine his parents for not getting him into school.

The threat appeared to work.

Mailk started to come into classes before the school bell rang each morning and stayed put at his desk. He used the toilets during break and lunch times. On the face of it all was well. Malik's behaviour had improved and he was showing no other signs that anything was going wrong for him.

It was later that year I received a call. Malik had spoken to his pastoral worker Joe and told him that he had been seriously assaulted. I was asked, along with my research team, to review his case. Malik hadn't only told Joe about the assault. He had also explained why he had been truanting from school. It had nothing to do with his family at all.

Malik described how once he started to attend more classes the bullying escalated and resulted in him being assaulted in his community. Before then, Malik had been avoiding classes where he would see the boys who were bullying him. On other occasions he was late to lessons; waiting to hear the sound of a teacher addressing his classmates before he'd dare to enter the room or for silence to descend in the school corridors before he'd emerge from under the stairs and scuttle to his class. He also asked to be excused from classes to use the toilets while they were empty – avoiding being assaulted in the cubicles as they filled with other students at break times.

Just like Sara, Malik had learnt the rules of the social fields he was in and developed behaviours and techniques to survive while in them. Like Sara,

Malik was harmed in contexts where adults had a presence – but their presence in many cases was insufficient to keep him safe. There were caveats to this. A teacher being present in his classroom, for example, did halt any potential attack. However, when a teacher wasn't in sight, the general presence of staff in his school, and the wider student body, did not create a more protective set of social rules within Malik's school culture. Like Sara, Malik believed that seeking help from professionals would increase risk – and in his case, professional intervention did escalate risk significantly.

The social field that Malik described, the normalisation of violence in his school corridors, toilets and stairwells, informed the behaviour of a number of young people in the case – not just Malik. Joe knew the boys who had assaulted Malik – he knew their dynamics as a group. Some of these boys had also been bullied at school. Over time they aligned themselves to the person bullying them, Connor, to avoid being victimised. Being close to Connor gave these boys the social networks they needed to stay safe at school. They protected their social position by demonstrating loyalty to Connor – and they did this by bullying Malik.

However, during the review it was apparent that we couldn't simply isolate harm to the peer group who assaulted Malik. The wider student body were aware of the influence that Connor had; his power was felt (and unchallenged) throughout the school. Ineffective responses to bullying within the school further contributed to these social rules, sustaining the perception that disclosing concerns to staff would not afford young people safety and could in fact make matters worse.

Years later I would be sat on my living room sofa and memories of this case would come flooding back while I watched the US drama, *13 Reasons Why*. Just like the Malik's, the school in show was awash with social rules that normalised sexual assault by those students with social status, silenced those they harmed, and where the threat of being ostracized by ones' peers motivated, created and sustained the social conditions for abuse to flourish.

Beyond staff and students at his school, the local police knew Connor. He, and some other young people in the community, had been involved in a number of violent scuffles. Connor had himself been victimised in his community as a younger child – he'd had his bike stolen in his local park, and when he started to travel to school alone his phone was quickly taken from him too. He came to believe, quite quickly, that the police couldn't stop this from happening to him. In the absence of another route to safety he learnt the cultural codes of conduct on the streets, and networked with older people in the community who used violence, to protect himself.

In this heady mix of school, community and peer social fields, where peer-violence was normalised and protective adults appeared absent, Connor and his peers assaulted Malik. As was the case with Sara, adults were present in many of these contexts, and to some degree were aware of the way young people were behaving. But neither their physical presence, nor their awareness of violence, could be equated with protection. A blindness to the social rules to which these behaviours aligned, and an incapacity to see how a lack of available protection from adults contributed to these rules, left young people unsafe.

## From case exerts to a contextual evidence base

The stories of Sara and Malik bring to life the nature of social fields in which young people in England have been abused, and how the dynamics of adolescence interact with the rules at play within them. Stepping into these social fields is essential to understanding, and seeking to change, the evidently contextual dynamics of young people experiences. In 2017, I wrote a detailed account of each social context featured thus far – schools, peer groups, neighbourhoods and families – and how they related to young people's experiences of peer-abuse (Firmin, 2017c). Since this time I have asked similar questions of abuse that young people experience from adults unconnected to their families – including sexual and criminal exploitation. The same themes are evident regarding the nature of abuse, the social fields associated to that abuse and the challenge that adults face when seeking to intervene and protect young people. In particular, a contextual examination of international research, media and state inquiries into abuse in adolescence offer consistent messages that are exemplified by the cases presented thus far. Firstly, this evidence base indicates that when abuse occurs in extra-familial settings/relationships – particularly sexual and criminal exploitation, youth violence and peer abuse – it is informed by the social fields that operate in young people's schools, neighbourhoods and peer relationships. And secondly, that the social rules at play in these extra-familial contexts can present particular challenges to professionals and parents when they interact with the dynamics of adolescent development.

### *Interplay between the dynamics of adolescence and extra-familial social fields*

While the specific age-window is the subject of going dispute, 'adolescence' is widely acknowledged as a period in human development (from the age of about 10–12 right through to our mid-twenties) where individuals go through physical, emotional and social change (Blakemore, 2018; Coleman, 2011; Hanson & Holmes, 2015). It's a time where we react to risk, and enjoy the feelings of taking a risk, in a different way to when we are younger children and also older adults – although this engagement in risk-taking is thought to be quite socially informed (Blakemore, 2018). Our brains are still developing, particularly in the field of consequential thinking. This, combined with relatively minimal life experience, means that during adolescence we tend to be the motivated more readily by short, instead of long, term gains. Thanks to puberty our emotions are all over the place; we fall in love for the first time, and tend to fall hard; we can be overly tearful without explanation, feel frustrated, angry, low, excited and everything else in-between (Blakemore, 2018; Coleman, 2011; Hanson & Holmes,

2015). And to top it all off we have an increased desire for autonomy during adolescence; we want to take some responsibility for ourselves, make some choices and express our sense of self while we work out who we are.

These four dynamics of adolescence come together, and often play out, in extra-familial contexts and away from parental supervision. From parks, stairwells and shopping centres, to fast food outlets and social media platforms young people will often gravitate towards locations collectively, where they can socialise and form relationships; even if these are locations where some have experienced harm. Consider a shopping centre where young people are being groomed into criminal exploitation. Why might they continue to go to a shopping centre in the face of such risk? For some young people such risks may not be evident. Further to this, however, the shopping centre is just where 'everyone' goes. It's where hook-ups and hang-outs and everything in between happens. Young people in the local area acquire cultural capital by being there. The trainer shop that 'everyone' goes to in order to try on the latest status symbol and all talk about how they are definitely going to buy this coveted item of clothing that few of them can actually afford. It's the clinical white and brightly lit toilet cubicles that make the perfect back drop for the latest selfie, filtered to its last inch and uploaded simultaneously across all social media platforms so everyone else knows exactly who was there – and importantly who was not. It's the place where you can get access to Wi-Fi in order to upload said images for the cost of a burger split across eight of you. It's the route to being in on the jokes. It's the whisky and cigars room for the 21st-century teenager.

In addition to the places they self-select to 'hang-out', young people also need to access a number of extra-familial contexts just to get through the day: they have to enter school buildings to access their education, often use public transport or walk down high streets to get to school and home again, and so on. What happens in these settings informs young people's sense of safety and opportunities for personal development. What economic, social or cultural capital[1] enables a young person to safely navigate their local park, school or high street? How does their capital inform the choices that they then make in those settings? The value of capital will vary related to the social rules that operate in any given context – and as has already been indicated in the cases of Malik and Sara, the capital that matters at home will not necessarily be the capital that matters in extra-familial contexts.

At its most mundane, things which carry social clout in young people's school, neighbourhood or other peer community during adolescence will not necessarily be similarly valued by parents. Sam's parents don't like the music currently blaring out of the docking station in his bedroom. Charmaine's parents think her choice of school shoe is impractical. These battles between parents and their children is common place amongst many a household. It's all part of growing up – we have been told – as young people strive to develop a sense of self; a personal identity of their own. As John Coleman noted in his guide for parents everywhere:

In the majority of cases parents are seen as being the ones to turn to when it comes to education, careers and jobs, health matters, money and questions of morality. Where it is a question of social issues, where there are concerns about intimate relationships and where such things as clothes, music and leisure are discussed, then friends become important

(Coleman, 2014:99)

And so the idea that social preferences in families, peer groups, schools and neighbourhood contexts vary is only one part of the story. The weight of influence between these social norms during adolescence may also be unequal – depending on the matter at hand. Living in a safe family home does not necessarily transfer safety into extra-familial contexts (Catch 22, 2013; Firmin, 2017a; PACE, 2020). The norms of Sara's family did not translate into her peer relationships, or the neighbourhood settings she socialised. Sara behaved in accordance with peer norms, rather than familial ones, when spending time in her community. A pattern described by this young person, interviewed in 2013:

That's what I believed. I'm of age now. Sixteen, seventeen, I'm of age. Yeah, I would still go out and stay out, but they would still phone to make sure, wherever I am, to make sure that I'm safe. … I'm a man now; I'll stand on my own two feet. Do what I have to do. They were still parenting me and I was still listening, I wasn't rebelling in that way like that, I still had manners towards my mum and my dad. You know, maybe you might have the little arguments for whatever it may be, but I'll still listen to them, because obviously they're my guardians innit, so I'll still listen to them and that, but when I go outside, that's my time. When I'm inside, it's their time'.

(Rhys, African Caribbean, male, 14–17)
(Catch 22, 2013:39–40)

This position is reinforced by multiple studies into parents of young people who are abused extra-familial settings (Catch 22, 2013; Ewell Foster, et al., 2017; Hudeck, 2018; PACE, 2020; Scott & McNeish, 2017). Whether they are relatively protective, or experiencing some additional challenges, the safety young people experience within their family home will not necessarily keep them safe once they step outdoors or online: an invisible wall, or very visible front door in some cases can demarcate a parent's reach.

Building a sense of cultural capital, hanging out in spaces and with people that can maintain or boost one's social capital are just some ways in which young people can gain status – thereby belonging and, where also relevant, safety – in extra-familial contexts. And if you don't have the money to hang out in those places, and buy the trainers that everyone is looking at, then the 23-year-old who buys them for you and then asks you to hold some weed in your bedroom for them might just give you the economic capital you need to boost your position. This desire to feel safe and to be able to look after yourself when you are out and about, can twist and turn in certain contexts and situations to tragic consequences. From young people who grouped together and stabbed a peer to death over a fight about who had the right to stand in a milkshake shop, through to the young woman who, sexually abused from infancy, was sexually exploited in exchange for 50p from her peers on the estate so they would hang out with her, to the kids being trafficked to move drugs over train lines to earn some money and respect from those around them – the interplay of capital, social field and adolescence can appear tragically irrational, destructive and self-made (Allnock, 2019; Berelowitz, et al., 2013; Catch 22, 2013; Firmin, 2017c; Harding, 2014; Hudeck, 2018; Jay, 2014). Are you wincing as you read this – I am as I am writing – but such words illustrate what parents, practitioners and wider society have said when encountering someone like Sara (Barter, 2006; Eaton & Holmes, 2017; Turner, et al., 2019). I for one will never forget the moment during a site visit for the into Children's Commissioner's Inquiry for Sexual Exploitation in Gangs and Groups when a children's services manager informed me that they didn't really have any child sexual exploitation in the area: 'just a couple of girls prostituting themselves up and down the high street for vodka'.

The evidence presented thus far pushes against such a blaming, pathologising and simplified account of the choices young people make. We have to understand why certain forms of cultural, social and economic capital matter during adolescence – and in which contexts they matter the most.[2] If young people felt safe at school, valued in their communities, or that they belonged to their peer groups would they need to draw upon ultimately painful forms of capital to achieve 'safety' within those settings – a form of safety which often results in harm?

### *The contextual dynamics of abuse in extra-familial settings and relationships*

It is not simply that Malik had to go to school or Sara had to use the bus to get home that facilitated their abuse in these spaces. As has been illustrated, the social rules at play in these extra-familial contexts can be positively or negatively associated with abuse. Studies into bullying in schools, for example, routinely identify how school cultures are themselves informed by the attitudes of staff, students, and the curriculum and so on (Cowie, 2011; Taylor, et al., 2013). And it is the social rules, often unwritten within these contexts, which create the social conditions in which young people like Malik and Sara will be abused by young people like Connor or other adults.

Many young people affected by, or involved in, exploitation and other forms of abuse will be exposed to more than one set of social rules as they traverse different social contexts. The social rules of Malik's school and Sara's neighbourhood were not the same as their families. Social status and safety within Malik's family was not determined by whether he or his relatives were friends with Connor. Connor bore no social weight in his family home, and if anything association with Connor made Malik's life at home harder. Association with Connor and other young people who were committing criminal offences in the local neighbourhood was not something that Malik's parents would have welcomed or encouraged.

Research into different forms of extra-familial abuse has evidenced how the nature and influence of rules in a range of social contexts, sets the parameters in which young people act. Therefore to understand the actions young people take we have to also understand the contexts in which they occur. Jenny Pearce, for example, has called for a social model of consent to be used when conceptualising the decisions of young people who are sexually exploited. In this model Pearce thinks about choice in relation to poverty, fear, actions of professionals and social rules that normalise harm in certain contexts. Through this contextual lens Pearce argues that:

> A social model of consent would address the social and environmental features that impact on young people's ability to consent and help practitioners to assess the different ways that a young person's capacity to concern can be abused, exploited and manipulated
>
> (Pearce, 2013:53)

Despite such calls for a contextual and social lens much of the evidence base that underpins practice responses to extra-familial harm focuses on individual and familial vulnerabilities. For example, a range of studies are increasingly supporting professionals to understand young people's current experiences of abuse by assessing earlier, and adverse, experiences that have informed a person's sense of self and emotional well-being as a teenager (Ellis & Dietz, 2017). Much work has also been undertaken to understand the actions of parents and the relationship a young person has with their parents to understand this decision-making (Catch 22, 2013; Ewell Foster, et al., 2017; Hallett, et al., 2019; Hanson, 2016). Both of these exercises are hugely valuable, and as research has shown for many young people they provide some explanation for the difficulties they face in adolescence (and this understanding in turn offers the evidence base to build a plan to reduce risk and increase safety). However, as Pearce (2013) and others have noted they are not the sole explanatory routes – and during adolescence there is a third relational domain which informs the capital that matters during this time in one's life. Relationships with peers are particularly influential at this point in our lives, to the point that the views of a young person's peers can outweigh those of their parents particularly in relation to social norms. From Finkelhor in the United States, Barter in the United Kingdom and Smallbone in Australia, scholars have recorded the traumatic consequences of victimisation and perpetration experienced during adolescence within peer relationships. Personal traits, familial and peer relationships afford young people social, cultural and economic capital. The combination of all three, in particular contexts can increase safety and/or inform risk – and it is all three that must be considered in a contextual account of abuse.

Some of the settings in which extra-familial harm occurs, such as parks and shopping centres, have minimal adult supervision. This is important. Think about what happens in your local area at 4pm each day. Do you know where young people go after school? You probably do – you see them in groupings dancing at bus stops or consuming vast amount of chips out-side take-away shops. And if you know where to find them so does anyone who wants to access young people and exploit them. Who has their eyes on young people when they are in these places? And what do those eyes see? Groups of anti-social nuisances that we want to move on? Or children who are vulnerable to being groomed, threatened or attacked, in a crowd where they are anonymous and without the threat of teachers or parents watching these interactions. What's more – some of these locations are characterised by material goods – alcohol, food, a lift home – which can be offered to young people in exchange for their involvement in harmful behaviours (such as the selling of drugs).

With this in mind it is critical to note that young people are far from the only ones involved in creating, embodying and practicing the norms of extra-familial contexts. A range of social actors, including adults, spend time in, manage and oversee extra-familial contexts such as parks, schools and shopping centres. These social actors all play a role in setting social norms and expectations, and have opportunities to disrupt or agitate against norms associated with abuse in those settings – as did teachers in the case of Malik and members of the public who were at the bus stop with Sara. Their inability to understand the behaviour of Malik and Sara, or to offer effective support to safeguard them, reinforced the harmful norms associated with the abuse they experienced rather than challenged it.

Social rules will vary context by context. And an individuals' ability to play the rules of any given context, and come out on top, will vary too. Therefore, once we recognise that extra-familial abuse is shaped by the contexts in which it occurs, and that these contexts are characterised by a range of social rules, we need to understand the processes by which rules are embodied – and why.

## The abuse of adolescents in extra-familial settings: it's all in the interplay

Malik and Sara were abused in their schools, neighbourhood settings and on online platforms – by their peers or adults who were not directly connected to their families. In this regard their abuse was extra-familial. From sexual harassment at school, physical abuse in their romantic relationships, coercion into drugs trafficking, through to grooming online and sexual exploitation by criminal groups operating in local neighbourhoods, young people experience a range of risks in extra-familial contexts during adolescence (Ashurst &

McAlinden, 2015; Barter, 2009; Beckett, et al., 2013; Lefevre, et al., 2017; Turner, et al., 2019). When these issues emerge these contexts are ones in which young people's welfare, wellbeing and freedoms are compromised; to address how/why this happens we need to understand this process.

Variance in both the norms of social fields and their weight of influence combine to colour the extra-familial dynamics of abuse in adolescence. It is not simply that criminal exploitation, teenage relationship abuse, sexual harassment between peers, or serious youth violence occur in extra-familial contexts. It is that: (a) the nature of these abuses are informed by the rules of extra-familial contexts; (b) the rules of extra-familial contexts do not always align to those within families; (c) the social norms of families often fail to penetrate extra-familial settings; and (d) the norms of extra-familial contexts can penetrate, and undermine, familial norms – resulting in conflict between parents, young people, communities and professionals.

And in the midst of this collision young people have been trying to resolve situations themselves. During adolescence our increasing desire for self-autonomy means we often try to work things out on our own. This coupled with a struggle to comprehend long-term consequences, positive associations with feelings of risk, and the intense emotions we are often experiencing – can result in attempts at problem-solving going awry. The decision to carry a knife to school can be a young person's attempt at protecting themselves while travelling on a bus route or walking through a park where they believe they could be threatened or attacked. A young person's decision to start selling drugs for local dealers has occurred in the context of their own exclusion of school and their inability to see other viable options for making an income in a world where money matters. Their decision to continue to sell drugs even after being arrested is also informed by the threat that their home will be fire-bombed or their younger sibling attacked if they don't make up the money they lost when their drugs were confiscated at the point of arrest.

Such patterns have not only been documented for young people who believe their lives, or the lives of their families, are in danger. A fear of social isolation has, for some young people, been the contextual norm motivating their decision-making. During interviews with my colleagues in 2016–2017[3] young people in seven UK schools stated that they wouldn't intervene if they witnessed sexual harassment at school as they didn't want people to turn on them. They wouldn't speak to a teacher as they didn't want to be seen as a snitch and risk being ostracized from their peers. It wasn't that they didn't recognise the harmful consequences of sexual harassment. It was rather that they didn't think the risks involved with seeking help were worth it. And the impact of this: school environments in which sexual harassment went unchallenged. A matter that hadn't gone unnoticed by staff when they reflected on whether young people would go to teachers if they were concerned about sexual harassment in school: 'There's no appetite for that, no whistleblowing appetite at all. Zero' (Firmin, 2019:8).

For all of the above, safety, support and belonging to ones' family would not guard against social isolation at school, threats from criminal gangs, and a lack of educational inclusion nor employment opportunity. Instead these contextual norms – the rules which influence the actions that will provide status or could result in risk – inform the decisions that young people make. When you sit with cases such as Sara's and Malik's, and see their lives reflected in international research, one thing is clear. These young people experienced abuse. When we place those experiences of abuse in context it helps us to see and understand why this abuse may have been hidden in plain sight for so long.

The abuse is often happening in contexts where we – adults – don't believe young people need to be. If it was associated to their homes that might be different. As Lloyd found in her study comparing professional responses to sexual abuse within and outside of families:

> The spaces that sexually exploited girls inhabit outside the home are understood by the social workers as not being physically boundaried and thus they are understood to have more freedom about whether or not to enter into those spaces, unlike girls sexually abused in the private space of home.
>
> (Lloyd, 2019:9)

We understand that to a certain extent young people need to be in their homes, and are dependent on their families. So if they are then abused by their families – those responsible for keeping them safe – then it is right that the state sees this as abuse and intervenes. It is much harder to adopt this position when young people are abused by their peers – or when abuse happens on the high street or in the park. People might think – 'well you shouldn't have been hanging around there' or 'why don't you just make new friends'.

Much of these narratives fail to recognise the social rules at play in those contexts, the weight they can have over young people's decisions and the immobilising effect of harmful social norms, peer influence and fear.

This lack of understanding appears more acute still when it applies to young people who have abused others. Our inability to recognise choices as constrained, coerced or limited is often at the forefront of this mental block. 'You made the choice, you deal with the consequences'. Or even more confusing – if you are going to do adult things then expect to be punished as one; as it abuse is some form of adulting. There is nothing adult about causing harm to another human being – there is a lot that is wrong about it, but that applies whatever our age. Putting these annoyances to the side, a central need to place choice, as well as abuse, into context is evident by the account summarised in this chapter. This is not to say that we excuse, justify or ignore the actions of young people who have abused others. We must recognise this behaviour has harmful and unacceptable. However, when we place that behaviour in context it allows us to see how those young people who abused Malik had also been victimised themselves – in different contexts – and to prevent such an incident occurring again (or to have intervened sooner) the harmful relationships and contexts those young people were navigating also warranted attention.

Seeing Malik, Sara and even Connor, as young people in need of support is one thing – being able to respond at the intersection of extra-familial contexts and adolescent development is another matter entirely; a matter which is the focus of the following chapter. In England the government acknowledged child sexual exploitation as a form of abuse (and not 'child prostitution') in 2001. Safeguarding guidance was issued for young people affected by gang violence in 2010. Inquiries, case reviews and public reports have called for welfare responses to teenage relationship abuse and harmful sexual behaviour amongst young people (Barter, 2009; Criminal Justice Joint Inspection, 2013; Jay, 2014). In various ways the situations described in this chapter have been recognised as causing significant harm to the well-being of young people for over a decade in England. Why then have statutory systems continued to struggle with mounting a consistently effective response?

To appreciate why Contextual Safeguarding has developed, it is important to understand two things: the first is the contextual nature of extra-familial abuse (detailed in the present chapter). The second is the child and family focus of child protection systems that have been mobilised to respond to such abuse since 2010. In one sense Contextual Safeguarding is about responding to the place where extra-familial contexts and the dynamics of adolescence meet; in another sense it is about resolving the clash that emerged when policy-makers charged child protection services with responding to a form of abuse it was never designed to address.

## Notes

1   See Chapter 4 for full theoretical framework for this book.
2   While beyond the scope of this book we also need to note that the influence that peers have on individual decision-making is thought to vary around the world – with the patterns identified thus far particularly evident in the United Kingdom, North America, Australia and some European countries (Warr, 2002).
3   See Firmin, C., Lloyd, J. & Walker, J. (2019). *Beyond referrals: Levers for addressing harmful sexual behaviours between students at school in England.*

# 3   A flawed equation

## A systemic gap

In 2017 the BBC aired a three-part drama documenting how children's services, the police, sexual health, and other services as well as families reacted to the sexual exploitation of children in Rochdale – a town in the North of England. It was May, and I was thanking my lucky stars for catch-up TV as the first episode aired. I was pacing a dark corridor trying to settle my eight-week-old baby in a sling. He had silent reflux and so struggled to sleep lying flat for the first four months of his life – and I in turn functioned on little to no sleep so he could rest on me. That night I had been desperate to watch the programme, but he had other plans. So as he fussed, wriggled, and enjoyed being snug on his mum instead of in his crib, I 'watched' the first show via the twitter reaction it received which set my phone ablaze. As I digested the cumulative outrage expressed by the shows' 8.24 million viewers I was transported back to being sat alone, at a desk, reviewing Sara's case. Members of the public reacted to their television sets as I had to those box files. They were angered to be point of incredulity. How could it be possible for a social worker to react to clear evidence of sexual exploitation by stating:

> If I can speak to that from a social services point of view; unless abuse is taking place within the family, it's not something we'd get involved in
> (*Three Girls*, 2017)

They must have got it wrong. This was clearly abuse. But according to the professionals involved in this case, as in Sara's, the sexual exploitation of these three girls and countless others was not occurring in their families; and this meant there was little that children's social care could do to respond.

Much of how the press reported on cases of sexual exploitation in Northern towns from 2010 onwards was built on an idea that services failed to act because those who perpetrated the abuse in this case were primarily of Pakistani heritage (Norfolk, 2011; Reid, 2010). The overriding message in these stories was that so-called community sensitivity had meant that when it came to child sexual exploitation, people from ethnic minority communities were under-policed – completely counter to the way many have found them to be over-policed for a myriad of crimes (El-Enany & Bruce-Jone,

2015). Academics and activists alike have criticised the racialisation of the system failure that was documented in responses to the sexual exploitation of children in Northern towns. As Professor Ella Cockbain has eloquently stated:

> The image of the Asian groomer has proved a seductive and enduring one, yet, as this article has demonstrated, the idea of a uniquely Asian crime threat is ill founded, misleading and dangerous. The construction of grooming as a distinct offence and a racial crime threat has been shown to lie on insubstantial foundations: misconceptions, anecdote, opinion and the deliberate manipulation of limited statistics of dubious provenance. Nonetheless, the greatest tension in responding to all this arises from the identification of Asians as the second-largest racial group among suspects of various forms of CSE in two major national studies, greatly overrepresented relative to the general population … Asians, like whites or blacks, do not commit CSE offences because they are Asian, white or black. This lazy, circular logic, verging on quasigeneticism, would label every Asian adult equally a groomer-in-waiting and fails to address the immediate precipitates of CSE, such as ready access to children and low levels of formal or informal surveillance to constrain deviant behaviour … . Nor should talking about race mean shifting full responsibility for CSE onto Britain's Asian population in a way that conveniently absolves the indigenous majority from addressing the involvement of their own. Child sexual exploitation is not an 'Asian problem', it is everybody's problem.
>
> (Cockbain, 2013:30)

The reality is that many of the professionals who were tasked with protecting children from abuse didn't see those three girls in Rochdale as needing protection. They were working in a wider system that sustained that mind-set. It was a system that looked to those three girls as the source of their own exploitation: their 'poor choices' got them into that situation and making better choices would get them out of it. The system didn't look to those who were abusing them, or the situations and contexts in which they accessed children – in this case take away shops and taxis – as a potential focus of assessment and intervention. As the Chief Prosecutor in *Three Girls* admitted in a discussion with a journalist who questioned the delay in getting the case to court:

- Why did the CPS drop the case? Was there an issue around the ethnicity of the perpetrators?
- There was an issue around the witness, not the perpetrators. What happened is that, initially, a CPS lawyer formed the view that the witness would not be credible. That's why the case didn't progress to court. I came here last year and I reversed that decision. I looked at it afresh and I formed a different view. That she was absolutely credible (*Three Girls*, 2017).

Hearing this statement on prime time television was music to my ears. The words electrified my sleep deprived mind and immediately triggered a memory of an email I had read during a case review of a 13-year-old young woman, Sabrina.[1] It was a prosecutor who, like in the cases in Rochdale, had decided not to proceed with charges following allegations of sexual exploitation despite evidence. She stated that:

[We] would be asking the jury to "make a decision between two conflicting versions that may be of equal merit"… Witnesses to physical assaults refused to give evidence … [there are] inconsistencies in [her] account – going to retrieve [bus pass] then this changes to going to retrieve mobile phone … Sabrina goes to a bedroom without question … Issues regarding credibility as she admits to lying about an incident to a youth offending service worker and blaming someone else for an assault … [she] willingly went to the house … voluntarily gone to meet him and consented, albeit unwillingly, to full vaginal sex … it does portray her as a person who is prepared to consent to sex albeit grudgingly … [robbery offences on her record] – these are offences of dishonesty … [her social media] contains four references that she is sexually aware and they are written in a bragging tone, not one of sorrow or anger … [she] did not voluntarily go to the police with her allegation and was spoken to following a disclosure from another victim … Sabrina admits to carrying weapons and drugs for the boys involved for fear of retribution … The case cannot process to charge due to lack of evidence. There is no evidence that sex took place. Parts of her evidence raise questions (and if this case were to proceed, I would ask for those questions to be put to her). Surrounding evidence of violence cannot be used. She has credibility issues. The defendants do not make any admissions.

(Email from a prosecutor in response to allegations made by Sabrina when she was 13 years old that she had been repeatedly raped by other young people when she was 12 years old)

(Firmin, 2015:250–251)

How do her words make you feel?

When I first read them I cried. I guess in many ways I reacted to this email, in 2013, how members of the British public did when watching *Three Girls* four years later. I was part way through my doctoral research (referenced in the previous chapter), working my way through box files full of paperwork that detailed how social workers, police officers, health professionals, teachers, and others had responded to nine cases of peer abuse in England. Written in an email in 2011, these words were confronting, clear, and some might think callous. I sat back and desperately reached for answers to explain how a person, whose job it was to prosecute those who commit crimes, could take this view of a child who has been abused? Not only that, but how could this position be supported, or at least ineffectively challenged, by the wider institutions with whom she was working? This was not just her opinion on how to respond to a child – 'Sabrina' – who was raped by other young people, on more than one occasion, when she was 12 years old. The system maintained this position. The police were unable to charge and the investigation ceased. The social worker supporting her gradually stepped back and then closed the case as Sabrina lost faith in adults to protect her and shut down.

During the case review process I spoke to one of the investigating officers who had worked on Sabrina's case. They explained to me that despite being horrified when the prosecutor emailed through their decision, they felt there was little they could do to affect a different outcome in the case. They were sure, with every fibre of their being, that Sabrina had been abused. They were equally clear – as were many of the professionals in the *Three Girls* show, that there was little more they could have done to protect her.

In many ways the question I asked in this case – how on earth could this have been the response – pertained to one of the children in *Three Girls* who was found to be pregnant by one of the men who had abused her, when she was 13 years old? How could abuse of this kind ever be framed as 'consensual' – legally, socially, or ethically? How can a child protection system – a partnership of professionals tasked with safeguarding the welfare of children – fail to act in the face of such evidence?

I could follow the media position of 2011 and the right-wing groups who jumped on their bandwagon and argue that the system failed due to an institutionalised sensitivity towards British Pakistani communities and an unwillingness to police them: but alas, child protection systems appeared equally paralysed across cases I have reviewed, despite the varied heritage of those perpetrating the abuse.

I could single out the prosecutor in the case of Sabrina or the social worker in the case of the three girls in Rochdale – making a series of arguments about their professional competency – or even basic knowledge about the legal definition of consent which was notably absent – to explain why children were let down by these few bad apples in a wider system that generally functions effectively. But doing so would offer little explanation for why Professor Alexis Jay found similar attitudes in her inquiry into sexual exploitation in the Northern town of Rotherham (Jay, 2014); or why Nicky Hill found services struggling to protect Corey Junior Davis before he was shot and killed in the street in Newham, London (Hill, 2019). Of course everyone who comes into contact with children in the course of their work has a responsibility to keep them safe. However, one has to explore whether the system in which these individuals work actually equips them to act effectively, in order to understand/critique the decisions they made.

Therefore, in this chapter I seek to understand the poor decisions made in these cases, and many others, by shining a light on the system in which they were made. Using England as a case study, while reflecting on international child protection systems including in Europe, Northern America, and Australia, I will single out the cogs, rather than people, in child protection systems that result in states falling short in their duty to safeguard children from abuse. I will also acknowledge the steps taken over the past decade to better recognise different forms of exploitation and extra-familial harms as abuse: arguing that such progress to *recognise* exploitation as abuse has ultimately unearthed the critical systems challenges that cripple *responses*.

## Seeing and saying

In 2016, England's public transport network introduced a new campaign with the phrase: *See it. Say it. Sorted.* At the time of the campaign launch the Rail Minister, Paul Maynard MP, stated:

> We want to send a clear message to anyone threatening the security of the rail network that there are thousands of pairs of eyes and ears ready to report any potential threat to BTP and rail staff who are ready to respond to these reports
>
> (British Transport Police, 2016)

Tannoy announcements and posters featuring this same slogan are now the wallpaper of my daily commute. They suggest that all we need to do is to look out for things that might worry us, and if we see such a thing, then there are a number of professionals that we can tell who are fully equipped to respond.

This same perspective has shaped much of the progress made in responding to the exploitation of children like Malik, Sara, and Sabrina over the past decade. In the wake of numerous public scandals, the media, politicians, and activists have committed to naming all manner of things that pose a risk of significant harm to our children as abuse.

From 2011 onwards, the issue of child sexual exploitation was high on the political agenda – with public outrage at the knowledge that teenage girls, like Sara, had been abused in Derby, Rochdale, Rotherham, and Oxford seemingly in plain sight of professionals who had referred to them as 'prostitutes' (Evans, 2015; Jay, 2014). At the time I was working at the national children's charity Barnardo's as their policy lead on child sexual exploitation and youth justice, and soon after was the policy advisor to the Office of the Children's Commissioner's Inquiry into sexual exploitation in groups and gangs. The newspapers were awash with statements from politicians admonishing the (in) action of social workers who had fallen short in their duties to safeguard (primarily) young women who endured years of sexual abuse. Reacting to a serious case review of responses to sexual exploitation in Oxfordshire, the then Prime Minister, David Cameron, held a summit for tackling the issue. The plans he unveiled focused, almost exclusively, on the need for improvement in professional practice. He announced a helpline for reporting bad practice;

a new joint inspection of services to tackle a 'culture of denial' in public services; and consequences, including legal sanction, for professionals who 'failed to protect' young people. Throughout this period ineffective practice was framed as the fault of individual professionals and their inability to recognise abuse; the Prime Minister's plans ought to rectify this. He stated that:

> Today, I am sending an unequivocal message that professionals who fail to protect children will be held properly accountable and council bosses who preside over such catastrophic failure will not see rewards for that failure.
>
> (Cameron, 2015)

A few years later, the BBC were reporting that 5,500 sexual assaults had occurred in UK schools (BBC, 2015). What followed was further parliamentary inquiries and calls for the government to step in on the grounds that girls rights to education were being compromised when exposed to sexual violence at school (EVAW, 2017; House of Commons, Committee, W.a.E., 2016). Schools themselves called for further support to address the issue. In a report produced by the National Education Union and UK Feminista, schoolteachers shared their concerns about the rates of sexual harassment within classrooms and corridors, as well as in their inability to respond effectively:

> In class boys talk about girls' bodies and what they 'would do to them', make female sex noises at the teachers and at girls, ask girls in class if a particular photo was them, have they got it shaved, what it looks like. Girls have cried in class several times due to abuse of intimate photos
> (National Education Union and UK Feminista, 2017:8)

And fast forward to 2017, a similar panic was brewing regarding the criminal exploitation of children. Media outlets were reporting that young people – this time primarily young men and often black young men – who had gone missing from UK cities were being found in houses riddled with drugs and money in seaside and rural towns. Charities advocating on behalf of their families stressed that these young people had been groomed or coerced, before being trafficked to move drugs via train routes or in taxis. They had been threatened with extreme violence, were fearful of drug debts, had been kidnapped, and some had been sexually exploited (APPG on runaway and missing children, 2017; Britain's Child Drug Runners, 2019; NCA, 2017). Their accounts reminded me of a young woman I had interviewed in a young offenders institution seven years prior, who explained how:

> … it was like that was my way to keep in with the boys without having to beat (have sex with) them. Like me, I'm this little Asian girl, what police is gonna think to stop me. I was running stuff from Birmingham

to London and back again for time and never got caught, even though
have a record of my own

(Firmin, 2010:57)

Like sexual exploitation in communities, and sexual violence in schools, the issue
of criminal exploitation too was quickly branded a form of child abuse by
national leaders and journalists – and enshrined as such in our public discourse.

Through all these storms of political hand-wringing, public outcry, and
policy development, the forms of harm outlined in the previous chapter were
being seen as abuse, and those with power and influence were calling it out as
such. Reminiscent of the 2017 #metoo movement to recognise sexual harassment in the film industry (Pivovarchuk, 2019), protests about sexual assault in
American college campuses (Keenan, 2015), and inquiries into the institutional
abuse of children by peers as well as adults in Australia (Royal Commission
Royal Commission into Institutional Responses to Child Sexual Abuse, 2017),
these efforts were disrupting public and political narratives about problematic
behaviour. Each time the clouds cleared, and the headlines shifted focus for
a while, young people like Malik, Sara, and Sabrina were seen more as children
who had been abused and less as young adults who had made poor lifestyle
choices.

In some respects framing these forms of harm as abuse may seem obvious. In
England, a term 'significant harm' is used to describe a threshold against which
services must act to safeguard the welfare of children. There is no formal definition of 'significant harm'; however, the Children Act 1989 provides a definition
for 'harm':

> Harm 'means ill-treatment or the impairment of health or development
> including, for example, impairment suffered from seeing or hearing the
> ill-treatment of another (e.g. domestic abuse);
>    'Development' means physical, intellectual, emotional, social or
> behavioural development;
>    'Health' means physical or mental health; and
>    'Ill-treatment' includes sexual abuse and forms of ill-treatment which
> are not physical'.

(Section 31(9) p111 of the Children Act 1989 as amended by the<br>Adoption and Children Act 2002)

It also sets parameters around which such harm might be considered
significant:

> Where the question of whether harm suffered by a child is significant
> turns on the child's health and development, his health or development
> shall be compared with that which could reasonably be expected of
> a similar child

(Section 31(10) p111 of the Act)

The harm described in the various public inquiries and high-profile cases listed at the outset of this chapter were indeed significant. Based on the definition of significant harm in England's child protection framework, it follows that the children featured in these inquiries, and in the cases I reviewed, had been abused.

But beyond the black and white clarity of policy documents is the messy grey place of application – also known as real life. The statutory definition of significant harm is not the barometer by which societies – or the public – understand abuse.

As painfully articulated by the prosecutor featured earlier in this chapter, it is the action taken by the child who is harmed, and how such action is perceived, that provides a lens through which abuse is seen. If societies focus on the 'choice' that Sara made to walk alongside the boys who raped her, then she doesn't appear to be abused. These are people who are 'old enough' to make decisions for themselves. They are not the vulnerable under-fives who have no control over the people they spend their time with (i.e. Lloyd, 2019). It is Sara's choice, rather than the conditions in which she made that choice, which are seen. Seeing the choice can then blind us to abuse.

The seemingly visible gains of money, status, friendship, phones, clothing, and so on that young people sometimes receive from those who exploit them further blur our vision. We focus on what young people appear to be 'getting' rather than what they lose, or have taken from them, in the process of abuse (Eaton & Holmes, 2017; Firmin, 2010; Hudeck, 2018; Pearce, 2013).

And to make matters worse these are young people who sometimes cause harm to others, commit crimes, or go against the advice of their parents, teachers, and others around them (Beckett, et al., 2013; Firmin, 2010; Pitts, 2013).

For all of the reasons above, the shifting public and political awareness to see these experiences as harmful has been significant. So too has been the further step to name sexual exploitation, criminal exploitation, and the threat of youth violence as forms of abuse. In this sense, a range of social actors have taken steps to increase theirs and others ability to *see* harm as abuse and to *say* it is so.

The UK government has taken it a step further and adopted the whole mantra from the aforementioned public transport campaign. In the wake of the inquiries and media reports outlined earlier in this chapter, the initial response of the government was to call on professionals or other adults to phone children's social care should they be concerned about the welfare of children (BBC, 2015; Community Care, 2015).

> Our statutory guidance is crystal clear that anyone who has concerns about pupils' welfare should refer to local authorities or the police if a crime is committed, and all schools must act swiftly on allegations (Government response to BBC investigation into sexual assaults in UK schools)
>
> (BBC, 2015)

As far as they were concerned there was a child protection system in place – and those who ran that system were ready to respond to these concerns. The blockage to responses had been the inability of professionals to see exploitation and other forms of extra-familial harm as abuse. Now that everyone's vision had improved, the professional response would be more effective than it had been in previous cases. In other words, once everyone knew what they were looking for, i.e. 'saw it', recognised it as abuse and called it that, i.e. 'said it', social workers, police officers, and others would 'sort it'. By taking this position, the government signalled that there was a child protection system ready to respond to cases of exploitation, just like the British Transport Police was poised and ready to disrupt potential acts of terror.

## Not quite sorted

Their calculation was as follows. Services are struggling to respond to exploitation, peer abuse, youth violence, and so on because they don't see it as abuse. There is a child protection system, and wider safeguarding partnerships, established in England to respond to the abuse of children. If these social actors recognise these forms of harm as abuse they will respond as such (Figure 3.1).

There was a flaw in this calculation.

The child protection system, as it operates in 2019, is based on the Children Act 1989 and 2004. As Bliston (2006), Hanson and Holmes (2014), Hallett, et al. (2019), and many others have detailed, this is a legislative framework for a system to safeguard children whose parents were failing to protect them or causing them harm. It was therefore, abuse + parenting, and not abuse in and of itself, that resulted in action being taken by children's social care. The association between abuse/significant harm, parenting, and the grounds upon which the state should intervene is evident throughout various stages of the child protection system in England. A child and their family or parents can be 'referred' into children's social care for support. When assessing a child's needs, a social worker will make

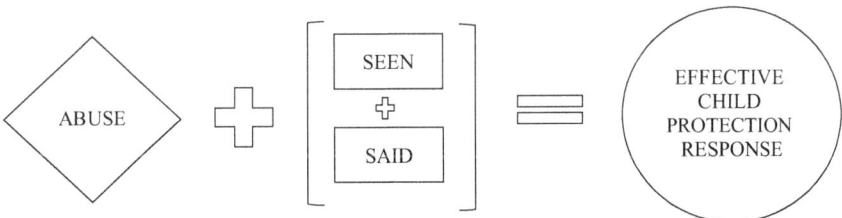

*Figure 3.1* Seen, Said, and Sorted Diagram

contact with a child's parents, and also gather information about a child and their family from other agencies (such as health services and schools), in order to assess their welfare. The assessment conducted is often referred to as a child and family assessment and the framework which guides that process pays particular attention to the capacity of parents to meet a child's needs and keep them safe (Figure 3.2). Should the assessment result in the development of a statutory investigation (Section 47 of the Children Act 1989) and a statutory plan (child protection plan), this process is built to:

- Ensure the child is safe from harm and prevent them from suffering further harm
- Promote the child's health and development.
- **Support the family and wider family members to safeguard and promote the welfare of their child,** provided it is in the best interests of the child (bold added by author) (HM Government, 2018:48).

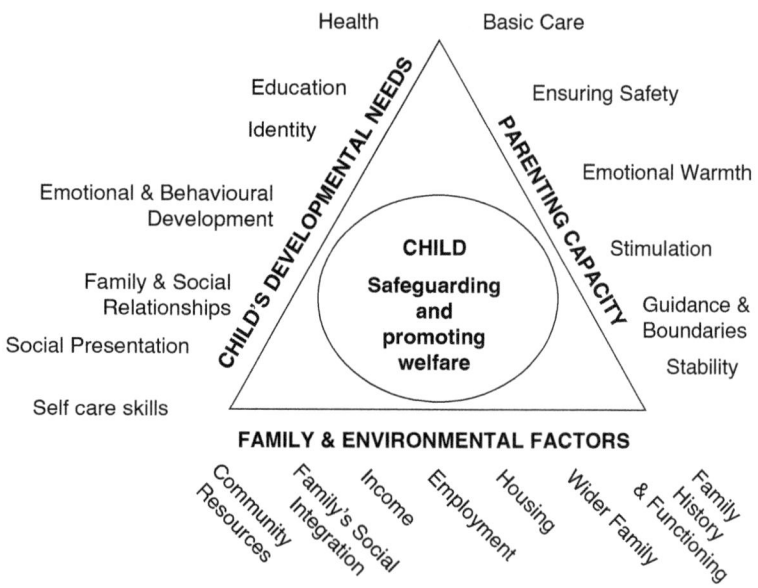

*Figure 3.2* Child and Family Assessment Triangle

The matter of attribution becomes increasingly important should children's services decide to initiate legal proceedings to place a child under the care of a local authority (the state) or under the supervision of the state. At this point the legislation requires that a court must be satisfied that:

a) The child concerned is suffering, or is likely to suffer, significant harm; **and**
b) The harm, or likelihood of harm, is **attributable to** –

  (i) **The care given to the child**, or likely to be given to him if the order were not made, not being what it would be reasonable to expect a parent to give to him; **or**
  (ii) The child's being **beyond parental control** (Section 31, Children Act 1989 – bold added by author).

As state intervention increases, so does the requirement that the harm experienced by a child is, in some way, *attributable* to actions taken by their parents or caregivers. Evidence of abuse alone is insufficient grounds to intervene.

The legislative framing of abuse as attributable to parenting, and the grounds for state intervention being in turn associated to this, is not unique to England. In many countries around the world 'child abuse' is defined as that which is perpetrated by a parent or caregiver (Gilbert, et al., 2011; Merkel-Holguin, et al., 2019). In Germany, France, the United States, Australia, and Canada, amongst other European or Anglophone nations, the policy or legislative framework which defines, and governs, child protection processes and parameters sets this tone. The Australian Institute of Health and Welfare defines sexual abuse as 'any act by a person having the care of a child that exposes the child to, or involves the child in, sexual processes ...' (Oates, 2019, p. 13); in France social services will commence an 'administrative intervention' where they have deemed 'a situation of danger is possible considering the situation of the child in his or her family setting' (Bolter & Seraphin, 2019, p. 79), and Dutch child protection systems are described as mobilising when either parents are culpable of abusing their children or on the grounds of 'capacity' to parent (Lopez, et al., 2019).

Beyond definitions of abuse, the target of such systems further reinforces a family-focus approach to child protection. For the most part, both punitive interventions and offers of support programmes are delivered to families; with the view that improved parenting will result in improved protection (Gilbert, et al., 2011; Lopez, et al., 2019), the limitations of which have been lamented by social work scholars for some time (see Rogowoski, 2012 for a summary – to be discussed further in Chapter 4). As such, regardless of whether wider systems adopt a family support style response to child abuse, take a more interventionist child protection stance or have an emerging child focused orientation to the delivery of services (Gilbert, et al., 2011), they all appear largely wedded to framing abuse through the lens of family. The variable philosophy of these systems do offer some opportunities to explore abuse through a broader lens (to be explored later in this book), but this does not negate their primary intention.

Back in 2010, Rowena Fong and Jodi Berger Cardoso noted this inconsistency with regards to child welfare responses to child sexual exploitation in the United

States. They argued that despite legislation which acknowledged the sexual exploitation and trafficking of children as abuse

> due to eligibility restrictions not all of these forms of sexual abuse fall under the jurisdiction of the public child welfare system. For child protect-ive services to become involved with the case, the perpetrator of sexual abuse needs to be responsible for the care and custody of the child.
>
> (Fong & Cardoso, 2010:313)

Nearly 10 years on this challenge, it appears, remains unresolved in many countries around the world, with responses to extra-familial harm sitting largely with voluntary and community organisations rather than via state oversight.

In some countries, therefore, the definition of abuse is itself intertwined with parenting. In England, a broader definition of abuse is employed – via the definition of significant harm – that can include extra-familial harm as in the United States; but the legislative and practice frameworks built around that definition narrow the lens to parenting. In all countries in question, states look to parents and families as the primary line of defence against abuse. The state intervenes to protect children from abuse when their families aren't able to do so. Furthermore, the system frames intervention as being with the family – rather than with the abuse – building the capacity of the family to be more protective or mitigating their harmful behaviours. The real life equation for responding to abuse therefore looked more like the one as showed in Figure 3.3.

And this equation simply doesn't work in many cases of extra-familial abuse– where the primary risk of harm is not a child's parents, or where the harm their child is experiencing can't be attributed to them (Hill, 2019; Hudeck, 2018; Lloyd & Firmin, 2020; PACE, 2020; Shuker, 2017). In these cases – like Sabrina, Mark, Sara, and the *Three Girls* – there is a 'computer says no' or 'cannot compute' response. The resultant vacuum is one in which despite *seeing* exploitation as abuse, and *saying* that it is abuse, the abuse cannot be, and is not, '*sorted*'. Across my team's research programme (detailed in Chapters 2, 5, and 9) the outputs from this malfunction are identified in three primary response pathways.

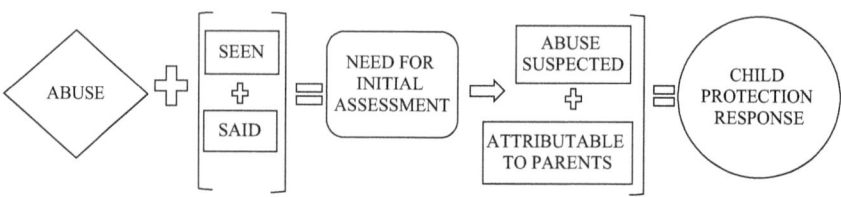

*Figure 3.3* Seen, Said, and Sorted Version 2

Response Pathway 1: No Further Action or voluntary 1:1 engagement with the young person

In these cases, parents are assessed as doing all they can to support a child who despite these efforts continues to be criminally exploited by adults in their community, is being sexually harassed at school, or has been groomed via an online gaming platform. Children in these situations may be at risk of significant harm. However, the practitioner assessing their case recognises that the parents are not the source of that harm and so questions the extent to which a social work plan with the parents can affect positive change for the child. Instead the social worker closes the case and may in some cases refer the child for further support from a specialist exploitation service or the youth service. These services may support the child through mentoring, lessons on healthy relationships, consequential thinking, and so on as means to increasing safety.

There are many potential benefits in this route. It rightly recognises that in some cases the parents cannot be a child's primary source of protection from extra-familial harm when they are not the primary source of the risk. Furthermore, this approach has the potential to work with the increased desire for autonomy that young people display during adolescence; focusing on working with the agency they want to exert as a route to safety. Most importantly, much of this work offers a young person a relationship with an adult – both within professional and familial settings. Young people have routinely identified that trusted relationships with adults who care about them are an important source of support (Lewing, et al., 2018) and this approach can sometimes provide this. Due to these potential benefits, the limitations of this work do not sit with the work itself, but the context in which such work takes place.

Firstly, if Response Pathway 1 is the *sole* action taken in a case of exploitation, then the young person becomes the focus of the plan: changing their behaviour – and importantly their choices – through education and support is situated as the route to risk reduction. Such an approach can facilitate the very victim-blaming narratives alluded to throughout this chapter – implying that if you can change the child, rather than the situation that they are in, then the abuse will cease.

Secondly, the decision to remove social work oversight in these cases can signal to a wider partnership that such exploitation is not a child protection issue despite being a form of abuse. Partner organisations, such as schools, have reported wanting these cases to be progressed by social care but have been told that they do not reach a 'threshold' for a statutory plan (ITV News, 2018; Lloyd & Firmin, 2020). In these cases, schools may believe a child's life is at risk (due to youth violence for example) but as parents are fully supportive and do not pose a risk, the referral into social care does not proceed. Such decision-making raises fundamental questions about who should step in if a child is being abused outside of the family – who should coordinate a plan if social care do not?

And finally, solely working with a young person affected by exploitation independently of the peer relationships, school, or neighbourhood settings in which they are being abused fails to disrupt the source of harm. If the source of harm were parents they would feature in a plan to increase safety – however when the source of harm is adults or peers in extra-familial settings, the individual young person is the source of the plan rather than the situation they are in. This creates a risk that the abusive situation will persist, and threaten the welfare of other young people connected to the same peer group, school, or community space.

> Response Pathway 2: Statutory Plan focused on parenting as a source of protection

In Response Pathway 2, young people who are being exploited or at risk of other forms of extra-familial harm are placed on statutory social work plans. The decision-making in these cases can be split into two broad camps that share a similar sum.

In camp one, a child is referred into children's services because someone is concerned that they are being exploited. An initial assessment indicates that (a) the child is being exploited, (b) their parents/carers are struggling to protect them from this abuse, and (c) their struggle to do so is due to domestic abuse at home, or a parent who is addicted to alcohol or drugs, or a parent who is not home often as they are working three jobs to cover the rent, or a parent with a history of poor interactions with statutory services and therefore is unwillingly to seek help from them on this occasion and report their child missing, and so on. In short, the assessment finds that there is a problem at home for this child, as well as exploitation beyond the family's front door, and for this reason the case is progressed to a social work plan.

In camp two, a child is also referred into children's services because someone is concerned that they are being exploited. However, in this case the initial assessment doesn't surface any concerns about parenting and finds that the parents are doing all they can to keep their child safe. Unlike Response Pathway 1, the practitioner taking Pathway 2 still recommends that a social work plan is developed for this child because the evidence suggests they are at risk of significant harm despite parental intervention. This process has been evident in a number of local areas following the national outcry that social workers did not intervene in places such as Rochdale and Rotherham. Cases that previously would have resulted in a service following Response Pathway 1, now follow Response Pathway 2: especially in areas where a strategic decision has been made that all children who are being exploited must have an allocated social worker who has oversight of their case.

Whether a family is in camp one or camp two of this pathway, however, the sum of the process remains the same. A plan is developed for the child and family to reduce the risk of extra-familial harm faced by the child. In camp one that plan often focuses on the evident concerns the assessment has found – such as requiring mum to leave an abusive partner or requiring parents to reduce their alcohol consumption etc. The plan focuses on whatever the parenting concern is and an assumption is made that addressing risks within the family will mitigate risk external to family. If no familial difficulties are evident, however, the plan may feature the offer of a parenting class to further build a parents' capacity to set and enforce boundaries for their child, and through this process stop their child from spending time with the people who are exploiting them.

There are two main benefits to following Pathway 2. The first is that it provides a multi-agency partnership with route to recognise that (a) this child is being abused, (b) children's services are concerned, and (c) they will coordinate a response from partners. It therefore maintains, rather than pushes against, the public narrative that exploitation is abuse and state services must sort it when they see it.

Secondly, it speaks to the evidenced relationship between risks and adversities experienced by families and the increased vulnerability of young people in those families to exploitation in community contexts. As noted in Chapter 2, while any child can be exploited, or come to harm, in extra-familial settings it is widely recognised that a young person who has been exposed to violence in earlier childhood, has experienced familial abuse, or has a fractured relationship with their parents may be particularly vulnerable to grooming and other forms of harm with which this book is concerned (Catch 22, 2013; Ewell Foster, et al., 2017; Hallett, et al., 2019; Hanson, 2016). Research into adolescent development has also suggested that parents with previously close and stable relationships with their children might be better equipped to push against negative peer influence during adolescence, than parents who try to repair or build those relationships during the adolescent period (Coleman, 2011). All parents might experience an increase in peer influence while their children are teenagers, but secure relationships provide a more solid foundation for parents to mount an effective counter offer to negative peer influence.

As such, building the protective capacity of families is an important mechanism for buffering the reach of extra-familial risks. However, there are multiple difficulties with this approach. Firstly, if exploitation is already established, then removing the risks of domestic abuse or neglect within a family will not impact the drug debt owed by their child. Until that threat to their safety is addressed and their community is a safe place for them to be, the risk of exploitation will remain in place even if the family becomes safer. Secondly, for parents where there is no evidence that they could do more to protect their children, social work intervention can be experienced as isolating, judgemental, and damaging (Catch 22, 2013; Hudeck, 2018; PACE, 2020; Shuker, 2017). Parents have reported feeling blamed by professionals for their child being groomed. Some have felt that professionals have looked for a problem in their family, or with their parenting, to explain the issue at hand, rather than considering that the abuse of their child may not be linked to their parenting ability. Given the frameworks upon which child protection systems are built (outlined previously and explored throughout this book), this focus is somewhat unsurprising.

Finally, this response pathway focuses professional attention on parents and arguably away from the primary source of harm in cases of extra-familial abuse. In some respects this is understandable. Societal and political pressure to respond to exploitation as abuse, coupled with a system designed to focus on parenting and risks caused by parents when responding to abuse, creates organisational conditions and cultures favourable to Pathway 2 – as will be explored in further chapters throughout this book. Work with families is what social workers have been trained to do – and if they are required to lead a response to exploitation then they may go to where they think they are best placed to affect change – families. However, a push back from parents who feel judged and unsupported, coupled with a growing realisation that a statutory plan can't create safety for a context in which it has no reach, has raised significant questions about the efficacy of this response pathway (Firmin, 2017; Hallett, 2017; Scott & Botcherby, 2017).

> Response Pathway 3: Relocation

What do you do if the choices of a child and the protective capacity of their parents are being constrained by the community or school they are in? The answer in many cases has been to move that child – and sometimes their family – away from the context in which they have been exploited (Ellis, 2018; Firmin, 2019; Hudeck, 2018; Shuker, 2017). When professionals take this approach, they demonstrate that the risk of harm is significant, acknowledge that work with parents will be insufficient at reducing risks, and confirm that should the situation persist 1:1 work with the child is unlikely to yield safety.

However, this third Response Pathway, that is relocation, also comes with multiple challenges. Firstly, the above achievements are made by disrupting a young person, rather than the abusive situation they are in. As such the abusive situation remains, which may pose a risk to multiple other young people also spending time in that locality or peer group (APPG on runaway and missing children, 2017; Hickle & Roe-Sepowitz, 2018; Shuker, 2013). Analysis of cases I had reviewed across multiple studies also demonstrated that relocation was primarily motivated by a desire to secure the physical safety of a young person, but often undermined their psychological and relational safety (Firmin, 2019). As such young people often return to the places they have been moved away from – to visit family, friends or to feel a sense of belonging. While embedded in children's services departments I have heard about young people hanging about outside a school they have been excluded from, as they still want to be there and see their friends – despite being the risks that they will be violently attacked by other young people who are looking for them.

So vexed have we been by this 'wicked problem' that in late 2018 my team secured funding to conduct a three-year grant to study the rate, cost, and impact of relocations in response to extra-familial harm. At the point of writing this book, we had surveyed 13 local areas to capture a snapshot of the number of young people they moved away from home in a one-month period, when faced with risks of extra-familial harm. The results, so far, have been staggering. Areas had up to 45 young people living away from their home local authority who were at risk of extra-familial harm in September 2019; whereas others had no children living out of their local authority having made a conscious decision not to do this. We will continue to explore this variance, but initial follow-up interviews with participating sites have already told us two things. Firstly, when relocations are used, it can be as a last resort when a young person is in crisis and it isn't clear how they can be kept safe in the area where they live. And, secondly, that little is known about the efficacy of these actions, despite their significant financial cost and the conditions in which they might increase safety compared to those where they might exacerbate risk.

## The (II) logic model of child protection and extra-familial abuse

In many ways the system failures outlined in the *Three Girls* drama and outlined at the start of this chapter feel illogical. How could people get it so wrong – how could they let children down so badly? However, in this chapter I have provided an account of child protection systems which demonstrates that while responses we have witnessed are jarring, upsetting, and in many respects unacceptable, they are also logically aligned to legislative frameworks.

The failed responses to young people and families have followed a system logic. Children's services departments have gradually recognised the limitations of this equation; in response they have developed more varied and nuanced approaches to work around child protection system, or append approaches to it, that grapple with the challenges that contemporary and extra-familial harms present to child protection systems (Firmin, et al., 2019b; Hanson & Holmes, 2015; Holmes, 2018; Ofsted, 2018). In 2019 the President of the Association of Directors of Children's Services, Rachel Dickinson, stated that:

> The Children Act 1989 received royal assent 30 years ago. I want to use my year as President to celebrate the successes of the Act and to

**reflect upon the modern challenges facing children, families, social work and children's services that the Act simply could not have foreseen** … The lived experiences of some of our children and families today, wherever they live across the country, are not a million miles away from Billy's. The South Yorkshire of today has new opportunities, having been transformed with new industries, but are they opportunities for Billy?

Billy experiences domestic and emotional abuse, largely at the hands of his older brother Jud. The hunger pangs in Billy's belly drive him to steal. **Are we sure that our response today would be to consider Billy or Jud as children first and criminals second? I think we are much, much better at understanding the impacts of adverse early childhood experiences but I do worry that the Billy's and Jud's of today face multiple risk of exploitation in this digital age – complex, contextual, extra-familial risks in addition to** their poverty, uncertain job prospects, narrow school curricular, less money in schools for pastoral care, less money in wider services to intervene early to provide support, more fixed term exclusions from schools. I do worry that despite our schools being truly aspirational they are hampered from delivering that aspiration to all children, to children like Billy. So what of their life chances? (Bold added by author)

(Dickinson, 2019)

The thoughts in this speech reflect the increasing concern shared by many professionals working at the front line of England's child protection systems. They are working to a legislative framework that was designed by people who never had in mind the abuse that Sabrina, Malik, or Sara endured. While awareness raising has got us to a place where we are better equipped to see them – like Billy who is referred to in this exert – as children first, it isn't clear that this alone will resolve the shortcomings of system design and intention. The additional, contextual, and more complex extra-familial harms that young people face, in addition to those that were in mind in 1989, require further attention than this.

And it is such attention to which this book contributes – by firstly summarising the consequences of a mismatch between the intention behind England's child protection system and its current use. In a bid to recognise extra-familial harm as a child protection issue, children's services departments have broadly followed three overarching response pathways when cases of extra-familial harm meet child protection systems in England. There is a risk that a similar set of pathways would emerge in any cultural context in which child protection systems, designed to respond to abuse within families, are required to safeguard young people from exploitation and other forms of abuse within community, peer, and other extra-familial settings (Fong & Cardoso, 2010; Merkel-Holguin, et al., 2019). A recognition of this risk as systemic, rather an individual, is important. Too often case reviews and inquiries have focused on a lack of information sharing about, or recognition of, abuse lying at the heart of

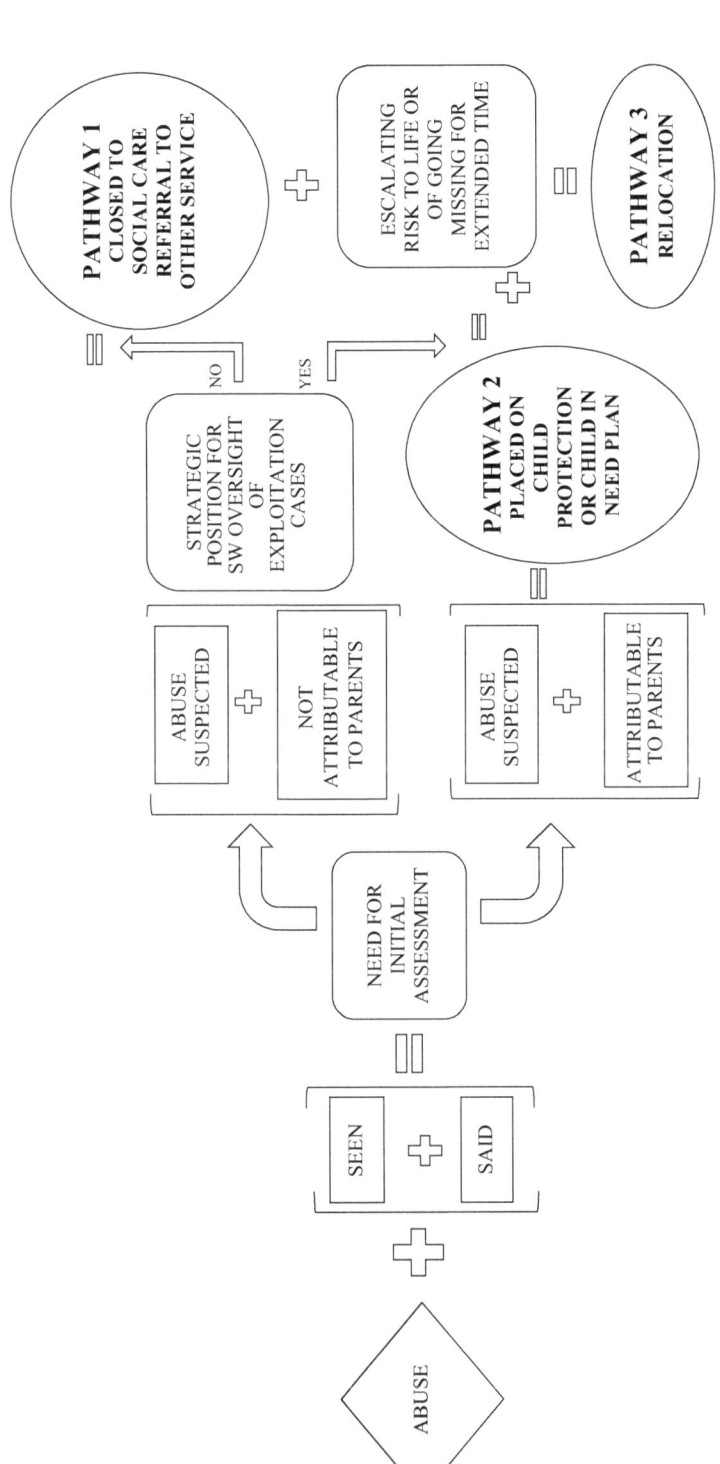

*Figure 3.4* Seen, Said, and Three Pathways Model

ineffective practice: if only we had been made aware that exploitation was abuse, or seen it as abuse, we would have responded differently. The evidence in this chapter suggests that even when abuse is seen and stated the systems' ability to sort, it is shoe-horned into three dominant response pathways – none of which creates the safety and protection our children deserve (Figure 3.4).

There are of course exceptions to these three response pathways. Our work in areas around the country has surfaced numerous examples of alternative practice. These alternatives have informed the development of Contextual Safeguarding and will be detailed in remaining three parts of this book. They are excluded from the equations thus far as they have developed in spite of, rather than due to, the dominant system structure, national guidance, and legislative frameworks. The three dominant pathways explored thus far are in keeping with the overarching reach of child protection systems – assessment of, and case work with, individuals to change their behaviour as a route to achieving safety. Those responses that work against or around this narrative move us beyond work with individuals and towards a contextual response (Firmin, et al., 2019b; Holmes, 2018).

There is a mounting practical and conceptual critique of individualised child protection systems to which these identified pathways adhere; some of which hark back to 40-year-old debates about radical social work, social justice in social work and community or patched-based provision. Contextual Safeguarding speaks to, and is built upon, many of these debates that provide a home for challenging the above logic model. In the following chapter I detail these traditions, including community and systemic approaches to social work, ecological, and situational theories of crime and human development, and calls for social models of child protection and crime reduction. Presenting them within a broader theoretical framework from Pierre Bourdieu, I will build a hybrid set of specs through which we can see a different way of safeguarding children abused beyond their homes.

### Note

1   Name changed to protect identity of the young person.

# 4   A contextual lens

Podcasts often accompany my morning routine. From the uplifting Oprah Winfrey's *Super Soul Sunday,* to the classic *Desert Island Discs* by Radio 4 and the gritty suspense of *Serial,* they set the tone to my day, and often remind me that the work I do speaks to, and is deeply connected with, varying facets of the world around me. At first I introduced them to my mornings to punctuate a point in the day that was truly my own – where I could mindfully and peacefully get ready in the bathroom before my two-year old came hurtling towards me, packed lunches were hurriedly put together and my husband and I reeled of the days to-do list. But within a couple of weeks I quickly came to realise that wherever I looked people were talking about social contexts – and how we needed to understand them – to make sense of the world and our place within it.

One morning in 2018, I was listening to an episode of *Super Soul Sunday* where Michelle Obama was discussing her book '*Becoming*'. In conversation with Oprah she stated:

> I was taught to understand this about my grandfather very early on so that I could have the compassion and the empathy for him because as I said what's important in this book is context and I try to put context in this book because everybody's life has context – there's context – you can't judge them body or know somebody just based on their actions you have to know the full breadth of their experience's and my parents taught me that.
>
> (Michelle Obama, Super Soul Sunday Recording, 2018)

Two of the most powerful women in the world sat together and aired to millions of people that 'there's context'. They know it: somehow, somewhere, a lot of us understand that the experiences of Sabrina, Sara, and Malik are all about context too. The challenge is that our systems, services, and policy frameworks often fail to apply that contextual lens to some of the very issues that require it – and instead opt for a single vision dissection of deviant, troubled, and problematic individuals that blur our sight and render our services ineffective.

In this chapter I take the logical but somewhat ineffective child protection processes outlined in the previous chapter and begin to visualise how they might look through the eyes of Michelle Obama. To achieve this I will take building blocks from sociology, social work, criminology, and health to build a hybrid conceptual framework – also known as a set of glasses – through which we can start to see how effective responses to extra-familial harm might look. Such an approach speaks far more to the realities that Sabrina, Sara, and Malik faced when they were abused in their schools and communities than the systems they encountered. In doing so, we get one step closer to creating systems that reflect what people need, rather than fixating on creating people that fit our systems.

## Let's get sociological

If there is one thing I love about sociology it is that it gives you the tools to get deep about things many of us intuitively know to be true. What do we actually mean when we say that context matters? Why does it matter? How does it matter? How do we understand why it matters? What are the nuts and bolts of that mattering and what might that mean to everything else we do with our lives, services, and structures?

I stumbled across French sociologist Pierre Bourdieu thanks to one of my doctoral supervisor, John Pitts, and stuck with him in large part thanks to Australian criminologist Anastasia Powell. The year was 2012 and I was trying to organise my thoughts. I had spent the previous five years in various jobs speaking to young people affected by violence. Right back in 2008 – running focus groups in a London radio station studio and way before I had reviewed any case files – a young person had said to me

> It depends on where you're brought up as well, your environment … cos like you could have a good family background or whatever and your mum could have brought you up well, but it like depends on where you live as well cos when you step outside of your home, there's other people there, school's a big influence, and you get peer pressured in to doing bare stupidness

(Firmin, 2008:29)

This message had been reiterated in interview after interview, and their reverberations came flooding back when I spent the first year of my doctorate reviewing all that international research had to offer on the issue of violence and abuse during adolescence (much of which I outlined in chapter 2 of this book). Numerous academics had said what young people had told me – peer groups, schools, communities are relevant to how we experience abuse. But why?

I was sat in the canteen of my university with John Pitts and he casually said to me, 'well it's like Bourdieu said you know it's all about the Social Field'. John often weaves theory into chats like most of us do commentary about the morning news – matter of fact, with ease and as if we all do (or should) know that this has been said. And so started my journey into the world of Pierre Bourdieu, the concepts of Social Field, Habitus, Capital and Symbolic Violence, and to unpicking the 'mattering' of context.

Fully embracing my inner geek, I snapped up every Bourdieu publication I could get my hands on – *Masculine Domination, In Other Words, An Invitation to Reflexive Sociology* – and then sat with my head in those same hands as I struggled to make much sense of anything he was saying. I found the text dense, floral, and without enough punctuation – but mostly I struggled to think how I could apply it to the reality of young people's lives. It definitely didn't feel as accessible as John Pitts had made it seem.

So it was to my great relief to find a special issue on Bourdieu published in 2008 by the Journal of Sociology. It featured a collection of papers by scholars who had applied Bourdieu's ideas to all manner of social and political questions: one of these scholars was Anastasia Powell. She had used Bourdieu to understand why context mattered to young adults in Australia as they navigated their sexual relationships and interactions. Through Bourdieu's ideas, Powell was able to identify and articulate the (unwritten) rules of sexual contact between participants in her study. According to Powell, young adults were operating in a context in which a number of social rules informed the decisions they made – such as if you don't have sex with your partner when they want you to they might end the relationship. The dominance of such rules, and the way that people adopted them, was evident in how young adults talked about negotiating their relationships. It also resulted in young women, in particular, having sex on occasions when they didn't want to, and young men sometimes knowing that this might be the case – raising significant questions about consent. According to Powell, educating people about healthy relationships was an insufficient route to behaviour change. The underlying rules to which those behaviours conformed needed to be rewritten. The context in which these sexual relationships formed needed to change:

> Yet the persistence of entrenched social 'rules' in the field of sexual encounters – which are reproduced across social institutions such as education and the family – means that the extent to which this alternative discourse alone represents a significant challenge to the existing rules of the game, and how easily it is likely to be taken up at the level of everyday practice, remains questionable. Questionable, that is, without concurrent interventions in the reproduction of gender across various social institutions. Preventing sexual violence is a community-wide issue and it requires a community-wide response
>
> (Powell, 2008:180)

Even though she was writing in a different country, and looking at a different age group of people, with one reading I understood exactly what Powell meant, and how this might make sense of the ideas I was grappling with. Did the contexts of peers, schools and neighbourhoods, and the institutions that influence those contexts, matter to young people's experiences of abuse because the social rules of those contexts facilitated, enabled, or failed to challenge the behaviours they experienced?

With this accessible introduction at the forefront of my mind, I returned to my mountain of Bourdieu texts and to my delight could now understand what he meant when he said

> Because the foundation of symbolic violence lies not in mystified consciousness that only need to be enlightened but in dispositions attuned to the structure of domination of which they are the produce, the relation of complicity that the victims of symbolic domination grant to the dominant can only be broke through a radical transformation of the social conditions of production of the dispositions that lead the dominated to take the point of view of the dominant on the dominant themselves.
>
> (Bourdieu, 2001:41–42)

Like Powell, Bourdieu was arguing that you couldn't rely solely on educating behaviour change within contexts or institutions that promoted opposing social rules. When spending time in contexts, individuals embody the rules of that space and act accordingly – and the more they spend time in that space, the more they become accustomed to those rules even when those rules were to their detriment. As such the rules with which people are engaged require attention – and radical transformation – and not just their response to those rules, to support a process of behaviour change.

In terms of abuse and extra-familial harm therefore, it is not enough to teach young people about the signs of a healthy relationship or the risks of carrying weapons – if they spend time in contexts in which the dominant social rules oppose the content of such lessons. The rules of those contexts require attention.

Bourdieu employed key concepts to help us build, understand, and better communicate this position. He talked about:

1. Social Fields – the identified fields or social rules in any given context.
2. Habitus your feel for the rules at play in social fields.
3. Capital – the economic (financial), social (networks and relationships), and cultural (understanding of the cultural cues and characteristics relevant to the field) resources you could draw upon in any given Social Field which combined gave you're your symbolic capital.
4. Symbolic Violence – your engagement with the rules of a social field which may ultimately be to your detriment but through which your engagement maintains/sustains your position in that social field and thereby gives you status.

For Powell, this meant that young adults were spending time in social fields where unwritten rules of sexual engagement were in operation – these included rules about needing to have sex with your partner whenever they wanted to avoid being dumped. Young women demonstrated their feel for these rules by making up other excuses to avoid having sex – such as saying that they had a headache, rather than state that they didn't want to have sex in a given situation. Others described not physically interacting with their partners during the build-up to sex hoping that this would signal that they didn't want to have sex without them having to say it out loud. However, young men also described rules of the social field which meant that unless someone actively said 'no' to sexual advances then they had consented. In this context, young women and young men were drawing upon their cultural capital (their knowledge of these various social cues) to navigate sexual interactions. However, in the process, young women in particular experienced symbolic violence as they were exposed to abusive and non-consensual acts that were sustained by the wider rules of sexual interaction in the contexts they were in. Despite physically demonstrating that they didn't want to have sex, a wider requirement for them to say no meant that sexual interactions were happening that they did not want. For Powell, therefore, the social rule that required a clear 'no' for sex to stop needed to be changed to a rule that required an enthusiastic 'yes' from all parties to know sex was wanted and consented to. Powell's position speaks to similar attempts to change the social rules of sexual interaction in college campuses in America (Keenan, 2015), which have sparked political and ethical debates about sex, consent, the law – and what the rules of sexual interaction should be.

Back in the world of extra-familial harm and young people in England these concepts provide a helpful framework for articulating why context matters for how abuse happens and how we might respond. Returning to Sara and Malik's stories from chapter 2 will help illustrate this point.

Sara and Malik were spending time in social fields in which a suite of unwritten rules was associated to the abuse they endured. Through their time in these contexts, they embodied these rules and through their behaviour demonstrated that they understood them. They did not seek help from professionals – their cultural capital (understanding of what happened to people who 'snitched' in their social field) meant they believed they may be more unsafe if adults intervened. They aligned themselves with those who were harming them, hoping that this may build some social capital that could disrupt the harmful situations they were in. Both of these decisions utilised the capital that they had while simultaneously maintaining a status quo in their parks, schools, and high streets that was ultimately to their detriment: they experienced symbolic violence through this process.

The logic models of child protection presented in the previous chapter do not seek to change the rules of abusive social fields. Rather they seek to change the way that children and families interact with, or navigate, abusive social fields – and where required, build up their capacity (or capital) to make 'safer choices' in unsafe spaces. The closest the system gets to recognition of the limits of such an approach is to move individual children and families out of social fields in which they have encountered harm. However, such activity disrupts people but maintains and can even strengthen the rules of abusive social fields. If our only option is to move children away – we send a message to others that remain that there is little we can do about what goes on here, the best we can do is to get you away from it. The rules are there – and they are there to stay.

And yet Bourdieu was no way nearly as deterministic as this approach to practice (Lawler, 2004). Although he didn't write about social work or child protection explicitly, he was keen to emphasise a 'reflexive' relationship between social fields and the individuals who spent time in them. Social fields informed individual behaviour, but individual behaviour informed the rules at play within a social field. So when Sara walked alongside the boys who raped her, the rules of that social field were maintained. Who could have disrupted this process – was it only Sara? There were a number of other social actors around Sara who could have stepped in. For starters, the professionals who listened to her accounts and decided to focus on her, instead of the situation she was in, also maintained the rules of that social field. If they had responded differently, recognised that the risk sat in Sara's peer group, school, and park, and not in her, they could have taken the first steps to unsettling the social rules that dominated Sara's life.

As noted in chapter 2, Jenny Pearce has called for a social rather than medical model of consent to be employed: in doing so she recognised the different dynamics of social fields which could interplay with young people's decisions (and their capacity to exercise choice freely). Social fields coloured by poverty, violence, or attitudes that normalised abuse within peer relationships would all negatively inform sexual encounters. In the cases of Sara, Malik, Sabrina, children exploited from Rotherham, Oxford, CJ who was shot in Newham and so on, these dynamics, to varying extents, were evident – as was what Pearce refers to as 'condoned consent'. Young people made decisions that maintained the status quo of abusive social fields in parallel to professional decision-making which shut down, or failed to offer, rule-changing intervention.

And so, with Bourdieu's glasses on we can see, at varying levels, why context matters to how we understand abuse. Context creates the social conditions for abuse. Young people's decisions in abusive contexts reflect the capital they have access to in which they can make the 'best' out of terrible, and sometimes life threatening, situation. A lack of attention to context in how we respond to abuse shuts down routes to protection. We are all (potential) social actors in the contexts of abuse.

And so Bourdieu's concepts help us to understand not only why context matters to how we understand abuse but also provides a lens through which we can see the limitations of mainstream responses. But Bourdieu didn't write about child protection – and he rarely wrote about young people's experiences of violence. To make best use of his theory, it needs to be coupled with attempts that have already been made to build context in (a) social work practices and (b) responses to crime and violence. The remainder of this chapter will do just that.

## Ecological, social justice, and systemic practice: when social work and community meet

While Bourdieu didn't write about child protection, a handful of social work scholars have noted the value of his ideas for advancing social and contextual approaches to social work (Frost & Hogget, 2008; Gray & Webb, 2013). Their commentary sits within a broader field of debate about the reach, intention, and ethics of child protection systems, and the role of social workers within them. Since the 1970s, there has been mounting critique of social work practice and child protection systems that locate risk in individuals rather than in the social situations and networks those individuals navigate (Featherstone, et al., 2018; Fenton, 2016; Gray & Webb, 2013; Parton, 2014; Woodward & Mackay, 2012). These scholars promote systems that target the social conditions in which families live; noting a relationship between a lack of community support and health services, and exposure to crime and unemployment, as inextricably linked with child abuse.

Resolving the relationship between structure, human agency, and social work has been debated for over 30 years (Fenton, 2016; Ferguson & Woodward, 2009; Gray & Webb, 2013), in a range of traditions. From theories for creating 'structural social work' in the United States (Wood & Tully, 2006), through to traditions of critical social work in Australia (Allan, et al., 2009), and social theories of child protection in England (Featherstone, et al., 2018), they continue to the present day. While the individual positions have varied over time, they are all broadly concerned with locating individual experiences within wider structures, and importantly see social work as playing a role in addressing these broader structural issues that undermine or negatively affect human welfare. For them, social work is about changing the material and social conditions which enable harm. And yet, as Gray and Webb summarised, in practice this has been a struggle as 'mainstream'; social work has become 'largely about maintenance, fixing and engineering, and not social change' (2013:9).

Far from being a conceptual dream, their positions are built on empirical evidence of the value of community-driven support and community social work promoted from the 1970s onwards. In the 1990s, a community approach to safeguarding was trialled on the Canklow Estate in Rotherham, England (Eastham, 1990). The project involved patch-based community social workers collectively supporting children who were in receipt of support from children's social care across the estate. Their work involved building community support such as helping to establish community and youth groups, and create opportunities for adult education classes. The project was evaluated over a five-year period and appeared to demonstrably reduce the numbers of children on that estate who were open to children's social care. Reflecting on this project and a series of others, Jack and Gill (2010) have noted the evidenced value of community development methods for safeguarding the welfare of multiple young people and families. They argued that this collective evidence base pointed to three building blocks for effective 'community-orientated safeguarding: 'developing a culture of listening to children and adults; recognising and supporting the safeguarding activities of local people; and promoting partnership approaches to extending local provision' (2010:88), such as schools, youth clubs, and sports provisions.

Across the arguments made by Jack and Gill, various examples were provided of young people's friendships, as well as family relationships, being nurtured. This position was echoed by Rogowoski (2012) who lamented responses to sexual exploitation that focused on increasing parental supervision of young people and their need to set stringent boundaries. He queried why there was, at that time, a reluctance to work with groups of young people who were being exploited together, identifying ways that they could act as a positive means of support for each other, given that many of these experiences went beyond the control of their parents. Such arguments are supported by wider ecological theories of human development, that situate individuals within families, and families within wider social systems – and note the need to engage with these systems to achieve safety (Bronfrenbrenner, 1979; Ungar, 2002).

Authors who promote ecological ways of working, however, also note their limited take-up in child protection systems around the world. For example, landmark inquiries that have informed the design of England's child protection system largely excluded 'meaningful consideration of community-level factors' that may have informed these incidents (Jack & Gill, 2010:86). A recognition that trafficking and sexual exploitation are forms of child abuse did not result in child welfare services supporting young people affected by those issues in the United States (Fong & Cardoso, 2010). Managerialist approaches to child protection have required an individualised focus (Gilbert, et al., 2011; Rogowoski, 2012). The many countries that have moved in this direction since the 1980s effectively screened the bigger picture, in which individual cases sit, out of the social work view (Parton, 2014). Consequentially, even approaches that strive to be anti-oppressive can focus 'more on changing the language, behaviour and attitude of individuals than the materials conditions of their lives' (Pease, 2013:23)

Countries whose approach is more aligned to supporting, rather than policing, families arguably have a greater opportunity to recognise the value of community engagement in abuse prevention (Gilbert, et al., 2011). The impact of poverty, unemployment, or mental illness may be better attended to in these systems, and so offer some routes to engaging with more community-driven support. Furthermore, in many countries voluntary support is provided by community organisations, rather than via statutory social work services, increasing the potential for sustained and embedded support for families in need (Merkel-Holguin, et al., 2019). And yet, because all of these systems also largely frame abuse as something that happens within families, the support offered doesn't appear to reach the extra-familial contexts of abuse with which this book is concerned (something to be explored further in Part 4).

In many respects arguments to put the 'social' back into social work, and see families in context, calls into question the separation of extra-familial and intra-familial abuse upon which this book is premised. Many critiques of individualised child protection systems are primarily concerned with how such systems respond to abuse that has been constructed as 'intra-familial' – neglect, maltreatment, physical abuse – when they are informed by extra-familial factors – such as poverty, unemployment, crime within neighbourhoods, housing, and so on. Other scholars have noted that these contextual factors appear to be particularly relevant to neglect, emotional, and physical abuse, but appear less associated to familial sexual abuse (Wilkins, et al., 2019). They contend that sexual abuse occurs across boundaries of poverty and class, while being informed by wider structural issues such as sexism and racism.

Putting these debates about abuse within families to one side, these traditions of social work research support the development of contextual responses to extra-familial harm; providing a home for resolving the challenges in chapters 3 and 4 of this book. With the exception of a few examples noted above, however, much of this research field has focused on the general functioning of child protection systems, and how they individualise harm that occurs within a family setting. In this book I build upon, and extend this argument, alongside Rogowoski (2012) and Jack and Gill (2010), to consider abuse experienced outside of the family setting – extending the potential reach of child protection in the process.

## Beyond social work – contextual offers from policing and health

Proponents of community-based social work are not alone in recognising the relationship between context and harm. Schools of policing, particularly those informed by environmental criminology, and public health advocates also have much to offer in pursuit of a contextual response to children like Sara and Malik.

Victim, Offender, Location, Theme – also referred to as the VOLT model, has underpinned many a police investigation. It informs the problem analysis triangle used to understand crime trends (victim, offender, location) and has supported the development of problem-solving policing in the United Kingdom and the United States amongst other countries (Eck & Spelman, 1987). Police practice guidance in England and Wales references the problem analysis triangle as a way of utilising the 'SARA' model to police a range of harms or crime-related issues (College of Policing, 2013). SARA is an acronym for the following four stages of an approach to crime prevention or intervention:

- Stage 1: Scanning – using data to identify/profile the issue in an area.
- Stage 2: Analysis – using the available information to understand the nature of the issue, including any trends in terms of time, location, and probable causes.
- Stage 3: Response – building a response to the issue.
- Stage 4: Assessment – reviewing the effectiveness of the response.

Such an approach is built on the idea that in order to prevent harm we have to know who it might affect, who might perpetrate it, where it might happen, and what time of day it might occur. In the case of Sabrina – she was vulnerable, those who harmed her were the boys she met in her school and local community, they abused her in the park and at bus stops, and most of this occurred in the 15:30–18:30 window after school.

Understanding crime – and wider forms of harm – in this way has resulted in attempts to 'design out' opportunities for harm, or disrupt the situations which make harm/crime more likely. Post office desks were re-designed to include screens in a bid to reduce weapon-enabled robberies (including the use of bats and hammers). In the years that followed post office robberies decreased significantly (even though there was a slight increase in the use of firearms, robberies overall reduced) (Ekblom, 1988). In the 1970s, the reduction in levels of carbon monoxide emitted in gas cookers reduced the extent to which gas ovens could be used to assist suicide. Suicide by gassing dramatically decreased as a result of this change – but more notable was the fact that suicide by other means didn't appear to increase. By taking carbon monoxide out of the equation, scholars argued that there had been an actual reduction in suicides (Clarke & Mayhew, 1988).

Around the world, criminologists and psychologists have been able to locate an increased likelihood of crime to an area – and even to a street – based on the physical, cultural, and social dynamics of the place. In 1989, scholars spatially examined over 300,000 police calls for service in a US city over a 12-month period to 'hot spot' street addresses associated with crime. They found that 3% of 'places' were responsible for 50% of calls to police. These results led them to argue that:

> If future crime is six times more predictable by the address of the occurrence than by the identity of the offender, why aren't we doing more about it? Why aren't we thinking more about wheredunit, rather than just whodunit?
>
> (Sherman, 1995:36–37)

Scholars in Australia and the United Kingdom, including Richard Wortley and Stephen Smallbone (2006), Stephen Smallbone and Susan Rayment-McHugh (2013), and Ella Cockbain (2013, 2018), have applied a situational lens to sexual abuse, exploitation, and trafficking. Smallbone and colleagues, explored two locations in Queensland, Australia affected by peer-sexual abuse. They identified familial, peer, school, and neighbourhood dynamics that were associated with peer-sexual abuse and set about developing a suite of interventions to change the dynamics of those contexts. Their work was led by a team of clinical psychologists who, alongside local community members, worked well beyond the traditional 1:1 therapeutic interventions with individuals who had displayed abusive behaviours to build guardianship and safety in the social contexts associated to those behaviours (Smallbone, et al., 2013). I visited their project in 2017 and was particularly impressed with the partnership they had developed with local rubbish collectors. The clinical psychologists in the project informed me that each morning when they come into work they literally had a report on rubbish collected the night before in their inbox. Rubbish collectors would tell them where they had collected evidence of alcohol consumption, drug use, or sexual activity (condoms), so that outreach work could be tasked into those locations. It also gave the psychologists an indication if the parks they have previously worked in were still locations in which harmful behaviours were occurring or if the lack of rubbish suggested they may have ceased.

In a similar vein to situational crime prevention, public health responses to harm reduction have looked at harm thematically, rather than individually. The potential relevance of public health approaches in responding to child abuse has been explored in England since the early 2000s, when the then government broadened the 'safeguarding' agenda to focus on abuse prevention (France & Utting, 2005; Parton, 2014). Looking across populations, risk factors associated with different types of harm were identified, and prevention efforts sought to target those identified factors as a means of reducing the likelihood of abuse.

In the 2000s, this thinking was particularly used to shape responses to young people's experiences of street-based, and serious youth, violence. In Scotland, a Violence Reduction Unit (VRU) was established in 2005 to address the significantly high rates of fatal violence taking place in the city of Glasgow (Violence Reduction Unit, 2015). The VRU adopted a public health approach and sought to address the causes of violence – framing it as a 'disease' across communities. Over a 10-year period, it undertook a range of activities including significant amounts of work to address alcohol addiction which they found underpinned much of the violence they were witnessing. Interventions associated to domestic abuse also featured, as did bystander intervention programmes rolled out across schools to build student and staff capacity to challenge harmful attitudes associated to violence. The extent to which the work undertaken by the VRU is primarily responsible for reductions in violence in Glasgow has been debated (McVie, et al., 2018), and further data are required to resolve these tensions. Nonetheless, the apparent impact of the VRU in Scotland has led to funding for the creation of VRUs around England in 2019, through funding from Central Government and the London Mayor's Office of Policing and Crime.

An interest in addressing harm, such as exploitation and youth violence, by understanding and intervening with the causes has informed policy in England for decades. In the early 2000s, David Farrington's work to identify risk factors associated with youth crime in England (Farrington, 2000) was used to shape early intervention services for young people thought to be 'on the cusp' on harm. The past decade has witnessed a snowballing interest in 'adverse childhood experiences', and their impact on the latter vulnerability of young people and adults (Ellis & Dietz, 2017; Spratt, et al., 2019): the suggestion being that early experiences of adversity can result in trauma, which in turn can increase the prevalence of other harms being experienced in later life – such as substance misuse and mental illness.

Seeking to understand the causes of harm by looking across populations for trends, should, in many respects leverage a more contextual response. They have the potential to offer a birds-eye view of how different forms of harm are public issues shared by many, rather than private troubles of a deviant few. And yet, caution and criticism in how public health approaches are applied are abound. Population-wide trends have been individually interpreted. For example, living in a marginalised or disadvantaged community has been associated to young people's experiences of youth crime. One way to interpret this could be to intervene with those living conditions, increasing inclusion and opportunity, so communities are less disadvantaged. Another way to respond to this issue would be to profile which young people live in disadvantaged communities, identify them and target them with interventions to build their resilience for living in adversity, assign them a mentor, and so on. In this latter example, population-wide knowledge is used to intervene with people – and not with the contexts in which those people live their lives. The same concern might be raised about seeking to address alcohol addiction as associated to violence: do we target the causes of alcohol addiction such as providing appropriate mental health support in communities, and identifying why alcoholism impacts violence in certain settings and less so in others – or do we solely identify people with alcohol addiction and offer them addiction treatment? As much as alcohol addiction might be linked to violence, we must also ask what social conditions are linked to alcohol addiction. Such a concern has been flagged by Nigel Parton in his overview of public health approaches to child protection (2014), in which he argued that:

> While the explanation of the risks to be addressed is often at the broader environmental level the actual preventative interventions introduced are usually at the secondary level.
>
> (2019:60)

Secondly, concerns have been raised about the use of adverse childhood experiences to understand and prevent ongoing harm. Recognising previous adversity as associated to current harm is important – and can leverage a move away from victim-blaming narratives. However, if an awareness of adverse childhood experiences across populations leads to us profiling individuals with those experiences so as to intervene with them to prevent the future harm we can end up on a slippery slope to determinism (Spratt, et al., 2019). Such calculations neglect the relationship between contexts and individual experiences, and fail to consider which relational and structural factors cushion individuals and communities against the negative future impacts of past adversities (Ellis & Dietz, 2017).

Public health, situational, and population-wide accounts of harm therefore have much to offer in developing responses to Sabrina, Sara, and Malik. They locate their experiences in a broader context; identify routes for environmental, relational, and individual intervention; and can situate (in the case of this book) extra-familial harm as a social issue, requiring a social response. Each of them alone, however, does not necessarily leverage the contextual response required in cases of Sabrina, Sara, and Malik – nor do they offer a clear roadmap for achieving such a response within a child welfare, as opposed to criminal justice, system.

## Meeting in the middle: a Contextual Safeguarding lens

On their own, each of the frameworks presented thus far has something to offer when seeking to understand and address either the reality of Sara and Malik's lives (chapter 2) or the limitations of child protection responses to extra-familial harm to date (chapter 3). When combined, they provide the building blocks of a hybrid framework for creating more effective safeguarding systems.

Bourdieu's concepts of Social Field, Capital, Habitus, and Symbolic Violence have a dual function. Primarily they provide a route to understanding how context shapes abuse in extra-familial settings, including how young people's actions inform, and are informed by, those contexts. Secondly, they offer us a way to think about what might be possible for creating social change – that all of us are potential agents in social fields, and so could affect the rules at play in them.

Theories of public health and situational responses to crime and violence offer some routes to intervening with the social rules of abusive contexts. They demonstrate that it is possible to change the nature of places or disrupt situational themes, and that this work can have an effect on individual human behaviour.

When I embarked on a journey to understand how extra-familial abuse had been addressed in the past, and how we might improve that in the future, I was primarily concerned with how children's welfare was safeguarded. I was not driven to understand abuse solely as a crime, a social phenomenon, or as a health risk. This book, therefore, asks first and foremost how do our child protection systems adapt to support children and families impacted by extra-familial harm. Associating all of this with ecological theories of social work and child development therefore is integral to the success of this project. Social and community theories of social work offer a means of responding to extra-familial abuse within child welfare systems (rather than positioning such harm as solely a health or crime issue). There is clearly an appetite and narrative within social work that sees contextual work as part of abuse prevention. If the lead agency for safeguarding the welfare of children and families has room for practices that locate safety in contexts, rather than solely in people, then there is a place for the sociological theories of Bourdieu, and the interventions of public health and situational crime prevention into extra-familial contexts, to come together.

Figure 4.1 depicts how I have brought these perspectives together to frame everything that will develop in the following three parts of this book. It illustrates that the newness in this work is not to tell you, the reader, that 'context matters' – we know this, nor is it to say we need to think about context when we respond to abuse – as this chapter has demonstrated there are many theories that have already evidenced this too. Instead the newness is what a hybrid of these approaches offer to developing child protection responses to extra-familial harm – and the contexts in which that harm occurs.

Bourdieu's social concepts provide a language for exploring and understanding the contexts (and social rules of those contexts) in which harm occurs; as well as actions of young people, their parents, and professionals as they draw upon their capital to engage in those contexts. Theories of social justice in social work provide a welfare-based organisational framework in which to hold the approach being developed; and to articulate the relationships of support between professionals, young people, and parents during responses. Both public health and situational responses to crime and violence provide a contextual language to describe abuse, and exemplars of interventions that can create contextual change. When these interventions are fused with family support and child protection systems, they can be utilised to safeguard child welfare rather than solely reduce crime.

As such, the lens through which Contextual Safeguarding can be realised broadens, or deepens, established schools of thought. Calls for social, community, or ecological models of child protection have been primarily focused on harm that occurs within households or familial relationships: the theoretical framework proposed in this book applies those questions to abuse that is largely instigated and experienced outside of familial relationships. Theoretical approaches that have contextualised community violence or abuse in young people's peer relationships are utilised in this framework – but with child protection and child welfare systems in mind, rather than health, community safety, or policing practices. Through this fusion the rules of child protection, as well as the rules of abuse, are contextualised – and potentially up for change.

As I close this part of the book, I have established that (a) context matters in cases of extra-familial abuse; (b) traditional models of child protection do not account for these contextual dynamics; and (c) there is a kaleidoscope of theoretical frameworks that can help resolve this tension. The remainder of

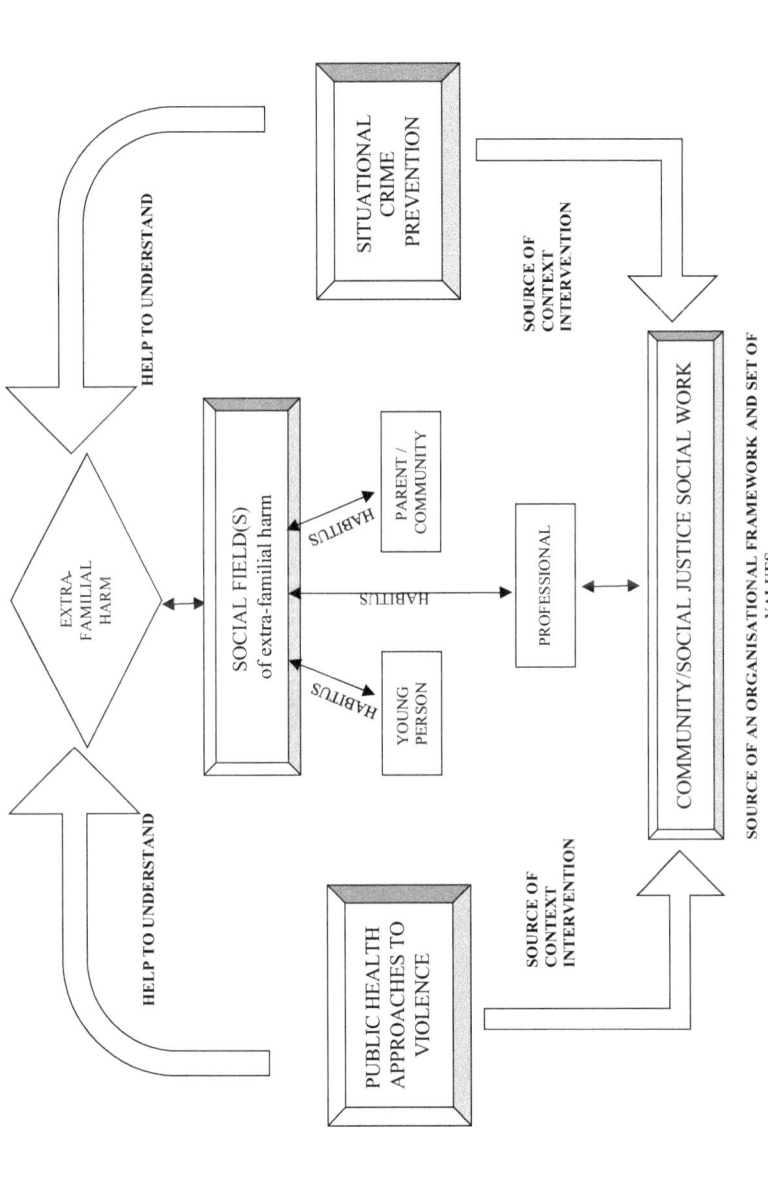

*Figure 4.1* Social Theory Foundations for Contextual Safeguarding

this book sets out a map for how we might, and are already on the road to, achieve this. In the three parts that follow I will outline the steps I have taken, alongside colleagues in the University of Bedfordshire and practitioners in England and Wales, to apply this lens and advance safeguarding systems. In doing so, we have started to build processes, approaches, resources, and most importantly communities (of practice and of places) who are re-writing the rules of what states can, and should, do to keep children safe.

# Part 2

# Establishing the building blocks for change

# 5 Crystallising ideas

## When tweaking is insufficient

By August 2013 I had a lot of questions.

I had spent two years reviewing cases of peer-on-peer abuse for my doctoral work, and had been advising a national inquiry into sexual exploitation in gangs and groups for the same length of time. I was acutely aware that extra-familial abuse was contextual (chapter 2). I was also beginning to understand the square peg that this issue presented to the round hole of child protection systems (chapter 3). But as I wrote up my thesis I was left asking:

- Were prosecutors, like the one in Sara's case, aware of how dire the situation had become and were they resolved to it or incensed by it? In other words, were practitioners aware of the system limitations they were working with – and did they recognise these as problematic?
- Was it possible to do things differently, when young people were abused in their peer groups, schools, and communities?
- Was it possible to act before such abuse occurred?
- If it was possible for practitioners to act differently (both in terms of prevention and response) what would leverage this change?
- What was preventing us from taking a different course of action?

And so I set about on a three-year journey to answer these questions. This chapter will detail the answers I gathered along the way.

### Setting off: understanding practice responses to peer-abuse in 2013

From 2013 to 2016 I based myself, and one other team member – George Curtis, in 11 parts of England; a process I then repeated in a further three areas in 2016–2017. In each area we spent time understanding how professionals were responding to peer-on-peer abuse.[1] We used a contextual lens to examine the different methods or tools practitioners used to refer concerns, assess them, plan, and then deliver a response – and the structures that managers used to support and quality assure these activities.

*Reviewing local procedures and structures*

Back in 2013 most local areas in England had developed siloed responses to different forms of extra-familial harm. For example, in the wake of public outcry related to response to child sexual exploitation (CSE) in 2010–2012 many areas set up specific strategies, procedures, and meetings to coordinate their response to this issue. Some forms of CSE were perpetrated by adults and on other occasions young people instigated this harm. Peer-on-peer abuse that was sexually exploitative was addressed through this strategic and practice framework. In other instances young people were physically harmed through acts of youth violence or weapon-enabled crime. Some of this violence was linked to, or driven by, local street gangs or organised crime groups. In response some areas had developed serious youth violence strategies, others had strategies for 'ending gang and youth violence' – informed by a national policy document of the same name around that time (Home Office, 2011). Peer-on-peer abuse that was characterised by weapon-enabled violence between young people was often managed through policies and procedures linked to an area's youth violence agenda. This response was once again distinct from abuse that young people might experience in their own romantic or intimate relationships. In 2012 the UK Government amended national guidance to acknowledge that young people (aged 16 and upwards) could experience domestic abuse.[2] National policy changes related to domestic abuse in 2012, amidst a government realisation that young people could be abused in relationships before their 18th birthday, meant that these experiences were also being incorporated into local violence against women and girls, or domestic abuse, strategies. And so on.

You can see the mess right? Far from being reserved to paperwork, issue-specific, siloed approaches filtered into multi-agency meeting structures in local areas. For every form of harm in which peer-on-peer abuse could feature, local services had established strategic and operational meetings. At the strategic level, senior managers discussed trends related to that form of harm, any training or services that were being commissioned to address that form of harm, and any barriers to practice that required attention. At the operational level, panels were meeting to discuss these 'complex' cases which often challenged their traditional safeguarding methods (as detailed in the Part 1). Lists of children currently thought to be affected by that particular issue – whether it was CSE or youth violence for example – were discussed and interventions or services allocated where further support was needed.

To disentangle this web of siloed policies, procedures, and meeting frameworks, George and I looked at them each individually and then collectively for each local area.

The content of each policy, procedure, or meeting, related to peer-on-peer abuse was analysed[3] through the lens of two questions:

1. Does this document/meeting link to, attempt to integrate with, or in any way connect to other documentation/meetings related to other forms of peer-on-peer abuse: in other words what ways does this document/meeting evidence an integrated approach to peer-on-peer abuse in the area?
2. To what extent does this document/meeting recognise/address family, peer, school, or neighbourhoods associated to peer-on-peer abuse: in other words does it propose a contextual or individualised response to peer-on-peer abuse?

Documents and meeting structures were supplemented in local areas by practice tools for assessing risk, planning interventions, and recording their success. All of these were compiled and organised into a table according to their siloes, before George and I assessed them for (a) integration (Table 5.1) and (b) recognition of extra-familial contexts.

Reviewing policy documents gave George and me our first peek through the windows of local responses to peer-on-peer abuse. Being sat in rooms where these written procedures were turned into practice (or in some respect where practice was developing ahead of, or in spite of, limited procedures) was invaluably enriching. In a bid to capture the tone, focus, outcomes, and levels of engagement in each of the meetings we observed, we used an observation log.

*Table 5.1* Organisational framework for policy reviews in local sites

| | Child sexual exploitation | Domestic abuse | Serious youth violence | Harmful sexual behaviour |
|---|---|---|---|---|
| Strategy and action plan | | | | |
| Strategic group | | | | |
| Guidance | | | | |
| Protocol | | | | |
| Multi-agency operational meeting | | | | |
| Assessment | | | | |
| Intervention plans and available interventions | | | | |
| Case management | | | | |

The log recorded: who was at the meeting; the matter discussed; the language used in meetings to describe the issue and children affected by it; the actions that were agreed and the partners that were involved. George and I also recorded our personal reflections about these meetings; anything we noted as related to the capacity of professionals in that meeting to engage with the holistic and contextual dynamics of peer abuse: factors that would restrict their capacity or enable it.

Listening to what was said, and importantly in relation to context what wasn't; agreement and disagreement, and between whom; and the significant harm that were being grappled with, shone a light on both the opportunities and challenges that lay ahead. They soaked us in real-time conversations that up until that point I had largely only read about when undertaking case reviews. I could see the eye rolls, hear the exasperated breaths, the silence that fell when people were out of ideas and the way that shoulders dropped a little and jaws loosened around a table when a child, who had been in trouble, was thought to now be safe.

Policy documents, reviews of practice tools along with all observation logs were analysed (both manually and using ICT software) to identify the extent to which they facilitated or illustrated integrated and contextual responses to peer-on-peer abuse (Table 5.2).

### Reflective workshops and targeted focus groups with practitioners

As well as observe how professionals were organising their response to peer-on-peer abuse George and I met with them, and provided them with space to reflect on the successes and challenges of their approach. We did this primarily in two ways.

*Table 5.2* Site audit data collection activities

| Years | Local authority/ site | Policies and procedures reviewed | Meetings observed | Professionals focus groups | Professionals interviewed |
|---|---|---|---|---|---|
| 2013–2016 | 1–6 Site A | 25 | 19 | N/A | 7 |
| | 7 Site B | 11 | 5 | N/A | 10 |
| | 8 Site C | 11 | 5 | N/A | 8 |
| | 9 Site D | 14 | 10 | 1 (12 attendees) | 7 |
| | 10 Site E | 32 | 10 | 1 (15 attendees) | 6 |
| | 11 Site F | 24 | 13 | 1 (17 attendees) | 8 |
| 2016–2017 | 12 Site G | 40 | 14 | 1 (3 attendees) | N/A |
| | 13 Site H | 28 | 10 | 2 (12 attendees) | N/A |
| | 14 Site I | 21 | 10 | N/A | N/A |

The first was to use semi-structured questions to run focus groups with practitioners. These groups generally comprised a mixed representation of different service areas, and participants took part in focused discussions about how their different sectors worked together in response to peer-on-peer abuse.

Secondly, George and I met with practitioners and with senior leaders to reflect on emerging findings. In these reflective workshops we would share an observation from a meeting or series of meetings, or ask questions about a specific policy document, to sense-check what we were finding and the extent to which local professionals felt it was illustrative of practices or policies more broadly. This applied to practices that struck us as highly siloed or individualised, such as calling a 14-year old who had been stabbed 'a little gangster', or initiating a child protection meeting about an unborn baby of a 16-year old who was being sexually exploited in which that 16-year old was held wholly responsible for the potential risks posed to her child. It equally applied to practices that appeared more coordinated or contextual. Examples of the latter included: ad hoc attempts to map young people's friendship groups in meetings; a proposal to intervene in a shopping centre where young people were being groomed by increasing social work and youth work presence there after school; attempts to refer whole peer groups into the youth service for a collective intervention; and analysts profiling forms of peer-on-peer abuse associated with different educational settings as a means of targeting intervention with affected schools. Each of these activities were discrete, and atypical, rather than representative of a whole service or locality response. It was important for us to understand how they had emerged, why they hadn't been mainstreamed, and any challenges that professionals could foresee should they be adopted as common practice.

George and I used information from the discussions at focus groups and workshops to fill in some of the gaps in our understanding that emerged when reviewing policies or observing meetings. These conversations also signposted where we may need to observe meetings on multiple occasions to account for potential variance in tone or focus. More generally they gave us a practice-informed way to frame our analysis and report writing – offering us an opportunity to reflect on whether practitioners were aware of the challenges/successes we were identifying; believed their responses required adaptation; and had any views as to how best enhance practice in the future.

## Switching lanes: developing contextual activities

George and I spent 6–8 months across the first 11 areas, building a picture of their current responses. The vast majority of assessment frameworks, intervention planning documents, and commissioned services they could draw upon zoned in on children and families: all the contextual knowledge displayed in those meetings faded into the background once their 'case work' commenced. Some of our work tried to bring these contexts back to the fore – by more officially and routinely recording information about locations or peers into casework documents: recording information about contexts during assessments or when referring a child to a service for support.

As noted earlier in this chapter, George and I had already encountered examples of practitioners who were initiating contextual interventions. They were working with peer and friendship groups who had been exploited when they were together. They were building relationships with security guards and store managers in shopping centres where young people were being groomed – and were getting to know the young people who hung about there to drink milkshakes after school at the same time. However, the toolbox practitioners were using didn't feature these approaches as standard practice – even in the areas where they had been identified. Instead these were examples of practitioners addressing contextual harm in spite of, or by working around, local processes rather than in accordance with them. In addition, all sites had services that engaged with peer group and community contexts – such as schools, youth services, neighbourhood policing, park wardens, housing caretakers, and community sector services. But knowledge and skills across these professional groups were rarely integrated into the design or development of plans to address extra-familial harm.

A key task, therefore, was to make contextual interventions a standard feature of a practitioner toolbox, and build the partnerships needed to design and deliver such interventions.

The wider strategic environment in which these assessments and interventions sat also needed attention. The procedures and protocols in the local toolbox required far greater integration. It wasn't clear in any site what a practitioner should do if a young woman was being physically abused by her boyfriend, of the same age, who was affected by gangs himself and had been stabbed on the high street. Let alone when that same young man had seemingly got her out of house where she, and her friend, had been taken against their will and where rape was a real possibility. Similar disjointed scenarios had emerged during meetings. The young woman in this case was initially discussed at a domestic abuse meeting, the young man had been discussed at the serious youth violence meeting, and the house had featured in other cases discussed at the sexual exploitation meeting. But in no meeting was the case and all its contextual features addressed holistically. The fact that the young man appeared to be victimised, and was perpetrating harm against a young woman he had also safeguarded, were incongruous with the structures that were drawn upon to 'hold' his case. All sites had relatively limited resources to support, and address the welfare needs of, young people suspected of abusing their peers. They also had limited provision for boys and young men more generally – both those who had abused, and/or been abused by, their peers.

We compiled what we had found into a report for each locality and presented our findings to a range of local leaders who made up the safeguarding partnership in each area. At the time every area in England had a Local Safeguarding Children's Board – established in the Children Act 2004. They featured senior representatives from local authority children's services, police forces, health services, education, community safety, probation, housing and wider council services, and voluntary and community organisations – and were chaired by an individual independent of those services. The report was presented, in person, to this group and the recommendations that we had made were discussed. We asked the safeguarding board to identify which recommendations that would like us to prioritise and pursue with local professionals over the 12–18-month period that would follow.

Each local board, in consultation with service managers and other key stakeholders, identified the activities they wanted to prioritise. In total 15 activities were agreed across the 11 sites; and they could be broadly organised into six categories (Table 5.3).

Cumulatively, these activities sought to leverage a more integrated response to peer-on-peer abuse by breaking down the siloed approaches they had developed for different forms of abuse and responding to the shared challenges that extra-familial harm presented to current working arrangements. Our work also provided practitioners and leaders with routes to more explicitly recognise and engage with peer group, school, and neighbourhood factors associated to abuse in their local area. This happened in many ways. For some practitioners it involved challenging individualised language and terminology being used in assessments, meetings, and training sessions to describe harm that was actually contextual – that is, children groomed into drug dealing being referred to as streetwise and children who were sexually exploited described as sexually active. For others it involved bringing those people and organisations who could influence extra-familial contexts into intervention planning – such as community-based groups, youth workers, and schools – rather than solely those whose primary function was to intervene with individuals and families affected by abuse, such as child and family social workers and youth offending officers.

Being involved in both the reviews of local practice and subsequent activities that practitioners developed meant I spent vast amounts of time on trains during those three years. The shires, towns, and urban boroughs that George and I were working in were spread across different parts of England. Working in these geographically distinct areas crystallised ideas that had emerged while I was reviewing cases. Despite differences in their landscapes, population demographics, and service structures these areas encountered similar challenges in mounting a response to peer-on-peer abuse. And while pursuing different activities to address those challenges, the work each site undertook led us to the same conclusion about what safeguarding systems required in their response not just to peer-on-peer abuse, but to all forms of extra-familial harm.

In the remainder of this chapter I will detail what local site work told George and I about: how practitioners felt when challenged in their response to peer-on-peer abuse; whether it was possible to respond differently; and what would leverage this change. Answering these questions didn't resolve the challenges posed in Part 1 of the book however. In the process of resolution other, and more fundamental, questions rose to the surface. Questions that

*Table 5.3* Local site activities

| Thematic category | | Activity |
|---|---|---|
| Coordinate, and where possible merge, local policies, procedures and meetings to provide a structure for an integrated response to peer-on-peer abuse specifically and/or safeguarding adolescents more generally | 1. | Arrange meetings between chairs of different multi-agency meetings to identify opportunities for information sharing across meetings and avoiding duplication |
| | 2. | Establishing an overarching safeguarding adolescents' strategic group to which issue-specific panels could report. This was seen as a stepping-stone to integrated individual panels over time |
| | 3. | Producing a briefing paper identifying and recommending ways to coordinate strategic documents, which in turn were used to inform the commissioning of new protocols and guidance safeguarding board for integrating all its documentation |
| Create opportunities for leaders, managers, and practitioners to know about, and understand, the contexts associated to peer-on-peer abuse in their local area | 4. | Reviews of cases of peer-on-peer abuse to identify the contextual dynamics of those incidents and convert them into case studies for use in training across the area (three areas) |
| | 5. | A seminar series for a group of analysts who were developing profiles of CSE and youth violence in their areas. Seminars explained datasets associated to school or community contexts that could enhance their profiling work (which to date had largely been built on data about individuals) (six areas) |
| | 6. | Coaching a team of analysts to build references to context into an existing problem profile related to peer-on-peer abuse |
| Identify and test opportunities for including consideration of peer groups, schools, and neighbourhoods when assessing incidents of, or a young person affected by, peer-on-peer abuse | 7. | Develop and pilot a form to record information about peer relationships when a young person is referred to child protection or youth offending services |
| | 8. | Identify ways in which the revised youth justice assessment can be used to reflect on peer group, school, and neighbourhood dynamics of offending |

| | | |
|---|---|---|
| Consistently involve educational providers in building a response to peer-on-peer abuse | 9. | Revise the paperwork used by schools when they refer a child to a meeting (Fair Access Panel) who they are seeking to exclude or move to another school so that any information about peer-on-peer abuse associated to the move is captured and addressed |
| | 10. | Enhance existing commitments to develop whole-school approaches to specific forms of peer-on-peer abuse by identifying methods by which they could take a more holistic approach to harm/abuse prevention (two areas) |
| Explore ways to engage voluntary and community sector organisations in the identification of, and attempts to address, contextual harm | 11. | Build training capacity in a range of organisations who can go on to train/inform community organisations in understanding the contextual dynamics of abuse and self-identify opportunities to play a role in responding |
| | 12. | Hold awareness-raising session for community organisations on the contextual dynamics of peer abuse in their local areas |
| | 13. | Examine the role of detached youth work in creating contextual safety for young people in the local area, and seek to capture the contextual impact of this work (outcomes beyond 1:1 engagement with young people) (six areas) |
| Develop responses for young people suspected of abusing peers that engage with family, peer, school, and neighbourhood dynamics that were associated with the abuse | 14. | Develop and test a framework for holding and recording meetings for young people suspected of sexually harming a peer – where the contexts associated to that behaviour feature in the discussion and can be the subject of actions |
| | 15. | Work with organisations already supporting boys and young men to identify opportunities to work with whole peer groups (rather than 1:1 work) who share harmful attitudes to gender, consent, or relationships |

I attended to further along the road to Contextual Safeguarding – and that I address in later parts of this book.

## Three years, 11 areas, what we learnt on the road to contextualised practice

The activities for each local area had been agreed. Senior leaders and local practitioners were set to work alongside George and I to change how they had been responding to peer-on-peer abuse. And despite the many differences between each area, and their plans, the wrongs we were trying to right were common across teams, services, and postcodes. Individual social workers, youth workers, and others could name the stairwells, parks, shops, transport hubs, educational settings, and even public service buildings where young people had been groomed, robbed, or assaulted. They knew their young people. Because of this they knew the bubbling friendships that might warrant concern, and which ones presented an opportunity for protection – or both. I lost count of the number of meetings I observed where the reams of paperwork and scored checklists were pushed to one side and in their place appeared a flip chart paper and box of markers. Workers dumped all that local knowledge held in their heads onto the page and in what felt like a matter of minutes they had mapped the places and connections in which individual young people were vulnerable.

But how does one translate this knowledge into actions that actually increase safety for young people? Practitioners were dipping into a toolbox that was no match for the abuses they had identified, the children affected or their parents. The activities we trialled were an initial attempt to fill that gap.

### *Practitioner reaction: engagement and exhaustion*

A mix of emotions was stirred and came to the surface as we set about implementing the agreed activities. From excitement and enthusiasm to apathy and exhaustion. From reflection and future-orientation to defensiveness and retrenchment. Enabled to disabled: to just plain stuck.

And when you think about it that makes a lot of sense.

There was much about the work we did in those early days which spoke to what practitioners already knew to be true. By bringing their knowledge of contexts and relationships to the fore, some of the activities made sense of the challenges they had hitherto faced. *I am struggling to engage this family because I'm focused on getting them to better control their child rather than on the factors that are pulling their child away from them AND the fact that I have been doing this is not because I am doing a bad job – it is because the system I work in isn't fit for purpose.* What had before felt like a 'private trouble' of that individual worker was now framed as a 'public issue' for senior leaders, legislators, policymakers, commissioners, and so on. And what's more, this same worker had a chance to shape the way forward as steps were taken to integrate and sustain their once ad-hoc, innovative responses to contextual harm. It is arguably easy to be enthusiastic when shortcomings you had attributed to your own practice can instead be associated with the system in which you deliver that practice. It is equally exciting to identify ways in which those structural barriers could be alleviated and that senior leaders who have the authority to make such changes are on board.

Some amendments to assessment tools that were trialled in local areas triggered these reactions. For example, the tools used by youth justice workers to assess young people who had committed offences already had features which could be used to record any extra-familial issues/contexts impacting a young person. Referred to as 'other controls' these sections were available to record factors outside of the young person that might impact risks of re-offending. Therefore, if a young person's offending was linked to them taking drugs, for example, and there was a local shop which was selling that young person 'legal highs', the existence of this shop – and the risk it posed to the young person – could be recorded in their assessment. Using this, a practitioner could explore which agencies might need to be involved in reducing the risk posed by that shop – such as licencing. By using the youth justice assessment in this way, practitioners could develop plans that recognised, and begun to address, the contextual characteristics of a young person's behaviour. Consequentially, workers no longer held sole responsibility for what happened in these cases – and neither did the young people they were supporting. Licencing and the local shopkeeper, in this example, also had a role to play. The 'problem' could be shared and the load carried by a broader set of shoulders.

Re-imagining the contribution that some roles/teams could make to safeguarding young people also yielded a future-oriented and reflective reaction from practitioners. Once they articulated why context mattered to how abuse was understood and responded to, they could also (a) reflect on how their role contributed to individualised practices in its current form and (b) identify how their role could be adapted to engage with or address contextual issues in the future.

This dynamic was evident in the various activities we undertook with analysts. Most sites that we were working with had allocated some resource for analysts to build a profile of the current scale, and nature, of different types of harm impacting young people. We brought together eight of these analysts from six different local areas to (a) collectively reflect on the contextual nature of their profiling work to date, and (b) identify datasets and methods that would further contextualise the profiles they produced in the future. At the start of the process, most analysts acknowledged that they built profiles on data about individuals, and produced profiles that were primarily about individuals. Through a series of workshops analysts heard about data available in education, health, transport, and community safety services, and thought about how they might use this information to build profiles about contexts, and not just people, affected by extra-familial harm.

Over the course of a year these analysts profiled patterns of peer-on-peer abuse as they related to peer networks, school contexts, and online platforms in particular – and worked with partners to plan interventions that could target these contextual dynamics of harm. For example, one analyst reviewed all cases of online forms of peer-on-peer abuse by the school of the young people affected. In doing so he identified patterns of harm within some schools that related either to specific online platforms or predominant pattern of harm. As a result, schools were able to provide parents with targeted information about any website names, phrases or apps that had been associated with forms peer-on-peer abuse that were particularly impacting their children.

Another analyst profiled different forms of online peer-on-peer abuse identified by the local authority, and identified that the predominant means of first contact between a young person and the person who had harmed them was 'meeting at school'. In 10% of cases the first contact was online rather than 'in-person', For the most part, therefore, young people personally knew people who later abused them online – they weren't 'strangers'. Knowing this was important to reviewing the relevance of education messages about online safety provided to young people up until that point, and challenged practitioner assumptions about the 'online' world being separate from the physical inter-actions young people had in schools, parks, or on high streets.

Developing contextual activities in sites, however, was far from this plain sailing most of the time. A number of activities that we commenced were met, at different points along the way, with a sense of apathy. Practitioners were often exhausted. They were well aware of how vulnerable some young people were. They had heard the details of the violence inflicted upon, and by, the young people they worked with. In some cases the threat was persistent – tick, tick, tick was the white noise in the background of many panicked meetings: meetings where the result was, *we just need to move this young person as far away from here as possible.* The work we were trying to develop required energy. It required space to think about how to do things differently, and to give those things a go in a measured and timely fashion.

On some occasions this proved too much for those we were working with. For example, work with community organisations to think about how they could integrate messages on gender, healthy relationships, and sexuality into their work with groups of young men required far more time than the project allowed. Many of these services survived on project-based funding – and this funding limited the scope of their work. Finding the capacity to build in add-itional work with young men was far from easy. In addition, there was an underlying fear that if some of this additional work commenced it could com-promise the work that was already underway. Supporting a young person to get a job felt like a more realistic goal than challenging any poor attitude that his peers held towards women and girls. The latter felt bigger than these work-ers and their projects – they were structural and beyond their reach. In other words they felt there was nothing they could do about society – they could only affect how that young person navigated that society.

### *Structural reaction: permitting and undervaluing change*

In addition to working with individual practitioners, some activities targeted strategic partnerships and structural frameworks as a means of contextualising local responses to peer-on-peer abuse. Efforts were made to merge siloed panels, amend paperwork that facilitated various meetings, and contextualise the way strategic leaders were measuring success. Through these activities we were trying to build shared objectives amongst strategic partners – and in doing so communicate to practitioners that it was possible, and permissible, to do things differently. These activities aimed to alleviate the anxiety that had built amongst some practitioners, put authorising structures around efforts to innovate, and capture the consequential impacts.

One example of this was changes made to a 'Fair Access Panel' (FAP) in one local area. FAPs operate across most local authorities in England, and are meetings to discuss children in need of an education place, and agree a placement for each child. Children discussed at FAPs include those: at risk of permanent exclusion from mainstream school; who have been permanently excluded; who are subject to managed moves between schools; and who are looked after young people being moved into the local authority and require a school place. Work across sites had shown us that children abused by, or who abused, peers at school were sometimes moved to alternative schools in response to incidents. It was important for local areas to understand the rate at which this was occurring locally, and whether the contextual dynamics underpinning incidents of peer-on-peer abuse had also been addressed.

One area agreed to revise the form that schools completed to refer to children for discussion at the FAP. The form was amended to explicitly ask whether the move was being triggered by an incident of peer-on-peer abuse, and what action the school had taken to address the impact of these issues on the wider student body (including affected peers) as a means of resolving concerns prior to, and if necessary following, any attempts to exclude. The amended form was trialled for a school term, during which time 32 referral forms were completed for consideration at the FAP. Because of improved recording in those forms it was possible to identify that over a third of the 32 cases referred to the FAP that term were related to peer-on-peer abuse. Analysis of the forms also demonstrated a noticeable improvement on the input of contextual data on some forms, for example, a park was mentioned in relation to risk experienced by one young person and a young man who was subject to a referral was identified as a 'leader' within his peer group when accounting for peer dynamics that he had experienced; information that informed ongoing profiling of risk and protection in the local area, as well as shaping ongoing support and intervention for young people. Increased and explicit recording of contextual information also evidenced the lack of provision available for young men displaying harmful sexual behaviours as a means of earlier intervention – informing strategic leaders of gaps in service provision to meet an identified need. Reflecting on this process the Head of Learning Access within the site commented that

> [the work undertaken had enabled] the local authority to create a data matrix of need around peer on peer abuse. The Learning Access Service has revised its procedures around the use of the following interventions: Pre FAP professionals' meetings, transition meetings between schools and restorative justice techniques to support pupils who have been identified as at risk to these issues.
>
> Firmin et al. 2016:29

Such work put structures in place where contextual concerns could be identified and contextual impact could be valued. It not only demonstrated that it was possible to do things differently, but it also evidenced why this was valuable.

Communicating the value of contextual work often required dedicated thought and action from local partners. In one site we wanted to build on contextual work identified during the initial audit of existing practice. Social workers, youth workers, and specialist sexual exploitation workers had been routinely visiting a shopping centre where concerns had been raised about adults approaching, and trying to groom, young people. The workers attended the shopping centre regularly – on the days and times associated to the concerns about grooming. Over time young people in the shopping centre got to know the workers, some came over to speak to them and in time expected to see them there. The practitioners also got to know local store managers, sales assistants, and security guards. These people became the eyes and ears for those practitioners when they couldn't be there – and would look out for the welfare of young people who were hanging out in the centre after school. We wanted to support those involved in the intervention to capture its impact on their ability to safeguard young people, and communicate this to commissioners and local strategic leaders – so we reviewed the terms of reference for the project, looked at their monitoring framework and reflected on the objectives they had agreed for the work.

Despite its highly contextualised method, and identified contextual need, the intervention in the shopping centre was driven by individual objectives and valued via individual impact measures. Practitioners were going into the shopping centre to identify individual young people who were vulnerable to grooming, to engage them into accessing 1:1 support and other diversionary activities available in the youth service. Success was measured on how many young people were engaged and accessed local positive activities as a result. I couldn't believe the extent to which the contextual value of the work had been missed. Firstly, there was the fact that while practitioners were in the shopping centre young people weren't being groomed and exploited – and this created safety in that context (albeit for a time-limited period). As a result young people could continue to socialise in the shopping centre, and spend time together in a location of their choice, without being abused in the process. Secondly, by building relationships with staff in the shopping centre, practitioners had built sustainable sources of protection within the shopping centre when they weren't there. Thirdly, young people had built trusted relationships with practitioners as groups, and practitioners were able to understand those peer dynamics. These benefits were not foreseen when the interventions were being designed (and so didn't feature in their objectives), and weren't monitored retrospectively as an example of impact. A significant shift in mindset was required amongst service commissioners, service managers, and strategic leaders for contextual value to guide decision-making.

This challenge was stark in one site where we tried to introduce a 'peer-group information capture form'. The form included prompt questions for social workers and youth justice workers to ask when a child, affected by peer-on-peer abuse, was being referred into, and assessed by, statutory services. The questions related to young people's friendships, and the proposal was that the practitioner leading the assessment contacted the young person's school or youth service they were working with to ask not just about the child's family but also about their friends. In particular, asking about the quality/protective nature of those friendships, and the role the young person played with peers (for example whether they led, followed etc.). The activity was proposed to the safeguarding partnership and immediately concerns were raised about information sharing. Partners disagreed on whether information about peers could be shared during assessments, especially as this wasn't a requirement in statutory guidance for child and family assessments. As a result the site proceeded with the activity for referrals into the youth justice service (related to peer-on-peer abuse only), but not within children's services. An inability to progress the action across services was tied to it being just that – an action – rather than the influence of peer relationships being recognised and embedded across safeguarding systems in the area. Many activities that we tried to introduce relied upon a wider acknowledgement of extra-familial contexts as relevant to safeguarding systems – and this level of system change was not the initial goal of the work being undertaken.

As such, we had started to learn that it was possible to change structures, and in doing so to inform intervention design, partnership working, and how leaders communicated success. And yet, without consistency – and a shift in wider values and cultures that framed such structures – it wasn't going to be easy to embed and sustain the change we had initiated. Furthermore, a contextual fair access panel didn't contextualise the broader practices and partnerships in place in a local area – it shone a light on a need for interventions within schools but those interventions were lacking. Likewise, the work in shopping centres highlighted a need to contextualise commissioning frameworks, but didn't impact them overnight. Tweaking elements of the system – be it direct work tools (like assessment forms or profiles), meeting structures, or intervention objectives – didn't a contextual system make.

## Going off-road: the insufficiency of tweaking

Successful attempts to contextualise discrete meetings or activities raised professional anxieties, exposed weaknesses in partnerships, and suggested that contextual intervention (whether that was trying to include peer relationships into child protection assessments or attempting to profile local risks with reference to the contexts in which abuse occurred rather than the demographics of the individuals involved) could not be sustained or embedded within child protection systems that remained otherwise focused on the assessment of, and intervention with, children and families. At best the contextual activities undertaken remained siloed from the wider system in which they sat; at worst they stalled altogether.

Returning to answer the original questions I had posed in 2013 (and at the start of this chapter), I now understood that practitioners were, in some respects, aware of the system limitations they were working with: a contextual lens supported them to further articulate this. And yet, they were so used to focusing on changing individual behaviour that even when they worked in a contextual way they weren't always able to value the group or location-based impact of their interventions. It was possible to do things differently when abuse occurred in extra-familial settings – the work in the shopping centre and with the fair access panels, for example, had shown this to be the case. Profiling work with schools had also illustrated that it was possible to act in a contextual way before abuse occurred. But for practitioners to consistently apply a contextual lens to both prevention and responses to abuse, the system in which they worked, and not solely to tools they used or activities they delivered, needed reform. A contextual system was required to leverage change: the absence of a framework to guide that change (and the legislative permission to work beyond the parameters of the system as it stood) prevented a different course of action.

It was evident that contextual activities enhanced elements of how sites were responding to peer-on-peer abuse. It was equally evident that these activities wouldn't outlive the project unless they could be integrated into wider structures, systems, and policy frameworks. And furthermore, that any advances in policy frameworks were tied to broader social expectations and legal parameters of child protection systems which were beyond the remit of any single local area. England's child protection system couldn't support or sustain the contextual change that had been initiated – without broadening the contexts/relationships into which the system reached. This broadening not only applied in cases of peer-on-peer abuse (which was where we had originally focused) but was likely to be also relevant when young people were abused by adults (unconnected to their families) in extra-familial settings. If harm was extra-familial, a contextual response held much merit – but could not be in held – in England's child protection system. As we wrapped up our work in 11 sites we had come to understand that the rules of the child protection system, and not just rules of the contexts in which abuse occurred, required attention. Our site activities provided the foundation and impetus for the development of a conceptual framework to describe a child protection system capable of protecting young people from extra-familial abuse: a framework introduced in the following chapter.

## Notes

1 We defined peer-on-peer abuse as 'physical, sexual, emotional and financial abuse, and coercive control, exercised within young people's relationships' (Firmin, 2015).
2 Policy before this had limited domestic abuse to that which occurred in adult (18+) relationships.
3 All written texts were coded using the qualitative analytical software, NVivo.

# 6   Articulating an ambition

## A Contextual Safeguarding framework

The ups and downs of trying to contextualise responses to peer-on-peer abuse had taught me one fundamental lesson: it was impossible. Or put more accurately, you couldn't contextualise activities, and sustain that type of change, if the wider system that hosted those activities remained focused on individual children and families. Our attempts to do so, as documented in the previous chapter, had resulted in variable levels of uptake. The systems we were working in struggled to hold activities that ran so counter to its daily mode of operation. The buy-in of practitioners who were eager to work with their gut, and the evidence base, by building context into their work, was overwhelmed by cultural, structural, legal, and policy-based barriers. From ICT systems that could only log information on individuals and information sharing policies that didn't account for talking about places instead of people, through to practice cultures that immediately looked for parental deficits to explain difficulties that children faced and statutory partnerships that lacked any engagement from local communities, businesses, or others who operated in contexts of concern: the system said 'no'.

The big picture, therefore, was clear. The child protection system itself needed contextual immersion. This wasn't about a nod here and there to peer groups when a child was being assessed or an ad-hoc mention about a corner shop that was selling legal highs in a practitioner meeting. In every fibre of its working, the system needed to be alive to peer relationships, school, and neighbourhood environments in the same way it was about children and their families. If you cut through the system, it needed to bleed troubled contexts and not just troubled people. Various shades of systemic social work practice provided a fertile ground to grow this type of change – but how to plant the seed, what conditions would enable it to flourish, and what would it look like in full bloom?

For three months I wrote up the findings from work in local sites, and reflected on the contextual approach I had called for when I had completed all of my initial case reviews a year earlier. George had moved on from the team and I had been joined by a brilliant geographer, Dr Jenny Lloyd. Jenny's arrival was perfectly timed. She was new to the field of child protection research, and the contextual methodologies we had been developing.

As such Jenny brought a fresh pair of ears that needed to hear about, and understand, what we had been trying to achieve to date and where it was going. At the same time Danielle Fritz also came on board to bring together the practitioners we had been working with over the previous three years, and form a virtual network to connect them: providing a space of peer learning as the work continued to develop. Both dialogue with this group of practitioners and discussions with Jenny over the summer of 2016 gave me the space to reflect on the big picture and convert it into a framework. As it was largely a conceptual process, albeit grounded in the knowledge that I had garnered from my work to date, it only took me so far. I was able to articulate what full bloom would need to look like for a contextual approach to be sustained. That was far enough – and that is what this chapter will detail. Sourcing the seeds, gardeners, and conditions required to get us there would be the job of many years to come.

## Contextual Safeguarding: four components of a framework

Stepping back it was possible to see four elements of the child protection system that prevented the adoption of a contextual approach. At each stage of the system it targeted children and families instead of the contexts that posed a risk of harm to those children and families. Where contexts were considered, and in some cases disrupted, this was primarily seen as a community safety and policing responsibility, rather than a matter of child welfare. The partnerships that formed in response to extra-familial harm largely comprised organisations with an expertise in, or primarily commissioned for, working with individuals.

Success, and the outcomes of intervention, were being measured solely in relation to the behaviour of individuals – how many were missing from home, how many were in education, and so on – without any way to understand if those individual measures were a sign of safety and for whom.

Each of these elements needed to be disentangled, and an alternative proposed, to build a framework for a contextual approach to safeguarding young people.

### *The target of the child protection system*

As detailed in Part 1 of this book, the intended target of the child protection system has been children and families. Sara and Malik, the choices they made, and the actions taken by their parents were seen as both the cause of the harm they faced/posed, and the route to achieving safety in the future: a position that ran counter to histories of community social work, social justice practices, and advocates of public health approaches to harm reduction. Observations of practice in local areas illustrated how such a focus was threaded through the operational workings of local child protection systems.

Let's start at the 'multi-agency safeguarding hub' (MASH) or what is more commonly referred to as the 'front door' of children and families services. This is the part of the system in England where all the calls come in. If a professional or member of the public is concerned about the welfare of the child and picks up the phone, it is the people in the MASH who take their call, screen the concern, and make a decision about initial next steps. If the concerns raised warrant further consideration they may gather information about the child and family from other services to make an initial screening decision. In some cases they may refer the child and family for a social work assessment; in other cases a referral will be made to an early help, partner or voluntary service; and in other instances they will close the case altogether.

In the light of increased public awareness and concern (chapter 3), children who were at risk of harm in their schools, communities, and peer groups were also being referred into children's services. However, the contexts in which they were being abused were not – and could not be – the subject of referrals. Therefore, if three friends were all being sexually exploited together, and by the same person or groups of people, each one would be referred into the system differently and split off at that point. We had made an initial attempt to combat this with some of the activities in sites – for example, introducing a 'peer group information capture form' that practitioners could use when taking a referral for a young person into social care or youth offending. However, as noted in the previous chapter this slight adaptation caused all manner of concern about information sharing agreements, data management, and insufficient ICT processes. In truth, the primary referral points into the child protection system could not accommodate contextual information – hugely limiting attempts to mainstream the adaptations we had trialled.

Moving through the system, the same patterns were evident in frameworks and tools used to conduct assessments in the areas we were supporting. While some services had started to map the relationships between young people who were being supported by different workers in their services, the vast majority of assessment frameworks had no space to hold, or draw information from, this type of contextual work. The exception to this had been the youth justice assessment tool – and we had started to document how that could be utilised to build contextual assessments. However, the assessments that sat at the heart of the child protection system were framed around children and the capacity of their parents to keep them safe. As a result, even peer group mapping exercises fell short and often resulted in individual actions with individual members of peer groups – rather than a plan for supporting a peer group as a collective whole. There was no framework in place to hold such an assessment in the system, and use it as the foundation for building safeguarding plans. Further to this, assessments of places – such as high streets, transport hubs, and housing estates were primarily driven by concerns about crime and anti-social behaviour. Detailed assessments of what was happening in these places, therefore, were either reserved for community safety and policing meetings or were addressed at child welfare focused meetings by tasking policing or community safety colleagues to take action. There was a complete absence of mechanisms to conduct a welfare-based assessment of contexts outside of families.

As a result, the plans to increase safety for children and young people focused on work with them and their families. Interventions with peer groups or in shopping centres identified during this phase of site work were anomalies rather than characteristic of the wider system that delivered them. Suggestions that they could be a core part of the response to sexual or criminal exploitation were met with concerns about resources. Threaded through these concerns was that interventions with places and groups were additional to, rather than a central feature of, responses to extra-familial harm.

Further to this, however, some of these interventions while on the face of it appeared contextual were primarily measured on individualised success measures. Take the example of the shopping centre intervention first introduced in the previous chapter. Social workers, youth workers, and workers from a voluntary sector sexual exploitation service had been routinely visiting a shopping centre where there were concerns about young people being groomed. The approach looked extremely promising. Practitioners had built relationships with security staff and store managers in the shopping centre – who were supported to 'look out' for young people when this team of practitioners couldn't be around. Young people also noticed the workers – some of them knew them already – and began to talk to them in the shopping centre. When managers described why this intervention had been successful they talked about the numbers of young people that they had engaged by being in the shopping centre – many of whom had successfully been referred into their local youth service. While this was an important outcome, those involved had missed the point that simply by being in the shopping centre and talking to young people who could have been the target of grooming they had disrupted this environment and made it safer – at least in those moments. Furthermore, by building relationships with adults who were in the shopping centre more regularly, and educating them to act as guardians in this space, they had increased the capacity for the shopping centre to be protective more generally. By engaging young people while they were hanging out with their friends, they had also created opportunities to see young people's peer groups, and understand some of the dynamics of those friendships. All of those contextual outcomes had been completely missed in a wider practice culture that was driven to measure success solely by assessing the impact on individual behaviour and engagement.

From referral, therefore, through to assessment, planning, and impact the system targeted individuals. Even attempts to target groups or contexts in the system had their potential thwarted by individualised cultural, legal, technical, and practical components (chapter 5).

To address the contextual dynamics of extra-familial harm, therefore, the child protection system needed to be able to *target* peer group, school, and neighbourhood's contexts. This targeting needed to be system-wide - from the point of referral onwards.

## *A lens of child welfare and child protection*

A number of systems have for a long time considered places, locations, and contexts as part of their every-day work. As noted in Part 1, policing and community safety services have been informed by theories of situational crime prevention in knowledge that it is often easier to predict the location where a crime is going to occur than the person who is going to commit it. It was therefore unsurprising that when reviewing cases and in the early days of local site work, some of the most contextual work Jenny, George, and I encountered was driven by those working in crime reduction.

In one case I reviewed, for example, a young woman, Lana, had been murdered by her ex-boyfriend who was also under the age of 16. During their investigations the police interviewed a number of their friends – in the knowledge that they were more likely to know what had been happening in the weeks prior to the murder, than either of their parents. They also spoke to shopkeepers and other business owners who worked on the high street where this group of young people used to hang out. This route of enquiry worked. Lana had disclosed to her friends in school as the abuse in her relationship escalated. Her peers in the community had also witnessed Lana being assaulted – not just by her ex-boyfriend but by other young men in the local area. Local shopkeepers were aware of how vulnerable she was – and she had spoken to one of them about feeling afraid. Lana's extra-familial community, and networks, was where she had sought advice in the days before her death. Engaging in these contexts was the route to understanding what had happened. They were also the contexts in which risks persisted after the murder. And this was a problem. As despite being a target for police investigations, Lana's peers and the high street where she had hung out were not subject to any welfare-based assessment. A number of her peers were physically assaulted by other young people after talking to the police – their welfare had not been considered by safeguarding partners. The risk, in many respects, was viewed as located in young person who lost her life and the young person who took it – and not the contexts associated to that violence. As such outside of the police investigation, a welfare response to these concerns was notable only by their absence.

In a similar vein most localities that were worked with had a 'locations' meeting, or community safety panels, who sat and identified locations in which anti-social behaviour or crime was a concern. These meetings were focused on crime reduction or crime prevention in local areas, and rarely fed into child welfare focused meetings on child sexual exploitation or serious youth violence. Even on occasions where there was some join-up between the two structures they didn't share the same tone, culture, and measures of success. In one meeting, young people were being described as problematic, anti-social, and a risk to the local community; in another meeting they were described as experiencing adversities, vulnerable, and at risk in their local community. Work done to address community concerns of anti-social behaviour were not connected to the individual welfare-based or social work plans for the same young people who were vulnerable in those communities. It reminded me of a case I had reviewed where a group of young men raped a young woman on a stairwell. In the weeks before the rape most of those young men had been served with behaviour notices due to anti-social behaviour – which did little to address their escalating and concerning behaviour. The vulnerability of the young man who ultimately led the assault, his experiences of violence on the streets, and the drivers for him being missing from home most nights were not being tackled by any welfare-based agency – or the influence he had on the rest of his peers who committed offences only when in his company.

It is also important to consider what child protection systems offer in a response to vulnerable children, families, and communities. A number of families will be supported by social workers who are not under a police investigation. A crime does not have to have been committed for social workers to be concerned about the welfare of children and families. Support to increase safety within a family setting may involve direct work with parents and/or with young people. It may also involve support from health, housing, or community organisations – amongst others: support which is brokered or coordinated by social workers on behalf of the families they are supporting.

When I suggest that in a Contextual Safeguarding approach professionals respond to extra-familial harm through the lens of child protection and child welfare, I do so with this reading of social work in mind. It would be remiss of me to suggest that this is always the approach taken in social work and within child protections systems more generally (a matter raised in chapter 3 and to be explored further in Parts 3 and 4 of this book). There has been a mounting critique of individualised approaches to child protection in recent decades. In many countries, including England, social work has been viewed as increasingly punitive: based on intervention rather than support, adversarial to families and operating a 'case work' approach which reduces engagement with the wider communities of which families are a part (Featherstone, et al., 2018; Fenton, 2016; Ferguson & Woodward, 2009; Gilbert, et al., 2011; Parton, 2014)

In many respects Contextual Safeguarding, as will be discussed throughout this book, re-centres community, support, and advocacy into child protection and social work practices. Case review and local site work both indicated the importance of holding responses to extra-familial harm within child protection and child welfare systems – and the potential risks of seeing contextual work as solely a community safety matter. If we agree that the sexual and criminal exploitation of children, weapon-enabled crime, and serious violence, and other matters than threaten young people's lives and welfare are forms of abuse then we require a child protection response. We need such a response to not only come into force when a crime has been committed and a child has been harmed. We need to be able to identify contexts, situations, and relationships in which young people are at increased vulnerability to ham and seek to build safety or increased support within those contexts.

This is not to say the Contextual Safeguarding approaches would not feature contributions from community safety and policing professionals. There is a place for enforcement and crime reduction work within a safeguarding agenda – but it cannot be seen as the lead or sole route for addressing safeguarding issues in extra-familial settings, for all the reasons outlined above. In some cases a peer group spending time and drinking in a local park where other young people have been groomed into drug dealing may need support from detached youth workers. In other cases, if agencies know who has been grooming young people then enforcement against those individuals might also happen. And in other cases, design work in the park to increase its use for positive activities, and involving this group of young people in designing those activities, might be all that is needed to safeguard their welfare. Or all of the above might be required. Through this work professionals might identify that some of those young people also have parents in need of support, or that they are experiencing other difficulties at home – but this may not be the case for all the young people in question. When the issue in the park is seen as a concern for community safety agencies alone, there is the risk that the dispersal of those young people, the serving of civil orders for anti-social behaviour, and/or their criminalisation for public order offences are seen as the route to restoring safety in the park. The difficulty in such an approach is that: it doesn't address the causes of the behaviour in the first place; it doesn't work with, or respond to, the group dynamics and the potential strengths that might exist within it; it fails to see young people as part of the local community who should be able to safely use the park; and it risks isolating young people even further from services and pushing them closer to those who can groom them into criminal activity because they have little to lose anyway.

### The partnerships involved in child protection

The anxieties that we had encountered in local sites often kept me up at night. Why was there such concern, and in some cases resistance, about social workers having oversight of responses to extra-familial harm? If this was abuse, and posed a risk of significant harm to young people's welfare, who else in a local area would coordinate responses? Discussions with local practitioners were critical to thinking through this first hurdle in the development of a Contextual Safeguarding framework. Quite quickly one word came to the forefront of those discussions – and for more than one reason – and that word was 'partnership'.

Firstly, social workers argued that they didn't have the right partnerships in place to leverage a contextual response to harm that was occurring in parks, high streets, schools, and stairwells – let alone via social media platforms. In many respects they were right. When we had observed meetings in local sites the agencies around the table were often all responsible for delivering 1:1 work with young people or families. From health, to social care and even policing and education – the interventions being offered and discussed were focused on individuals. We could put that child on this counselling course, and that parent on this course about boundary setting, and exclude that child from school or arrest that person, and so on. No one was stepping in to intervene with the high street or the park – as a whole – just with an individual who was a concern when in those contexts, and there appeared to be three features of this dynamic.

A number of agencies who were in, or could reach into, extra-familial contexts were not invited to these meetings. Local shopkeepers, housing officers, and neighbourhood policing, for example, were not on the attendance list for a safeguarding meeting about sexual exploitation in the local area. From a policing perspective, the public protection unit (often featuring a specialist branch operating complex child sexual exploitation investigations) may be in attendance, but these were not the neighbourhoods or schools' officers who worked in the contexts of concern. As a result, social actors who could play an active role in re-shaping the context in question were not formal partners in the design of many plans.

In addition to this, voluntary, community, and youth work sector organisations represented at these meetings had been increasingly commissioned to deliver 1:1 work with individuals, rather than with communities or groups. This de-contextualising of community support structures led practitioners down a dead-end in the search for partners who could leverage the contextual change required. In reflective workshops with youth workers across participating sites many commented on the how their contribution to safeguarding practices were being measured. They reflected how years prior their key 'partners' had been the guy who ran the launderette, the woman at the sweet shop counter, community groups, families. Fast forward to 2016 and these partners were the police and social workers – and they felt like the voluntary arm of 'case work' rather than a partner of the community. One commented that:

> We haven't got enough time to invest in the old style – going into the area and meeting with the neighbourhood and the parents. I often find myself these days more – almost like – like avoiding certain roads because I know that we'll walk there and the parents will be hanging out on their balcony … I know that sounds awful
>
> (Fritz et al. 2016:8)

I was struck by this insight. It echoed the position of many voluntary sector staff who would talk about the 'cases' of sexual exploitation that had been referred into them. They were commissioned by statutory services not to be a source of open support in communities but rather to accept referrals from statutory agencies for individual children and families who required intensive

1:1 or 'specialist' support around the form of harm they were experiencing. Every route to support was individual, referral, and case based – squeezing out the space for group and placed-based work.

This dynamic was particularly notable as there were a handful of sites that had retained a detached youth work service. We spent time with those youth workers, on the high streets and housing estates where they spent their evenings. They knew the guy who ran the local post office, the stairwells where people bought crack and the front doors behind which domestic abuse was escalating; and arguably more importantly the people in the post office, on the stairwell and behind those front doors knew them. They were an integral part of that community space and had built their place there over a five-year period. When walking with them, one evening they noticed a 13-year-old boy. They were immediately concerned. He was stood amongst a huddle of older boys who all nodded at us as we walked past. A number of the group were already caught up in drug dealing and carrying weapons. One of the workers walked over to the group and exchanged a few pleasantries. They asked one of the older ones how he had got on handing in CVs that week – he said he had an interview coming up. They also asked the 13-year old how he was – how things were going at school, how his mum was. They said their goodbyes and we walked off. I noted a number of things about that interaction and the conversation that followed. These youth workers were concerned – and not because they had received a 'referral' about a 13-year old or that he had displayed $X$ number of risk indicators on a checklist. They were worried because of who was with and when he was with them. They remained equally concerned about the welfare of those older young people and discussed what further they might be able to do with the group. They thought about the group dynamic – who they had, and could get, on side. They talked about the need to disrupt the connection that was forming between this 13-year old and that group. They had the trust of them all, and of their community, and believed they could make a difference.

In the absence of detached youth workers or community based/facing organisations, many social workers were reliant on partnerships with other individuals and organisations that had a presence in extra-familial contexts – such as schools and even high street businesses. While we were in local areas we were impressed to see a large range of potential partner agencies being trained in the signs of sexual exploitation. From hoteliers to taxi drivers, safeguarding partnerships were reaching out to those who operated in the places where harm was occurring. To an extent this was contextual – but only to an extent. Messaging in the training sessions mirrored the 'see it, say it, sorted' equation examined in Part 1 of the book. Posters were circulated around local areas calling on people to say something about sexual exploitation if they saw it. As such the training built the capacity of a wider group of people to spot the signs of abuse. What it failed to do was work with those agencies to think about the role they could play in creating safe spaces for young people to be – rather than just referring individuals who they thought may come to harm in an unsafe locality. Awareness raising certainly hadn't filled the community guardianship-size hole left when detached and community focused work was de-commissioned.

For these partnerships to reach their full potential, the interpretation of safeguarding being 'everybody's business' needed a re-think. Our time in local areas illustrated that to date this had been largely seen as it being everybody's business to look out for the signs of abuse (in this case extra-familial harm) and make a referral into social services if they spotted anything of note. However, in moving towards a contextual approach social workers required those agencies to move beyond referrals to actively participate in the planning for, and intervening in spaces, places, and relationships where they had some influence or reach.

Young people themselves, and their parents, were also a key partner in creating contextual change. Young people, as peers who could influence each other, played a role in creating safe and protective norms amongst friendship groups (Allnock, 2013; Barter, et al., 2015; Buck, et al., 2017; Gardner & Steinberg, 2005; Pawlby, et al., 1997). The increasing desire that young people have for self-autonomy during adolescence could also be harnessed in plans. Young people wanted to make decisions for themselves; creating contexts in which those decisions had less constraints, and where safer options didn't also increase contextual risk, was something to be explored in partnerships between professionals, young people, and their parents (Coleman, 2011; Gray & Manning, 2014; Warrington & Thomas, 2016).

And parents, who were often overwhelmed by the influence that extra-familial contexts had over their young people, required support to stand alongside other professionals in creating safety in school, peer, and community spaces. The fact that the harm in question was rarely instigated by parents didn't mean they had no role to play in creating safety: to the contrary, the protective role of parents could be utilised as an asset in contextual plans. And further to this, when families were experiencing additional difficulties – addressing these in order for them to also play a role in building safety in contexts beyond their front doors was equally important (Catch 22, 2013; Hudeck, 2018; PACE, 2020; Scott & McNeish, 2017; Shuker, 2017).

It was clear therefore that partnerships were required between social workers and a whole range of agencies that had a reach into extra-familial contexts for Contextual Safeguarding to be viable. Contextual change could not be realised through shifting the lens of social work to target extra-familial spaces. The partners who could create change in those spaces had to be involved, and resourced to engage, with the process. They also had to understand and identify their role in shaping the nature of extra-familial contexts and relationships. Central to both of these was the ability for safeguarding systems to recognise the value of contextual impact, relationships, and reach. This meant moving beyond counting the numbers of individuals within a service, or the number of individual indicators of risk they each displayed pre- and post intervention, to examining the environments in which their behaviour changed and which it did not.

### The outcomes of child protection systems

I remember sitting in one panel meeting where a social worker commented words to the effect of:

> we have placed her miles away from any train station – she is currently safeguarded.

I was perplexed. How did moving a 15-year old out of a relatively protective family and into a residential children's home miles away from all her family, friends, and any transport networks equate with safety? For sure she was now at a physical distance from a group of adults who had been sexually exploiting her. However, mobile phone technology, cars, and all manner of other 21st century quirks meant that this physical separation was under constant threat. Furthermore, she was now a socially isolated young person who desired connection – personal contact, friendship, the chance to socialise. Quite quickly she started to go missing from the children's home where she had been placed. Hitchhiking her way to train stations so that she could get back to see her family or friends – or to hang out with other young people in the area where she had been placed. She was unsafe again – and arguably even more so than before she had been moved, as no one knew where she had gone when she was missing. Her experience, like many others, exemplified what were emergent and are now persistent concerns about the use of care placements for children at risk of extra-familial harm: with the relational and psychological safety of young people compromised in a bid to place them at a physical distance from contexts and relationships in which they have been abused (Ellis, 2018; Firmin, 2019; Scott & Botcherby, 2017; Shuker, 2013)

And what was even more startling was that interventions ceased with relocation. The contexts that led to her being moved were not subject to intervention – and the fact that they remained a risk to other young people – did not inform how success or safety was measured: and herein lay the additional challenge. Some of the relocation work observed during this time did benefit individual young people. On some occasions whole families were moved to different areas, for example, and when those moves were successful the abuse their child had experienced was sometimes disrupted. However, the contexts in which they had been abused – the peer network, the high street, the park – still remained harmful. Movement, or other forms of effective intervention for an individual child, created a 'victim vacuum' that other young people filled. Likewise, young women who had been sexually assaulted in schools were moved onto other schools to get them away from the person who had assaulted them and the other students who were tormenting them for being 'a snitch'. These moves gave a message to the wider student body that if school professionals couldn't guarantee safety at school and you sought support, you might have to move. This in turn gave the green light to young people who were abusing their peers – no one will tell unless they want to get moved as well.

The use of relocation wasn't the only example George and I encountered during practice observation, focus groups, or case reviews, where the measure used to denote 'safety' or even 'success' was questionable. Like Malik's truancy (outlined in chapter 2), behaviours that practitioners were focusing on as a sign of risk were actually young people's attempts at safety. Running away to sell drugs miles away from home because if they didn't their younger sibling would be attacked at the schools gates; drinking alcohol to shut out the flashbacks of rape that often resulted in fits of violence and rage; stealing from others to avoid being stolen from; and so on. For young people in these situations not going missing meant a physical attack; not drinking meant them attacking someone else; not stealing phones meant repeat victimisation. Sure their behaviour could change but it didn't mean that they were safer.

The system limitation was therefore twofold.

Baseline assessments of safety were built on individual measures. We are worried about this child truanting or this child offending. We'll know our interventions have been successful therefore, when this behaviour changes. Areas weren't measuring the nature and number of unsafe contexts in which those behaviours were being displayed – and therefore didn't have a contextual focus for intervention or route to measuring impact.

Beyond baseline measures, strategic leaders only had access to an individualised account of need and demand in a local area. Work with analysts in some sites had indicated the value of profiling both risk and safety across cases – identifying how many peer groups, schools, and public places were in need of support (chapter 5). By 2016, most areas could give an account of the numbers of young people referred into children's services with concerns for sexual exploitation – but they couldn't tell you if they were all at the same education provision, linked via the friendships groups or were all groomed on the same high street. Understanding need in this way was critical for mobilising partners, and appropriately resourcing services that could reach into the contexts that were in need. As long as need and impact were measured solely at the individual level they only informed the commissioning, and evaluation, of services that could operate at that level. And the initial ripples, and even waves, of contextual profiling initiated in sites were gradually lost in a wider sea that valued individual impact over all other.

Work undertaken in sites by 2016 indicated that to sustain or embed any of contextual activities that had been developed the wider child protection systems in which they sat needed to recognise their value. While the system was largely measured on casework and individual outcomes, such work could not be integral to the measured impact the system made on extra-familial harm.

## Sowing the seeds of Contextual Safeguarding

Spending three years developing contextual activities within children's services had taught me that change was possible – but that it needed to be systemic to be sustained, and this type of change was not going to be easy. Contextual activities buckled within systems that were focused on intervening with individuals at risk of, or experiencing, abuse. To adopt a contextual approach to harm – particularly that which was extra-familial – child protection systems and wider safeguarding partnerships needed to:

A.  **Target** the contexts (social conditions) in which harm was occurring.
B.  Locate contextual work in the field of **child protection, child welfare, and safeguarding**, rather than crime reduction and community safety.
C.  Be built on **partnerships** that had a reach into the contexts where harm was occurring.
D.  Measure **success and outcomes** contextually.

These four areas for systemic development provided both the pillars for building a Contextual Safeguarding approach and the framework against which systems could be measured (Figure 6.1). In others words, when my team and I went into an area could we asked ourselves if we could see these four domains within child protection and safeguarding responses to extra-familial harm? And if we couldn't we explored how we could support an area, through action research, to get there.

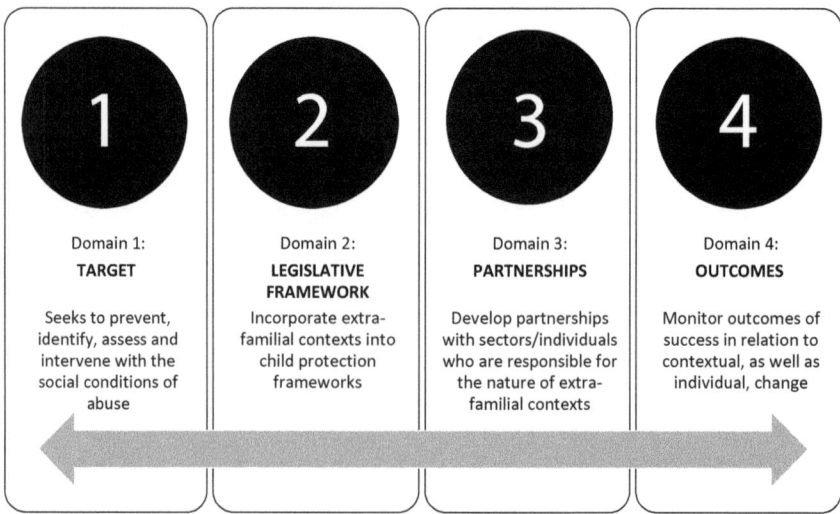

*Figure 6.1* Contextual Safeguarding Framework

Articulating this Contextual Safeguarding framework in 2016 (Figure 6.1) gave a vocabulary to describe what needed to happen to sustain the progress made when initiating contextual activities. When we launched an online network to connect practitioners who had been with us on this journey to that point, buy-in to the framework and associated resources was quick. Hundreds joined in the first few weeks and over the following three years membership would reach in excess of 6,000. But despite this enthusiasm for the approach, questions remained. To what extent was working in the way proposed, aligned to what regulators and government departments expected of child protection systems? What role could decision-makers play to support the development of practice in this direction – and what role could my team and I play in shaping such a policy framework?

From 2016 to 2018, we embarked on a programme of work with key decision-makers to begin to build an authorising environment for testing Contextual Safeguarding on the ground. The following chapter will document key developments in this area; in particular changes made to statutory child protection guidance that first signalled that a contextual approach was permissible in the eyes of the state. Over this two-year period, we would see the language of Contextual Safeguarding achieve far more wide-spread adoption – sowing the seeds for full systems testing and implementation in the years to come.

# 7 Creating an authorising environment

## Contextualising national policy frameworks

We were at an impasse.

A core group of practitioners was sold on the idea of contextualising their practice. They were mapping the relationships between children who were being sexually exploited together. They were packing up their laptops, leaving their desks, and familiarising themselves with shopping centres and bus stops, where children had been approached and coerced to sell drugs. As the clock struck 3:00 pm each day, the sounds of telephones and laptop keys were replaced by tram bells and Tannoy announcements. In other words they were engaging with the places and spaces where young people were vulnerable to abuse. They were mapping, observing, and assessing the physical and cultural fabric of those contexts – the social rules at play within them. And most importantly they were using that knowledge to problem-solve how best to increase safety for young people who spent time in those contexts. In thinking about how to sustain and mainstream their practice I had been able to develop a Contextual Safeguarding framework (chapter 6). This framework moved the discussion from how we could contextualise child protection and safeguarding *practices* to how we might contextualise the child protection and safeguarding *systems* in which such practices took place. If we wanted contextual practices to be 'business as usual' then the wider system in which they sat needed to be contextual too.

Growing that system was another matter entirely. Forging ahead on the sails of optimism and clarity of an idea would have led us head first into a brick wall. The conditions were not in place for a Contextual Safeguarding system to flourish – and pushback from individual practitioners and service leaders (chapter 5) was symptomatic of this fact. Ideas that social workers 'work with families not friends', or that 'drugs have always been dealt on that street and always would be', were not simply the views of some practitioners we met in some sites. The roots of these views required interrogation – and this wouldn't be achieved through the observation of local practice alone. I needed to understand the practice frameworks in which their decision-making (and associated views) existed. As much as there were differences between the local areas we had been supporting, this type of push back, anxiety, and blockage was shared across all 11: it was a national characteristic. And so I returned to the practice and policy frameworks guiding child protection responses in England (first detailed in chapter 3) in pursuit of national mechanisms that might leverage Contextual Safeguarding systems. In this chapter I will detail what I learnt from reviewing national policy frameworks in 2016 and the extent to which they appeared to enshrine an individualised narrative of abuse. I will also track how revisions made to key documents in this framework in 2017 and 2018 gave a national opening for the development of local contextual practices – and in doing so began to create the conditions for Contextual Safeguarding systems to take root.

## The child protection system in 2016 – a paper version

The lives of Malik, Sara, and other young people featured in the cases I reviewed had clearly demonstrated a mismatch between the operations of the child protection system in England, and the nature of abuse in extra-familial contexts (see Part 1). In failing to understand this mismatch political and media announcements wrongly positioned the child protection system, and the social workers within it, as ready to respond to all forms of extra-familial harm once they understood it as abuse. In reality, seeing exploitation and other such forms of harm as abuse didn't rework the functions and capability of the child protection system. The barriers faced when contextualising practices with local practitioners was further evidence of this fact.

*Working Together to Safeguard Children* (WTSC) provides England's statutory guidance about how a range of agencies should respond to (and intervene early to prevent) child abuse. While it refers to the roles played by numerous organisations including policing, health, and housing services, it centres children's services (and social workers specifically) as coordinating the protection of children in England. It has been subjected to four sets of revisions since its introduction into the child protection landscape in 2006 – growing and shrinking in size under different political administrations and their varying approaches to organising protective services for children. During this time, one thing has remained constant – the document, until 2018, guided service responses to/about/with *children and families.*

For example, To understand and identify significant harm, it is necessary to consider:

- The nature of harm, in terms of maltreatment or failure to provide adequate care.
- The impact on the child's health and development.
- **The child's development within the context of their family and wider environment.**
- Any special needs, such as a medical condition, communication impairment or disability, that may affect the **child's development and care within the family.**

- **The capacity of parents** to meet adequately the child's needs; and
- **The wider and environmental family context**.

(*Working Together to Safeguard Children*, 2010:37
Bold added by author)

When I sat down to review WTSC over a cappuccino in my local coffee shop back in 2016, I felt a little fizz of excitement. I might have been a researcher for some time, but policy has shaped by career from the outset. It has always fascinated me how the words on pages issued by Government departments can have such an influence over what happens in local areas, organisations, communities, and families – and yet in many ways have no influence over it at all. For decades, public policy scholars have investigated the policy-practice implementation gap (Pülzl & Treib, 2007): why do inconsistent local practices exist when national policy documents clearly set out what is required? The placement of children in care has been classic in this regard. National policy states that if a local authority places a child in care at a distance from where they live it is important that the local authority in which they have been placed is informed (HM Government, 2014; Ofsted, 2014): and yet national inquiry after national inquiry has found examples of where this hasn't happened (Jarrett & Harker, 2016). In other instances local practice appears to be miles ahead of national policy. Since 2013, I had been working with areas that were trying to integrate their local responses to youth violence, children who were missing from home, trafficking, and sexual exploitation – despite a notable lack of integrated policy from Government even in 2019. And yet there are other examples when policy and practice do intersect. Until 2011 no national strategies on gangs or serious youth violence had paid notable attention to the impact of these issues on women and girls. Following three years of research into the lives of women and girls associated to serious youth violence, we managed to get clear consideration of this issue into national policy documents, funding streams and local area assessments; which in turn impacted local responses – and the lives of women and girls who could access services that hadn't been available before then.

So whenever I set out to interrogate a policy framework, I am curious. Do the words on these pages mean anything to local practice, and if they do will changing them make any difference to the conundrum we face?

### *The nooks and crannies of child protection guidance*

In WTSC the link to local practice was clear. Firstly, I could see it on the pages I reviewed. And in testing these ideas out with practitioners during consultation events, and a practice survey, the significance of this association was confirmed.

In relation to WTSC, there were a myriad of ways in which the then 109 pages I reviewed in 2016 failed to consider the peer, school, and community contexts associated to child welfare and child protection responses to child abuse. For starters there wasn't a single mention of young people's friendships or peer relationships in the document at all. There were four references made to community contexts or community relationships in which families exist. Whereas family relationships were considered 'significant' throughout the text; repeatedly described as a source of both risk to and the protection of children. For example: With reference to early help and support:

Effective early help relies upon local agencies working together to:

- **Identify children and families** who would benefit from early help.
- Undertake an assessment of the need for early help; and
- **Provide targeted early help services to address the assessed needs of a child and their family** which focuses on activity to significantly improve the outcomes for the child. Local authorities, under section 10 of the Children Act 2004, have a responsibility to promote inter-agency cooperation to improve the welfare of children (WTSC, 2016:12).

To understand the purpose of assessment:

Whatever legislation the child is assessed under, the purpose of the assessment is always:

- To **gather important information about a child and family.**
- To analyse their needs and/or the nature and level of any risk and harm being suffered by the child.
- To decide whether the child is a child in need (section 17) and/or is suffering, or likely to suffer, significant harm (section 47); and
- To provide support to address those needs to improve the child's outcomes to make them safe (WTSC, 2016:19–20).

These varying and interlocking references to family, and particularly parenting, throughout WTSC situated families as the central focus of the child protection system. A child's 'family' was referenced 98 times, and parents were considered 70 times, in the text; creating layer upon layer of procedural and cultural norms that wedded the system to an assessment of and intervention with parents as a route to safeguarding children. In this process peer relationships were completely pushed out of the systems view – and the protective capacity of young people's friendships and/or the risks that they may pose was side-lined.

So peers were out – but did the document propose seeing the family in context? The Child and Family Assessment Framework promoted in the guidance suggested so. It recommended framing a child's needs and a parents' capacity to meet those needs in relation to wider environmental and relational factors.

To this extent, the assessment framework permitted consideration of the contexts associated to a family. Particular attention was paid to employment, access to community resources, the nature of housing, and wider family support. Given its centrality in the document – and the centrality of assessment in child protection processes more specifically – the inclusion of contextual factors in the assessment framework provided a route to contextualising child protection practices more widely.

The potential of the assessment framework, however, was limited by two factors that were threaded through the remainder of the document. The first was that most of the environmental and relational elements of the triangle were only really contextual if the reader wanted them to be. In other words – how contextual is the term 'employment'. This could be read as there are minimal opportunities for employment in the local area – or it could be read as the parents and wider family are not in employment. In the latter example it becomes easy to then individualise unemployment to being a characteristic of the family – and not the context in which the family live. Furthermore, even if matters are seen as contextual you still have to address the 'so what' in terms of its relation to parents, and their ability to safeguard, and meet the needs of, their children. Consider the reference to 'community resources'. I have lost count of the number of assessments I have reviewed over the years where social workers have recorded that 'there are no or limited community resources in the local area' or 'there are community resources in the local area' in an assessment – and that has been their sum assessment of this contextual factor. In other words, whether there are community resources or not bears little relation to what the parent is or isn't doing. If there are some community resources available the parents should draw upon them – and if they don't this is a further indictment of their approach to safeguarding their children. If there aren't community resources available then parents have to find other ways to safeguard their children, that is, better navigate a difficult situation. Both of these are individualised conclusions of a potentially contextual factor. A contextual conclusion would be – there are no community resources and consideration needs to be made for how to increase/bolster these in order to better support the family.

The potential of the assessment framework was further limited by the fact that the remaining 97 references to families in the document rarely coupled with the same consideration of context. So when agencies were asked to attend child protection meetings to share information about children and families – they weren't also asked to share information about the levels of crime, deprivation, or marginalisation that these same families experienced in their local community, for example. Schools weren't asked to account for whether their exclusion of this child from school was the first that year, or one in a long line of exclusions that were impacting the welfare of young people and families in that community. This series of omissions resulted in the social worker conducting the assessment being the sole route to contextualising (and accessing the information to contextualise) information shared about the child and family. The result was a policy framework that communicated little expectation that social workers, or the partners with whom they worked, would consider the nature of contexts beyond families when seeking to safeguard children – let alone consider that changing those contexts might be a route to safety.

Despite the absence of an expectation to contextualise in WTSC, the 2016 document didn't prohibit a contextual approach. In fact the document defines 'abuse' as:

> A form of maltreatment of a child. Somebody may abuse or neglect a child by inflicting harm, or by failing to act to prevent harm. Children may be abused in a family or in an institutional or community setting by those known to them or, more rarely, by others (e.g. via the internet). **They may be abused by an adult or adults, or another child or children**.
>
> (Bold added by author, WTSC, 2016:92)

Drawing on the 1989 legislation a child in need is not defined in a way that solely locates need within families, and recognises young people who have committed offences as in need:

> A child in need is defined under the Children Act 1989 as a child who is unlikely to achieve or maintain a reasonable level of health or development, or whose health and development is likely to be significantly or further impaired, without the provision of services; or a child who is disabled. Children in need may be assessed under section 17 of the Children Act 1989, in relation to their special educational needs, disabilities, as a carer, or because they have committed a crime. Where an assessment takes place, it will be carried out by a social worker.
>
> (WTSC, 2016:18)

In such respects risk does not have to be posed by a child's parents for the state to intervene and offer support. However, this broader interpretation of the role of the state narrowed in WTSC as the significance of the harm considered in the document increased. From the point at which a child is considered to be at risk of significant harm, and statutory assessments are required, the legislation and the guidance increasingly closes its focus on the risks posed by, and the capacity of, a child's parents. Section 47 enquiries, which form the basis of a statutory assessment of a child at risk of significant harm, only ask questions in relation to the child and family. Child protection conferences, meetings called to discuss the findings of the assessment and formulate a plan, are intended to:

> bring together family members (and the child where appropriate), with the supporters, advocates and professionals most involved with the

child and family, to make decisions about the child's future safety, health and development

(WTSC, 2016:43)

And should a local authority conclude that risk has not reduced, or continues to escalate, to the point that a child may need to be taken into care for their own protection, Section 31 of the Children's Act requires that the identified harm is attributable to the care or control afforded by a child's parents. From the viewpoint of escalation, therefore, the greater the risks faced by a child the greater the focus on parents. If at the point of early help it is evident that the risks faced by the child are not related to parenting – the system is designed to communicate that should these risks escalate (and still not be related to parenting) there is a point at which the social work system will struggle to respond given where it can target its clout.

### *The policy and practice implications of a familial lens*

The impact of WTSC 2016 (and versions that had preceded it) on practice was twofold.

Firstly, when surveyed in 2016,[1] practitioners reported a relationship between the usefulness of WTSC, the locations in which young people experienced abuse and their confidence in responding. For example 92% were confident that they would identify risks faced by adolescents at home and 84% felt that WTSC adequately addressed how they could safeguard adolescents who were being abused by parents/carers. Whereas, only 58% felt they would be able to identify young people at risk in public places, and 39% felt that WTSC adequately addressed how they could safeguard young people at risk in public places. While those who participated in the survey were not statistically representative of all practitioners in England, the views they shared were echoed by those who were consulted in workshops we ran that same year and who we had met in practice sites the years prior. Practitioners directly referenced statutory guidance, the expectations it set and the permissions it gave, as associated to how equipped they felt to address extra-familial forms of harm.

Further to this, additional policy documents had been, and were being, created to respond to different forms of extra-familial harm. The Department for Education (previously the Department for Children, Schools and Families) who oversaw child protection policy, published additional safeguarding guidance in 2009 for responding to cases of child sexual exploitation (further updated in 2017), and in 2010 for schools to consider their role in protecting children at risk of gang-affiliation. These documents which served as appendages to WTSC were in some sense a recognition that child protection guidelines alone offered insufficient advice for dealing with harm beyond families. In other cases, policy documents, services, and funding streams grew out of government departments responsible for community safety, policing, and criminal justice – rather than that which oversaw policy frameworks for child protection. The Home Office (the government department for crime and policing) published various government strategies for addressing gangs and serious youth violence from 2008 onwards. Some of these documents detailed the role of local community safety partnerships in leading a response to violence (including that which impacted the welfare of children). Others committed funding for specialist services for young people affected by serious youth violence, made offers for government and peer reviews of local responses to serious youth violence, and detailed the local processes for government responses to the radicalisation of children and young people.

The Home Office also led the policy developments to recognise that young people under-18 could be in abusive romantic or intimate relationships, and consulted with local areas on how best to respond to this. Responses to the 2011–2012 consultation once again surfaced debates about the role of child protection systems in safeguarding young people from extra-familial abuse. Respondents varied in their opinions as to whether teenage relationship abuse could be held within local child protection systems – and indeed whether it should – or whether responses to abuse in adult relationships should be extended to young people affected by the same issue.

> Children under the age of 18 are being abused either emotionally, phys- ically or sexually, and the risks to them need to be addressed via the child protection systems.
>
> (North West, Other Government department)
> (Home Office 2012: 13)

> Child abuse is quite distinct from domestic violence. Lowering the age to include all those under 18 would confuse the differences between child abuse and domestic violence.
>
> (South East, Local Authority/ Local Government/ Local Council)
> (Home Office 2012: 16)

> We feel that the inclusion of 16 and 17 year olds in the Government definition should be a sufficient action. Extending to all those under the age of 18 will most certainly blur the boundaries between childhood and adulthood and raise concerns about when such issues should be viewed as child protection/safeguarding issues.
>
> (North East, Local Authority/ Local Council/
> Local Government) (Home Office 2012:16)

The increasing, and uncoordinated, policy documents that detailed England's response to extra-familial harm, coupled with the confusion displayed during practitioner surveys and consultations, evidenced that the shortcomings of WTSC mattered. WTSC 2016 was ill-equipped to guide local responses to extra-familial harm and the contexts in which such harm occurred. And while in some respects it didn't prohibit a contextual child protection response to extra-familial harm – it also failed to explicitly permit or enable such an approach to be adopted. The disorganised, multi-department policy response to different forms of extra-familial harm that grew to fill this gap had practice implications. In the sites we had been working, local responses to youth violence were often seen as community safety, rather than child protection or safeguarding, issues. Specialist panels to coordinate responses to child sexual exploitation, youth violence, radicalisation, and so on sat separately from, or appended to, child protection systems (rather than being integrated within them) and from each other: from separate assessment frameworks for each issue and specialist response teams (in some areas), through to issue-based plans (such as a CSE plan for a child) rather than an overarching child protection or child in need plan. And no one seemed to know where teenage relationship abuse sat with all of this – mirroring the responses to the Home Office consultation on the matter.

As I reflected on this tangled web of policy, structure, and practice with Jenny two things were clear. National policy frameworks were not enabling a consistent safeguarding response to extra-familial harm, or the contexts associated with it. And secondly, this mess was relevant to practice and therefore required attention: amendments were required for Contextual Safeguarding systems to thrive in England.

## The first steps to contextualising child protection policy: WTSC 2018

By assessing our national policy frameworks I could see how push back in local sites was aligned to the 'rules' of child protection; and that those rules were enshrined in legislation, guidance and policy. The child protection system operated in a framework that individualised child abuse, and located it within families, *systematically.* Only children and families could be referred into the system; they were the ones who were assessed; had information shared about them and a plan built around them. Added to this was a chronic under-recognition of peer relationships and the extent to which they influenced safety and risk during adolescence, as did the contexts in which those relationships existed. Issue-specific or criminal justice policies to compensate for this gap further divorced extra-familial harm from national child protection frameworks and the operationalisation of children's services on the ground. A Contextual Safeguarding framework provided a way to organise my thoughts about each policy framework, individually and collectively, to identify where change was most required.

### *National policy built through the lens of Contextual Safeguarding*

To sustain and mainstream contextual practices, local child protection systems, and wider safeguarding partnerships, needed to be capable of targeting the contexts (and social conditions) in which extra-familial harm occurred. Such targeting needed to be grounded in child welfare practices – framed as a means of safeguarding the welfare of young people rather than disrupting crime. To achieve this, social workers required partnerships with organisations and individuals who could reach into, and influence, extra-familial contexts. Success in such a system would be measured contextually: senior leaders would know how many local shops, parks, stairwells, and so on where their young people reported feeling safe/unsafe; as well as the numbers of young people who had been harmed when there. From a national policy perspective there was much to do.

WTSC was almost exclusively targeted at children and families and not the contexts in which extra-familial harm largely occurred. This policy framework viewed extra-familial abuse with a child welfare and child protection lens. However, its target meant that it utilised a series of partnerships for the purposes of identifying and intervening with children and families only. A whole range of partner organisations were listed in WTSC. All of them were required to identify children at risk of abuse, refer them into children's services, and share information about them as required by social workers. Risk, and its reduction, was the way in which WTSC measured success. As risk within families reduced so did any need for statutory social work involvement. And the assessment framework, outlined earlier in this chapter, primarily framed risk as something that was held within families – and in particular the ability of parents to meet the needs of, and protect, their children.

Some wider policy frameworks had paid greater attention to context. Developing government policies on gangs, serious youth violence, and exploitation identified contexts in which such harm was occurring:

> There is evidence that residential children's care homes and pupil referral units are being targeted. We also know of cases where gang members have been waiting outside schools to meet children.
>
> (HM Government, 2016:3)

But these policies framed extra-familial harm as primarily crime and community safety issues. Strengthening families or child welfare were not the foundational drivers of these strategies. Further to this, responses were often led by policing, community safety, and commissioned voluntary sector organisations, rather than featuring partnerships between children's services and partners who could affect change in extra-familial contexts. And finally, the success of these organisations was primarily measured individually (the numbers of young people in education or employment as a result of interventions) and with the ultimate goal of crime reduction (rather than safety).

And then there were the issue-specific strategies for sexual exploitation and gang-affiliation. Despite being focused on extra-familial harm, these documents primarily targeted individuals affected by those issues – rather than the contexts in which those issues developed. While to varying extents these documents were framed through the lens of child welfare, they acted as appendages to child protection documents rather than integral to them. The partners involved in delivering on these strategies and protocols intervened with individuals: delivering health services to them, policing them, or providing them with employment and training programmes. They weren't tasked with changing the contexts in which this abuse occurred. A proliferation of individualised risk assessments had accompanied the implementation of these strategies (Brown, et al., 2017). For the most part, these located risk within individual children (at risk because they are missing, truanting from school, using illegal substances). As with Home Office strategies, these documents also increasingly promoted identifying the locations (takeaway shops, taxi firms etc.) associated with exploitation. This work was delivered through policing and licencing disruption, and was therefore constructed as a crime prevention element of exploitation strategies.

Assessed against the four domains of Contextual Safeguarding (Table 7.1) each area of strategy development fell short.

Through the lens of Contextual Safeguarding framework, I could identify where policy was most limited – and just in the nick of time, as Contextual Safeguarding landed in draft revisions of WTSC in 2017.

*Table 7.1* Contextual Safeguarding framework assessment of national policy framework

| Policy area | Target contexts | Child welfare lens | Contextual partners | Contextual outcomes |
|---|---|---|---|---|
| WTSC | Red | Green | Red | Red |
| Home Office strategy – serious youth violence, gangs, and domestic abuse | Amber | Red | Amber | Red |
| Department for Education – sexual exploitation, gang affiliation | Amber | Amber | Amber | Red |

### *WTSC 2018*

I'd heard it through the grapevine.

The term 'Contextual Safeguarding' had been inserted into draft revisions to WTSC. Initially I took the news with a pinch of salt. I hadn't been in touch with government officials for a while – instead focusing on work in local sites, and starting to share what we were learning with national regulators and inspectorates. While I had developed a framework for the approach, at this stage much of Contextual Safeguarding was conceptual. From applied research we had come to understand what the system needed to be able to do – we were only just starting to test whether it could actually be achieved (to be detailed in Part 3).

So when the consultation document was released in October 2017, I admit I was little stunned. There it was – in the section about assessment – three paragraphs on responding to extra-familial harm titled 'Contextual Safeguarding'. I spoke with some local leaders – some who had been involved in the first stages of developing the approach and others who I had been in touch with for a matter of months. Down the phone line I received an unequivocal message from each conversation. Contextual Safeguarding made sense. The four-part framework was accessible. But more importantly, it provided leaders and practitioners with a language and framework to do two things. Firstly, to describe something that they already knew to be true – the child protection system was an ill-fit for extra-familial forms of harm. Secondly, to envisage what better might be. As such, many areas wanted to use the term to develop their practice and inclusion in statutory guidance gave the permission for areas to move in that direction.

In some respects, therefore, the inclusion of Contextual Safeguarding in WTSC was a positive step. But the text that had been inserted needed work – as did the need to integrate the approach into the broader document. At this point, it was referred to solely as an approach to assessment – rather than a recognition that to do Contextual Safeguarding the four domains would need to be evident – and woven – throughout the policy. Any attempt to do this in 2017 would have been premature. As mentioned previously we had only recently commenced full system testing and were not in a position to detail a bells and whistles account of implementation. But at this stage – going back to the Red, Amber Green (RAG) policy rating I had already undertaken – it was possible to make some initial recommendations.

I sat down with Jenny and we looked at the text itself. There were some positive elements to it. The draft document recognised that extra-familial harm was abuse that required a safeguarding response. Most importantly, the new text recommended that plans be developed to address the environmental factors associated to extra-familial harm – opening up the ability to target contexts through the lens of child welfare and child protection.

To strengthen this, we noted key places where the WTSC text could be contextualised. A notable issue had been the omission of any reference to peer-relationships in previous versions. Therefore we recommended that text be added to encourage that connections between young people who were peers, as well as those who were siblings, be considered by stating that information sharing was essential when 'multiple children appear associated to the same contexts or locations of risk'.

In terms of assessment, we attempted to disrupt the persistent focus on looking inside families as the sole source of risk. We did this by recommending the insertion of three words 'or faced by' in the section on assessment. This would result in the text reading that during assessment social workers needed to 'understand the level of need and risk in, *or faced by*, a family from the child's perspective'.

We wanted to think about partners. How could focus partners already named in WTSC to consider their role in *creating* safety in contexts rather than solely referring individuals out of them? We initially identified two ways to do this. Firstly, we recommended the insertion of bullet point in the list of arrangements all such agencies needed to have in place to fulfil their safeguarding duty. We recommended that, in addition to responsibilities around safe recruitment and risks posed by adults, all listed organisations had arrangements in place for 'creating a culture of safety, equality, and protection within the services that they provide'.

We also suggested a specific action for youth offending services – recommending that they identify contexts in which the young people they were supporting were also vulnerable to harm. This was important: given the overlap between young people who were harmed, and who harmed others, in extra-familial contexts it presented an opportunity to push against an often-false victim/perpetrator distinction that is ingrained in many practice and policy frameworks.

And finally, to avoid an impression that Contextual Safeguarding was about funnelling increased numbers of children into the child protection system, a comment was made about 'early help services'. In particular, the need for early help interventions to be offered into contexts where there were emerging, thematic concerns. It was our view, and still is, that if safety can be increased in one context (affecting the welfare of multiple children), then this could prevent multiple children being harmed in that context and being referred into the child protection system later down the line.

And to our surprise every single recommendation listed above was accepted as written.

And as a result of these somewhat measured changes, the RAG rating for WTSC immediately changed.

*Table 7.2* Contextual Safeguarding framework assessment of working together to safeguard children 2018

| Policy area | Target contexts | Child welfare lens | Contextual partners | Contextual outcomes |
|---|---|---|---|---|
| WTSC | Amber | Green | Amber | Red |

Extra-familial risks had been named as child protection issues in statutory guidance, and initial steps had been taken to permit a contextual response to these issues by children's social care – and their partners. Now the real work had to start. We had created an environment conducive with growing a Contextual Safeguarding system. It was time to operationalise the four-pillared framework and turn the idea into a reality.

# Note

1  120 professionals participated in the survey, although response rates to individual questions fluctuated between 100 and 120. Of the 106 respondents who provided their job title/sector, the majority were working in policing (22%), health (22%), or children's social care (13%), with the rest comprising professionals in safeguarding, education, mental health, voluntary sector, youth offending, and other sectors. The sample is self-selecting rather than representative, and so may comprise professionals with a particular interest in – or commitment to – safeguarding adolescents. The findings should therefore be interpreted with caution. Respondents also chose whether to expand on their survey answers by providing further written explanations. A relatively small proportion of those surveyed chose to do so for most questions, and this means we cannot generalise these answers to all the survey respondents, or to the wider population of professionals working with adolescents.

# Part 3

# Mapping and test running Contextual Safeguarding systems

# 8 The developers, their tools, and their roadmap

One of my two-year-old son's favourite books is called 'Roadwork' by Sally Sutton. We settle into the rocking chair I insisted on buying while pregnant, and rhythmically rock to the rhyming roadmap for how you lay a motorway. From marking out the road with pegs and tipping down stones, to raising the signs and planting trees we work through each step with the technicians, gardeners, and ground staff, until you can 'shout hurray the work is done – ready now let's zoom!'. And as we do I am reminded of what we had in place as we set out to grow our first Contextual Safeguarding systems and what we absolutely didn't.

We had the teams of developers; two sets in fact. There was an ever-increasing online network of practitioners – eagerly contextualising their own practices and championing that their colleagues, teams and where possible wider services, follow suit. And then there were our 'test sites': children's services departments in 10 parts of England and Wales who were working alongside my research team to implement Contextual Safeguarding across their systems. The first of these was the London Borough of Hackney – who secured a Social Care Innovation Grant from the Department of Education in 2017 to run the first system's application of a Contextual Safeguarding approach. A grant from the National Lottery Community Fund in 2018 allowed us to take the learning emerging from Hackney and re-test the approach in three further areas – which ended up being five: Bristol, Kent, Knowsley, Swansea, and Wiltshire. And initially through self-funded efforts and latterly through support from London's Violence Reduction Unit, we set up for testing in the London boroughs of Barking and Dagenham, Ealing, Merton, and Sutton. In each test site it was all hands on deck. We worked in partnership with frontline practitioners – particularly social workers, youth offending practitioners, and youth workers – as well as analysts, business support and ICT staff, lawyers, and senior leaders to grow a Contextual Safeguarding approach to suit each of their local contexts.

Those teams, however, were without a roadmap; and when we commenced in Hackney we didn't even have a blueprint. All we had was the four-part conceptual framework developed in 2016 (chapter 6) – upon which to build a Theory of Change. We knew where we wanted to get to – but we weren't entirely clear on how to get there. Unlike the technicians, gardeners, and builders from *Roadwork*, we weren't working from a roadmap. We were going to need to build one as we went – and this was where our embedded approach to research was vital. We knew that Contextual Safeguarding could never be converted into a manual; to do so would be an oxymoron. The approach would differ according to the context in which it was developed – interweaving with the opportunities that came with the partnerships, communities, and operational frameworks that made each area unique. But we also knew a four-part framework was insufficient to create the type of change we were seeking. Working as embedded researchers, the Contextual Safeguarding team had two key functions: to support practitioners to review approaches in light of the Contextual Safeguarding framework; and then to document their attempts to operationalise the Contextual Safeguarding framework (and the process through which they got there). By capturing the application of the framework, we were able to build practice 'toolkits'. These communicated to leaders, practitioners, and policymakers exactly what a Contextual Safeguarding system could look like – and what was required to develop and sustain it.

Through the research team, these two sets of developers (network members and practice site members) interacted, continuously deepening how Contextual Safeguarding was understood and advanced. Innovations by network members were shared with test sites via embedded researchers to inform their systems-change. And the resources being co-produced by researchers and practitioners in test-sites were accessed by network members for application in their own services/teams/areas. In this chapter I will detail the tools used within this process (research and practice methods), as well as their cumulative value – before documenting their impact on practice in the remaining pages of this book.

## A virtual practice network

When we launched the Contextual Safeguarding Practitioners' Network in 2016 our aim was to secure 100 members by 2018. These members would support each other via a virtual forum – sharing practices they were developing and challenges they were encountering. It was an attempt to diffuse the innovation we were developing across a wider body of actors, and give them the space to be at the forefront of practice change. By 2018 network membership was at 1,000 and by the point of writing this book in 2019 it had exceeded 6,000. With growth came both opportunities and challenges. Such a large membership compromised our ability to develop intimate and conversational relationships with all members: we didn't 'know' them, and couldn't support all members to participate in some activities such as our learning sets and events. However, when it came to reviewing and advancing resources being developed in test sites, having a large pool of practitioners who were seeking advice and guidance was extremely useful. Furthermore, as members updated us on their use of resources we were able to identify sites/teams to visit – and understand how they were implementing the approach without the research team working alongside them.

### *Membership and recruitment*

Initially the network was promoted to the practitioners who had worked with George and I to test contextual activities from 2013 to 2016. It provided a means for us to keep in contact with them once this initial phase of work came to an end, and importantly for them to connect with each other. In this sense, membership was opportune – it was not representative of practitioners nationally or by sector; it simply reflected those who were interested and wanted to remain in involved in the project. From 2016 to 2018 the network was promoted via word-of-mouth – with practitioners encouraging their colleagues to sign up – as well as at training events and keynote speeches delivered by the Contextual Safeguarding research team. It therefore remained opportune and reflective of individual practitioners who had heard of the Contextual Safeguarding approach, knew there was an online network and wanted to be involved. Network membership was free – as the resource was funded through trusts and foundations. Over time therefore it became evident that some members joined to share their practice, and actively discuss their work with others – whereas other members were at the start of their journey and had joined to learn from others. By the end of November 2019 network membership stood at 6,202. Where information was recorded and available for members, at this point regional ($n = 5920$) and sector representation (6,202) was as detailed in Tables 8.1 and 8.2, respectively.

### *Learning projects*

A key network activity used from 2016 to 2017 was learning projects and events; this activity appeared to work best with a smaller membership built on relationships between practitioners and the research team. Four learning projects were run in total. They focused on: responding to peer-on-peer abuse in educational settings; approaches to peer group mapping; developing holistic approaches to safeguarding adolescents (working across issue-specific responses); and responding to safeguarding concerns in local businesses and neighbourhood settings.

For each learning project a brief survey was issued to capture examples of practice (and the opportunities and challenge of developing that practice) related to the topic in question. For the first three learning projects, events were also held during the survey period, where practitioners could meet in person, discuss survey questions, and hear brief presentations of how these issues were being addressed in some local areas. Participation in each learning project is detailed in Table 8.3.

Practice briefings, which summarised the findings from each learning project, were published on the network website.

*Table 8.1* Network membership by region

| Region | Recorded membership |
|---|---|
| Channel Islands | 13 |
| East Midlands | 397 |
| East of England | 471 |
| International (outside the UK) | 111 |
| London | 1,465 |
| North East | 144 |
| North West | 607 |
| Northern Ireland | 10 |
| Scotland | 126 |
| South East | 878 |
| South West | 575 |
| Wales | 88 |
| West Midlands | 466 |
| Yorkshire and Humber | 354 |
| UK-wide | 215 |
| TOTAL | 5,920 |

*Table 8.2* Network membership by sector

| Sector | Recorded membership |
|---|---|
| Education | 1,778 |
| Social care | 1,721 |
| Health | 476 |
| Community safety | 445 |
| Voluntary sector | 396 |
| Youth justice | 311 |
| Safeguarding boards | 207 |
| Youth work | 187 |
| Policing | 142 |
| Crown Prosecution Service | 99 |
| Housing | 28 |
| Probation | 5 |
| Other | 407 |
| TOTAL | 6,202 |

*Table 8.3* Learning project participants and topics

| Learning project | Participant numbers |
|---|---|
| Responding to peer-abuse in education | 16 |
| Peer mapping | 13 |
| Holistic approaches to safeguarding | 11 |
| Business engagement in safeguarding | 11 |

### Resource testing and feedback

From 2013 to 2016 we produced a series of products from the contextual activities being developed by local practitioners. From 2017 onwards we continued to do the same in test sites. All resources were published on the network website. After the network was launched, whenever a new product was published all members were notified via an e-newsletter. At the time of writing, there were 29 practice resources on the network website. Those most regularly visited/downloaded were the implementation toolkit for children's social care, and in particular the toolkit for conducting neighbourhood assessments (explored more in chapter 10), as well as a self-assessment toolkit for schools developing their responses to harmful sexual behaviour between students.

Whenever a resource was published, practitioners were actively encouraged to contact the research team and update them on its use – including whether they made any adaptations tools or approaches.

Some members contacted the research team via the network to provide feedback. Others met members of the team at public events or training sessions and offered feedback in person.

### Blogs and podcasts

Through the above contacts members were encouraged to participate in podcasts or write blogs that captured their learning. Supported by the research team, members produced 73 blogs and 23 podcasts by the end of November 2019 that documented, and shared learning about, their developing practice. For the research team these resources also served as helpful case studies – indicating where resources/activities had been scaled up (and what had been required to make this happen) and where work undertaken in one locality may not have been easy to translate elsewhere.

### Site visits

In addition to virtual contact in the form of blog writing and recording podcasts the research team undertook a series of visits to document the work of members who were developing a Contextual Safeguarding approach. From 2016 until the point of writing the team visited 19 local areas in the United Kingdom. On some occasions, we initiated visits to see a particular example of practice: in one area we visited to learn more about their work with park gardeners and park wardens; in another site we learnt about (and observed) their newly formed panels where extra-familial contexts were being discussed and plans put in place to increase safety for young people who spent time in them. Fieldwork notes were taken during each visit and converted into a blog or case study, with practitioners from the area, to share via the network website.

In addition to generating evidence and resources for network members – all of the activities above informed the research team, who then took that learning into test sites.

## In-person practice development: test sites

It was May 2017 when 'we' started work in the London Borough of Hackney – I say 'we' as I delivered a keynote on the launch day with my 8-week-old baby cocooned in a sling on my chest and stayed on maternity leave until September that year. Jenny Lloyd was the embedded researcher; based in the site three days a week for two years. Jenny's role was to:

1. Capture and understand the extent to which Hackney's social care system addressed extra-familial risk prior to full implementation of the Contextual Safeguarding approach.
2. Monitor, record, and reflect upon pilots to embed Contextual Safeguarding practice within a child protection statutory framework in Hackney and the extent to which they applied the four domains of Contextual Safeguarding framework.
3. Co-create (with practitioners) a range of evidence-based Contextual Safeguarding tools and resources (systems, interventions, assessments, polices), and identify the workforce skills required, to enable the scale-up of the identified principles of practice into other geographic areas, using self-reflection and self-recording techniques amongst others.

Jenny was supported by a research assistant – first Ruth Atkinson and latterly Delphine Peace – who were initially charged with capturing evidence from the wider practice network that may be of use to the Hackney project, and disseminating learning from Hackney out to the network. I was the academic lead for the project – supporting the team two days a week – liaising with leaders in Children's Services in Hackney and providing strategic oversight for the implementation process. Collectively through embedded, strategic, and action research engagement, we worked as a group of researchers to identify the principles, structures, and mechanisms for contextualising a social care offer to young people at risk of harm in extra-familial settings.

As they had secured Department for Education funding for the work Hackney also employed a project team – comprising social workers ($n = 4$), youth workers ($n = 2$), a participation officer, and a clinical supervisor – who worked together to develop and test a Contextual Safeguarding system that could be scaled out across the wider service. They were supported by other practitioners in Hackney who were championing a Contextual Safeguarding approach in their own service areas but were sat outside of the core project team, for example: a manager working in the team who screened referrals into children's services developed ways for contexts to be considered during the referral process; and a staff member from business support identified ways to use Hackney's case management system to record information on contexts as well as children and families being supported by children's services. A wider project advisory group was also established to engage multi-agency partners in the development of the approach – many of whom also worked on topic-specific work streams to develop work in schools for example, or consider how the whole service would develop or use interventions for working with peer groups. The project team (practitioners and researchers), wider staff members, advisory group, and work stream members, worked together to operationalise a Contextual Safeguarding system; and convert this system into a suite of practice resources which formed an online toolkit.

This complex web of roles and responsibilities could not be replicated in the other nine test sites. The funding received was solely to resource the support from the research team and didn't extend to project teams within the local authorities themselves. From 2019 the research team in those sites comprised a lead senior researcher (Jenny Lloyd), an embedded researcher (Joanne Walker), a social work practice advisor (Rachael Owens), and a research assistant (Vanessa Bradbury). Rachael had been a social work manager in the original Hackney team, and Jo had worked with Jenny and me on a project developing contextual approaches to safeguarding in schools. Each test site we worked with developed its own structures for supporting the process. All appointed a single point of contact for the research team and established a steering group – bringing together senior leaders from across their partnerships. Some also appointed a project manager, but for the most part the practitioners working with the research team were doing so alongside their remaining 'day job'. In some ways this was a limitation as new test sites had less resource to dedicate to the project. However, this approach meant that staff who would be involved in sustaining the approach beyond the research period were actively involved in its development. As such the system revisions were being embedded as we worked, rather than after it had been created by a discrete team. Furthermore, much of the first two years in Hackney was spent creating the first Contextual Safeguarding Implementation Toolkit – the original attempt at converting the four-part conceptual framework into an operational reality. Once this had been achieved, all new test sites had a blueprint to work from, which meant the task of designing their own systems was much less labour intensive; although implementation in these sites, for which we are only at the start at the point of writing this book, is no less challenging.

### *System mapping – case reviews, observations, and document review*

We commenced work in all test sites by reviewing their existing response to extra-familial harm. To what extent did a local system already reflect a Contextual Safeguarding framework: was the system targeting the social conditions of harm, through the lens of child welfare, with the necessary partnerships, to achieve (and measure) increased safety in places and groups where harm was occurring? A range of qualitative methods were used during this initial review.

Observation of practice and meetings was an essential part of being embedded in test sites. Members of the research team observed teams as they managed and discussed cases of extra-familial harm – over the phone, at their desks, and even over video conferencing. Observing these conversations both within and outside of formal meetings gave us an initial sense of professional cultures and relationships as well as the practicalities of how risks associated with extra-familial harm were being managed. Through fieldwork diaries and observation templates we recorded whether, and how, the conversations we observed intersected with the four domains of the Contextual Safeguarding framework – and indeed if any of them appeared contrary to it. Topics discussed, actions agreed, and the language used throughout were all routes to forming such conclusions. For example, when observing a meeting between practitioners responding to a stabbing the evening before we would be looking out for the extent to which it aligned to the Contextual Safeguarding framework (Table 8.4):

*Table 8.4* Contextual Safeguarding framework application to a site observation

| *Domain* | *Observation* |
| --- | --- |
| 1:  Target the context (social conditions of abuse) | Did the practitioners identify/explore the peer relationships involved in (or associated to) the incident or the nature of the context where the stabbing occurred |
| 2:  Deliver response through the lens of child welfare and child protection | What role, if any, was identified for children's social care – was it viewed as a safeguarding issue or primarily a criminal justice or community matter? |
| 3:  Leverage the partnerships who have reach in to the contexts in question | Did social workers involved in the case have access to partners who could begin to reach into the peer group or location of the stabbing – were they involved in initial conversations or where more appropriate were actions agreed to liaise with those partners for contextual purposes |
| 4:  Measure success/safety contextually | What was the objective of the work moving forward – was there an intention to safeguard the group or place, as well as the individual involved, or was success solely measured around actions taken with individual young people and families |
| Across all four domains | Throughout – did the language used in the meeting locate the incident in context? Were the relevant contexts described or was risk located in the child – the child who was stabbed had been making risky choices for a while – or the child was in a risky situation for a while (which informed their choices) etc. |

In Hackney ($n = 17$) and across the five stage 2 test sites ($n = 54$) 71 meetings were observed during the system mapping period; as well as 30 informal conversations and reflective meetings in Hackney that occurred during embedded research days (that were logged in fieldwork diaries).

In addition to observations, review of local documents, tools, and policies provided us with insights into how sites practiced – at least on paper. Building on the audit methodologies used in earlier iterations of the research programme (chapter 5), documents were mapped to generate a conceptual web of practice: how did they all talk to each other (if at all) – when all were applied what did this say about how the area responded to extra-familial harm. In addition, all documents were viewed through the lens of the Contextual Safeguarding framework – and the same questions applied to them as those used to analyse data gathered during observations. Did the documents provide a sense of how the area targeted contexts, through the lens of child welfare, with the appropriate partners and with shared contextual objectives to measure success? There were multiple levels of document to be reviewed as illustrated in Figure 8.1.

Local strategies detailed overarching commitments of senior leaders with regards to specific issues impacting young people – such as serious youth violence or domestic abuse. Commissioning commitments were often outlined in these documents, and they were also where we regularly located an area's vision and measures of success. Underneath strategies sat policies and procedures. These documents detailed the nuts and bolts of local process – what was an area's policy for how it responds to serious youth violence or domestic abuse and were there procedures to be followed in this regard? The service area who oversaw strategies, policies and procedures for any given topic often produced findings related to domain 2 of the Contextual Safeguarding framework. For example, serious youth violence strategy, policy, and procedures were often overseen by community safety partnerships in local areas – whereas sexual exploitation documents were more readily developed by safeguarding partnerships and boards mirroring national siloes. From the outset therefore, responses to sexual exploitation were more aligned to the Contextual Safeguarding framework than responses to serious youth violence in test sites – and this division

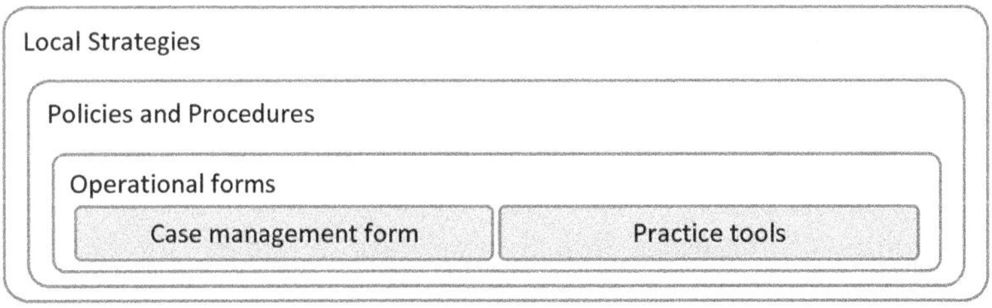

*Figure 8.1* Nests of Document Assessment in Local Sites

exemplified inconsistent (rather than holistic) responses to extra-familial harm. A series of forms and practice tools sat beneath policies and procedures – assisting practitioners in implementing a consistent local response to extra-familial harm: from forms to refer children into children's services for support and documents which detailed the various 'thresholds' for accessing support, through to assessment frameworks, and tools to use during direct work with young people and families. Each of these tools was considered against the Contextual Safeguarding framework – and the extent to which they assisted practitioners in targeting the social conditions of abuse, through the lens of child welfare, drawing upon relevant partnerships and with an objective of achieving contextual safety. Across Hackney ($n$ = 6) and the five stage 2 test sites ($n$ = 29) 35 documents were reviewed.

Case reviews – the method that underpinned the formation of Contextual Safeguarding – was used in sites to build illustrations of how all parts of the system that had been observed or reviewed on paper came together in response to an incident. The case review approach used in earlier studies was amended and abbreviated for the purpose of system mapping. Two types of case reviews were undertaken. The first, and most common, was 'dip-sampling' (Lloyd & Firmin, 2019) of referrals made into children's social care in all test sites that related to extra-familial harm. Initially in Hackney researchers sampled cases across a three-month period; in scale-up sites researchers' sampled cases from child and family assessments authorised in a one-month period. Focusing on cases of extra-familial harm that were assessed within that time period, we looked at the decision reached following assessment – whether the case received further social work support, was referred on to another service or closed altogether. The decision-making process in these cases told us many things about the approach taken to extra-familial harm in each site, including:

- Whether and how thresholds for accessing statutory support were being applied: was this based on the levels of risks faced by a child, or did this harm also need to be attributable to parents for a case to progress?
- To what extent did contextual, and not just familial factors, inform decision-making, and were peer relationships considered in this regard?

In total, 92 decisions featured in dip-sampling across five stage 2 test sites, and 67 were sampled across two occasions in Hackney by the end of 2019.

Dip-sampling provided us with an insight into case-handling at one juncture in a child protection system; the point at which children and families are referred (or not) for statutory support. More detailed case reviewing was used at opportune moments where cases were brought to the attention of the team during the system mapping process. These opportunities enabled us to build a start-to-end picture of how a case of extra-familial harm had been addressed – including the full assessment, plans, and interventions. They took the form of opportune case studies rather than in-depth reviews, but served to highlight occasions where services responded to extra-familial harm by targeting peer, school or neighbourhood dynamics.

Using these different forms of data collection the research team were able build an understanding of how systems were operating prior to the development of a Contextual Safeguarding approach in each site: identifying where the system already aligned with the Contextual Safeguarding framework and elements that required further attention. The research team produced two versions of a 'system-map' for each area – upon which the next stage of work could be planned. The first was a visual flowchart of a child's journey through the system as we had observed it; identifying various pathways, meetings, and so on available to practitioners who were overseeing those cases (Figure 8.2).

Each map was also annotated to identify where different practice tools were used and the extent to which they, and the processes identified, were aligned to the Contextual Safeguarding framework.

Secondly, we commenced a RAG rating process for each site at this point, to assist us in prioritising activities. The RAG was aligned to the Contextual Safeguarding framework and drew upon much of the qualitative evidence gathered through the above activities to illustrate the rating. For example:

> Language used to describe children experiencing extra-familial harm in the site demonstrated an awareness of the situations in which harm was occurring; how they considered the impact of this on a child's choice varied. Evidence had been found of the system targeting contexts at XXX meeting where XXX were discussed, and there was space to consider this in the record of the meeting. However the assessment framework being used didn't compliment this process and so there remains elements of the overarching system that target families alone. Site rated at AMBER for Domain 1: target.

Both the visual system map and the RAG rating table were produced for each site. When combined, they offered a starting point for the research team and practitioners in each site to develop their Contextual Safeguarding approach. At the point of writing this book all test sites had undergone this process. Once system mapping was completed a variety of action research methods were used between researchers and practitioners to build, test, and document emerging Contextual Safeguarding systems: by the end of 2019 this had only been realised in Hackney.

### Co-production and pilots

System mapping gave researchers and practitioners in each site an indication of where local practice or policy required development. In Hackney we created these developments from scratch. The project team worked together to design an approach to assessing schools, neighbourhoods, peer groups, and so on – drawing upon available research evidence on contextual practices and

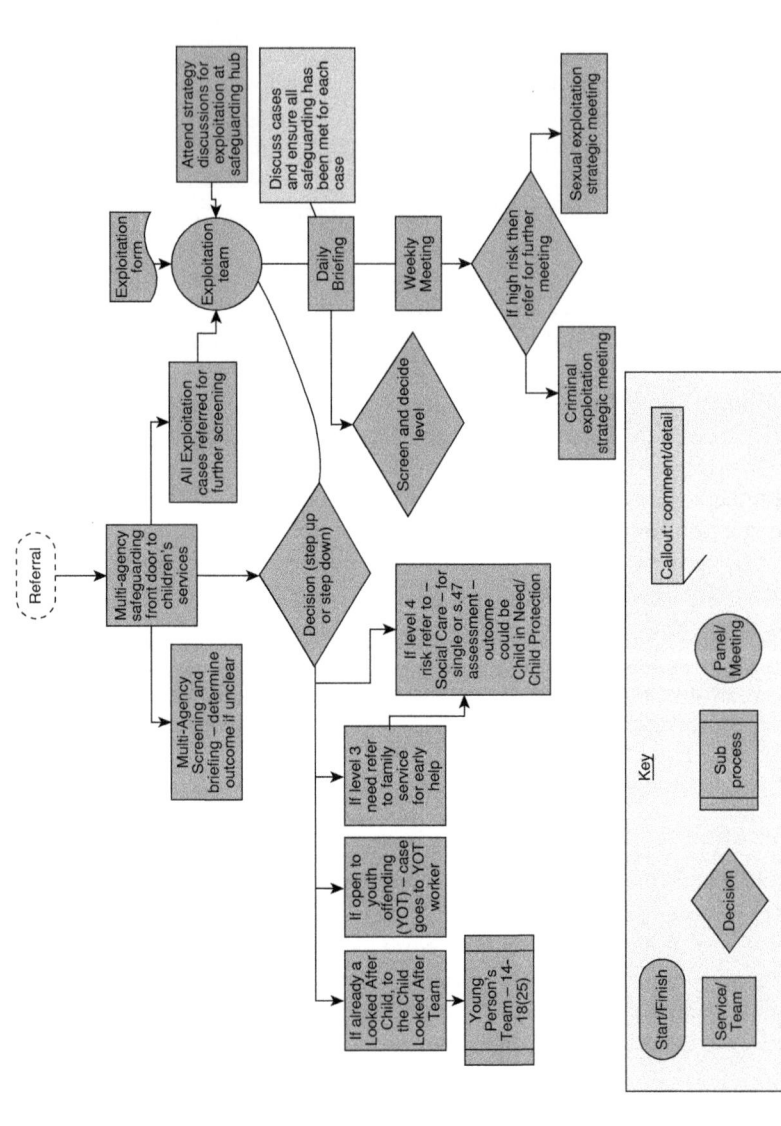

*Figure 8.2* System Map Exemplar

converting them for use in a social care setting. The details of these assessments and their impact are detailed in chapters 9 and 10. Whenever an approach or set of tools were created, practitioners then piloted them and researchers documented the piloting process – working towards a space in which the practice output was co-produced. In stage 2 test sites practitioners and researchers have been working from the Hackney blueprint, amending resources or creating further ones where they feel their local context or service requires them; the blueprint gave them a sense of the type of work they may have to do to contextualise their system. The process remains one of co-creation and piloting, and at the point of writing all stage 2 test sites were at this juncture in their development of Contextual Safeguarding.

### Reflective workshops

Following pilots, and as different policy frameworks or practice tools were being developed, researchers or practitioners facilitated reflective workshops with practitioners. Workshops were semi-structured and designed around a document or activity. The facilitator would introduce the focus of the conversation and invite practitioners to reflect on their use of a resource or engagement in a pilot. Reflections were drawn upon to further develop or amend the resource or practice in question – and therefore provided an additional route to co-producing their local Contextual Safeguarding approach. In this sense practitioners and researchers 'workshopped' a resource or approach together – identifying where further work might be required or identifying how best to embed the resource or approach across systems. Workshops provided a critical space for identifying the extent to which local practitioners understood, and were invested in, a particular element of the system. If their reflections surfaced anxieties about workforce capacity and/or skill sets, this provided an indication of whether the approach was sustainable in its current form. As the teams were seeking system change – rather than the introduction of a discrete intervention – practitioner buy-in, commitment, and confidence was critical: they would be at the forefront of the implementation process when the research team's involvement came to an end.

Reflective workshops were particularly useful for developing resources or policy documents that went beyond focused pilots. An example would be their use in developing 'threshold' documents (chapter 13). Every site had a threshold or equivalent document which they used to guide decision-making related to how best to meet the needs of children and families referred into children's social care for support. Work had to be undertaken to: (a) assess whether these documents appropriately engaged with extra-familial harm impacting children and families, and; (b) develop a threshold document to support decision-making related to extra-familial contexts in which such harm occurred. Draft iterations of these documents were produced by researchers and practitioners working alongside each other (see side-by-side learning below and chapter 13 for an example of the outputs).These drafts were then workshopped at a series of sessions with different practitioners and managers across children's services and partner agencies to get them to a point where they agreed to adopt the resource/approach.

### Side-by-side learning

Being embedded meant that researchers sat alongside social work and youth work practitioners in test sites. This provided a space for unstructured and iterative learning outside of more formal activities – like workshops, observations, and pilots. Practitioners could check in with researchers as they developed proposals; and researchers were given a timely indication of the challenges facing practice teams, the questions that were emerging in real time, and what research may offer to resolve some of them. This methodology was largely subtle, the learning captured through fieldwork diaries; but it provided the grounds upon which problem-solving could be tested, ideas could be co-produced, and relationships between practitioners and researchers could be built.

### Systems reviews

Implementing Contextual Safeguarding in any test site requires a series of discrete but interconnected activities. For example, from designing assessment

*Photo 8.1*

*Photo 8.2*

methods, reviewing intervention options, re-writing policy documents, updating ICT software, instructing legal advice, engaging parents and young people, training community representatives and building service champions, a host of different activities were completed by the research and practice team to design and test a Contextual Safeguarding approach. There were also a vast number of practitioners involved in discrete actions that related to their particular service area. System review sessions were run to bring these activities together and track how they were collectively advancing a site towards a Contextual Safeguarding Approach. I facilitated each of these sessions which occurred every 8–10 weeks in Hackney and are occurring three times a year in stage 2 test sites (following system mapping). Aided by blue-tack, flip chat pens, and markers I would scroll all site activity to contextualise: Referrals; Assessments; Planning; Interventions; and, Policy Frameworks.

An additional sheet was also used to document any pressing challenges or barriers identified by attendees. Not only did this process remind all participants what progress was being made, but it also provided us with a shared route of what to prioritise for the forthcoming 8–10 weeks. This meant that despite often working on separate tasks, each team member knew what we were working towards collectively for the coming period and what role we would each be playing in that regard. I found the system review process

*Photo 8.3*

energising – and other team members commented on the how much they valued them as way to check-in and re-focus. We were and continue to embark on such fundamental system change that it has been easy to forget how a change to an assessment framework (chapter 9) or attempts to train community guardians (chapter 10) fits into the wider picture – or whether it matters. Through system reviews we were reminded that not only did each activity matter, but also that it was integral to achieving the change we wanted to see.

## Change at two levels: the two tiers of Contextual Safeguarding

One year after launching the Contextual Safeguarding Practitioners' Network and six months after commencing work in our first test site (Hackney), I realised something quite profound, and yet obvious, about what each set of developers was trying to achieve. During sites' visits, in learning projects, via blogs on the network and in attempts to commence pilots in Hackney, the Contextual Safeguarding framework was being applied at two levels. The four pillars of the Contextual Safeguarding framework didn't, articulated on its own, get at the dual-levelled application that was starting to emerge in practice. Understanding this created a more sophisticated approach to combining, analysing, and presenting the emergent results of the activities outlined above.

When network members and practitioners in test sites set about implementing a Contextual Safeguarding framework they were firstly finding ways to integrate extra-familial contexts into existing work, or processes, which engaged with children and families. When they began making inroads in this regard, extra-familial contexts themselves emerged as a focus for work/attention. And when that happened, the developers needed to create new approaches for identifying, assessing and intervening with contexts themselves. At one level therefore, we saw adaptations to existing structures and resources. At a second level new structures or resources were introduced. Looking at how referrals into children's social care were being adapted is one way to understand what this meant in practice.

If a child had been stabbed at a bus terminus after school the police who attended that event may also refer that child into children's social care given the significant harm they had experienced. Traditionally the child would have been referred into the system with some detail provided about the incident, along with the child's personal details such as their home address and so on. If any other children were involved in the incident they would each be made the subject of their own individual, separate, referral. As Contextual Safeguarding was being picked up by network members and in test sites those receiving referrals began requesting and recording more information about the address of the stabbing as well as the address of the child's home; thereby building reference to the neighbourhood context into the referral. Some were also asking for referrals for multiple children associated to the same incident to be grouped so that those assessing the referral were aware of the potential peer relationships involved and the risks that might be shared within them. This was level 1 Contextual Safeguarding.

At level 2, however, the bus terminus itself might have been referred into children's social care as a context in which harm was occurring. This was happening in a number of ways. In Hackney work had commenced to identify how a referral about a location could be made into the children's social care 'front door' and formally recorded. Whereas network members, as well as other colleagues in Hackney, were also identifying concerns about locations in case notes and at multi-agency meetings and making 'in-system' or 'in-service' referrals about locations already documented in the records of individual children. Via either route level 2 Contextual Safeguarding was in train.

It seemed to us even then (at the end of 2017) that both levels, or tiers, of practice needed to be evident in a child protection system and wider safeguarding partnership for the Contextual Safeguarding framework to be fully operational. Contexts needed to be engaged with as a child and family were supported within child protection systems; and the contextual factors that these processes identified required attention (Figure 8.3). Only delivering the Contextual Safeguarding framework at level 1 meant that contextual factors could be recognised by practitioners, young people, and families,

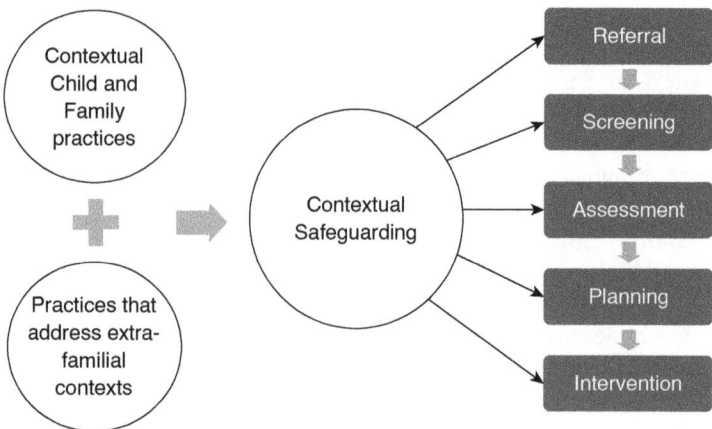

*Figure 8.3* Two Levels of Contextual Safeguarding

and inform direct work with them, but not necessarily be addressed. Whereas work at level 2 engaged with the contexts in which young people encountered harm, but didn't recognise the interplay between those environments and the individuals who were vulnerable within them.

Holding the interplay between context and individual at the heart of the Contextual Safeguarding framework, and its application, also maintained its alignment to Bourdieu's social theory (as outlined in chapter 4).

## Conclusion: a reflexive learning process

As we entered this stage in the development of Contextual Safeguarding, we had thought that learning about the approach would grow by taking initial learning from the network and scaling it across systems in test sites. In reality, network members have taken learning (and resources) emerging from test sites, applied them in their own practice and, via the research team, sent this back out for test sites to consider. It is this iterative process of creating, testing, sharing, testing, amending, and so on that has deepened the research teams' understanding of the levels at which Contextual Safeguarding can be implemented.

The various methods we adopted with each team of developers have been unique to their set-up: informed by both what they are expected to do in their team/role/system and our level of engagement with them. But collectively the process of working with each group of practitioners has created a developmental pathway for realising a Contextual Safeguarding approach: in other words we have learnt about what you need to do to gradually create that approach (and in creating it understood what Contextual

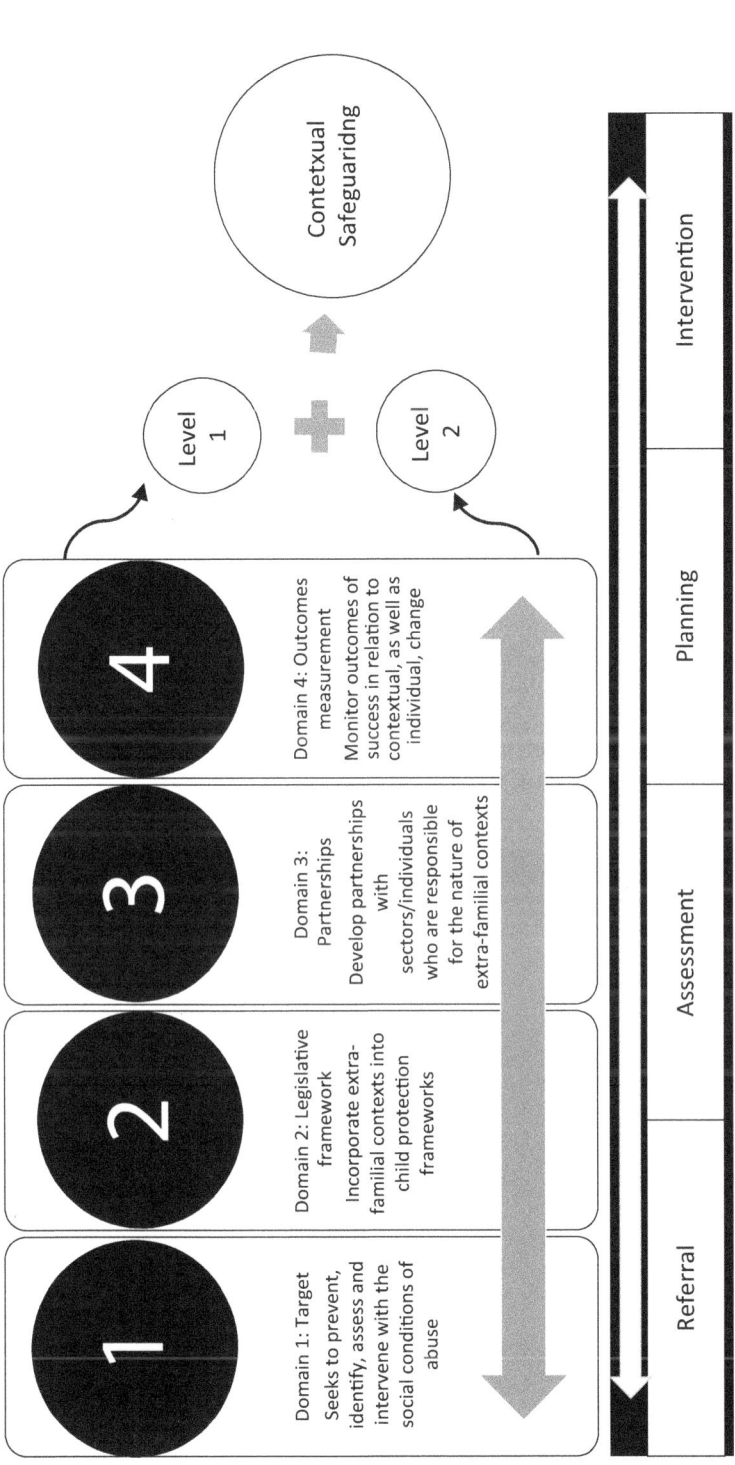

*Figure 8.4* Combined Contextual Safeguarding Framework for Testing

Safeguarding means), rather than simply generating it once and circulating the information around for mass replication.

In hindsight this has been a more realistic way of changing a system. It would have been difficult for network members to generate ideas from a four-part conceptual framework, largely independent of the team who were at the forefront of its continued development. However, network members were best placed to advise us on the feasibility of translating or using test site resources in their own practice, and whether such practices could be sustained in localities where the research team had no presence. Their ability, or not, to create Contextual Safeguarding approaches, has been (and continues to be) essential for sense-checking what broader systemic issues require attention – in terms of legislative and policy frameworks or commissioning priorities – for Contextual Safeguarding to be adopted wholesale.

Contextual Safeguarding as an approach therefore is best understood, investigated, and articulated via a combination of the four domains of the Contextual Safeguarding conceptual framework (chapter 6) and the two levels of Contextual Safeguarding implementation (Figure 8.4).

The remaining chapters in Part 3 of the book attempt to do this: firstly by dedicating a chapter to each level of implementation – using evidence from test sites and network members to illustrate elements of system change. After which I also consider issues related to policies and partnership that cut across both those levels and what this all is gradually telling us about the values which underpin a Contextual Safeguarding approach.

# 9 Bringing context into work with children and families

## Level 1 Contextual Safeguarding

When you look for it contextual practice is easy to see. It happens when a youth worker stands shoulder to shoulder with a Shaun in the waiting room of a sexual health clinic, knowing that if they weren't there that young person would probably feel too intimidated or afraid to stay put. It happens when a teacher knows that by sitting Ruth with Alexia and Susan the dynamic of that group will shift positively and all three will focus on the task they have been set in class. Or when a youth justice officer provides a comprehensive account of Michael's neighbourhood in his pre-sentence report before they go before the judge; using the opportunity to communicate how living on a street where drug-dealing happens in broad daylight is a constant risk to his safety. These, and many others, are examples of how individual practitioners recognise the impact of context on the decisions young people make. They see a young person in context and they see that context as relevant to how they practice.

Level 1 Contextual Safeguarding takes these individual examples of systemic practice and implements them across, and into the bones of, a child protection system. To do so isn't solely about shifting the actions of each individual practitioner in the system however. It isn't about everyone working like Shaun's youth work or Ruth's teacher. As previous chapters have already illustrated, the structures and processes of England's child protection system were wedded to individualised practice. Therefore, if all practitioners within the child protection system were told to 'place the child's experience in context' but their assessment frameworks, practice tools, measures of success or the information shared with them were all de-contextualised how far would into the system could such a message penetrate? The way children were referred into the child protection system, the systems that facilitated assessments, the way that plans to support children were developed, and the mechanisms for measuring their success all required attention for Contextual Safeguarding to take root.

Within six months of testing Contextual Safeguarding Hackney we realised that changes in some activities were pushing for change at this level. Before testing commenced I hadn't given this granular level of work much consideration. I was focused on what I thought was bigger system change – how to get the system to work with peer groups and locations (chapter 10) associated to extra-familial harm, for example. And that was the beauty of working alongside practitioners. They were far better placed than I ever could be to see what they and their colleagues would need to get to that level of system change. For the system to be at a place where working with parks or stairwells felt like second nature, they needed to be seen as relevant to work that was already underway with the children and families affected by, and affecting, those parks and stairwells.

As Level 1 resources and activities were designed in Hackney and shared on our virtual platforms; network members picked them up and tested them in their own areas and services. We were also able to mine information already available via our network members to inform efforts in Hackney. This diffusion of approaches and techniques deepened how we understood Level 1 change and I use this chapter to present the aggregated results of this process. Working through a 'system' I will document how context was integrated into referrals and assessments through to planning, interventions, policies, and wider cultures of practice; reflecting on the questions raised, as well as answered thus far, by the process.

## The stages of Level 1 implementation

In the text that follows the implementation of Contextual Safeguarding across a child protection system appears linear: the process of doing so is not. I had been sat in Hackney all but two weeks when a member of the project team asked to talk through an idea with me. They had been working on a resource to help young people, and the social workers who were supporting them, think about context. She showed me a map of the local area. Her idea was to create a series of talking points about the map, and encourage a young person to colour-code the map to illustrate where they felt safe (green), neutral (amber), and unsafe (red). I sat, eyes fixed on the screen when she asked – is this the type of thing you had in mind? I realised – I really didn't have anything in this level of practical detail in mind when I wrote the Contextual Safeguarding framework. But the practice I hoped it could lead to I absolutely did. Of course this resource was one part of developing a Contextual Safeguarding approach across a system: in and of itself it didn't create system-wide change. But no single activity detailed in this chapter would. What it did do was to give practitioners, young people, and families a tangible product that could assist them in being a part of, and working towards, a cumulative system impact.

This mapping exercise is explained below as an example of planning and intervention – therefore appearing much later on through the chapter. And yet in reality it was one of the first pieces of work to emerge from the Hackney team and to be picked up for further testing and development across the country by a series of network members – and has been used during the process of assessment, as well as a means of intervention. I have structured the chapter in accordance to a system as ultimately Contextual Safeguarding is achieved when all of these different activities work together – even if they originated independently and at different times. However, to replicate this process individuals and services can start at any point that makes most sense to them – working through activities until they coalesce to enable change from referral through to intervention – and all that sits in between.

### The front door

As noted in chapter six, each child's social care department across England has what is referred to as a 'front door'. This is where calls (and increasingly emails) are received when someone is concerned about the welfare of a child. Over time these have become multi-disciplinary parts of the safeguarding system where police officers, health professionals, and analysts work alongside social workers in a multi-agency safeguarding hub (MASH) to 'screen' and review referrals that have been made. Pulling together various pieces of information that they each might hold about a child and/or family, they are better positioned collectively, rather than on their own, to take an informed decision about any required action.

Testing of Contextual Safeguarding has shown us that there are great opportunities that come with integrating reference to context at this stage of a child's journey through the child protection system. The type of information that is shared at the point the referral is made, the forms used to record that information, and the way the information is screened all change when Contextual Safeguarding is implemented.

Let's start with the referral itself.

Going back to the case of Sara, whom we met in chapter 2. She was sexually assaulted on numerous occasions in a park, near a bus stop, and in a fast food restaurant. She passed these locations on her way to, and back from, school. She told a sexual health nurse about what had happened to her and where it had happened to her. Upon hearing this information the sexual health nurse phoned 'the front door' of her local children's services department and referred Sara into the system.

The referral was received and checks were made by the police, health, and other co-located agencies about Sara and her family. Social workers had been in contact with Sara and her family when she was a younger child, and based on what she had now said her case was re-opened to children's social care and a new assessment of her family commenced. From the point of the referral the park, bus stop, and fast food restaurant where she had been assaulted, and remained vulnerable to assault, faded into the background. And likewise her family, who rarely featured in the disclosures she made to a nurse, were at the foreground of everyone's concerns.

In testing Contextual Safeguarding therefore, practitioners in test sites and network members have been developing ways for parks, bus stops, and shops to feature as prominently in a referral as the child affected by them. As a basic starting point some front door departments are beginning to record the location in which the harm occurred (if known) as well as the living address of the young person who has been referred. In Sara's case these locations were buried in her case notes later down the line but didn't feature prominently when she was initially referred in for support. Acknowledging the need to do this has been a good first step. Full implementation has required practitioners to identify how to name a location – what is the appropriate 'naming convention' for example, for bus stop B on XXX road. Where can it be recorded on a system (linked to ICT changes detailed later below) and how to keep such recording consistent?

Additionally contextual information has also been collected in some areas about the schools attended by young people and the connections between them (when they are involved in an incident of harm together). This has required work with agencies that refer concerns as well as those that receive them. For example, in one local area when five young people were all groomed online they were each referred individually into the front door. At this point the fact that they were groomed together, and the risk they shared collectively, was lost. One child already had a social worker and so this new information was shared with them, one appeared to be living in some difficult circumstances and so an assessment was undertaken of him and his family. Two others were referred separately for support from an early help service and for the fifth there was decision to take no further action following referral. The impact that this had on them as a group was not explored. While individual support may have been required for some, the group dynamic of this incident did not inform the decision-making process.

As a result practitioners have started to explore methods to indicate connections between children referred separately but who are connected to the same incident – and have identified numerous routes. Some of this has been determined by the agency or individual who is making the referral in the first place. For example, each police force in England uses their own form to refer a child into children's services. In areas where Contextual Safeguarding is being explored the police are considering ways to indicate on these forms that the three children they have referred are connected. Alternatively other agencies use forms provided by social care – sometimes called a 'contact and referral form' or 'multi-agency referral form'. Children's services colleagues in some test sites have reviewed these forms to identify opportunities to record information about peer, school, public space, and virtual contexts associated to harm – and any connections between peers. In some cases this has resulted in schools trying to make single referrals for whole friendship groups for whom they have welfare concerns.

Testing of this in Hackney's front door has resulted in a significant transformation in the type of questions that are asked at the point of referral and the process that ensues afterwards. Figure 9.1 produced by a manager within this part of the service illustrates a before and after process of integrating context into referrals for children affected by extra-familial harm to make informed decisions about where support is most needed.

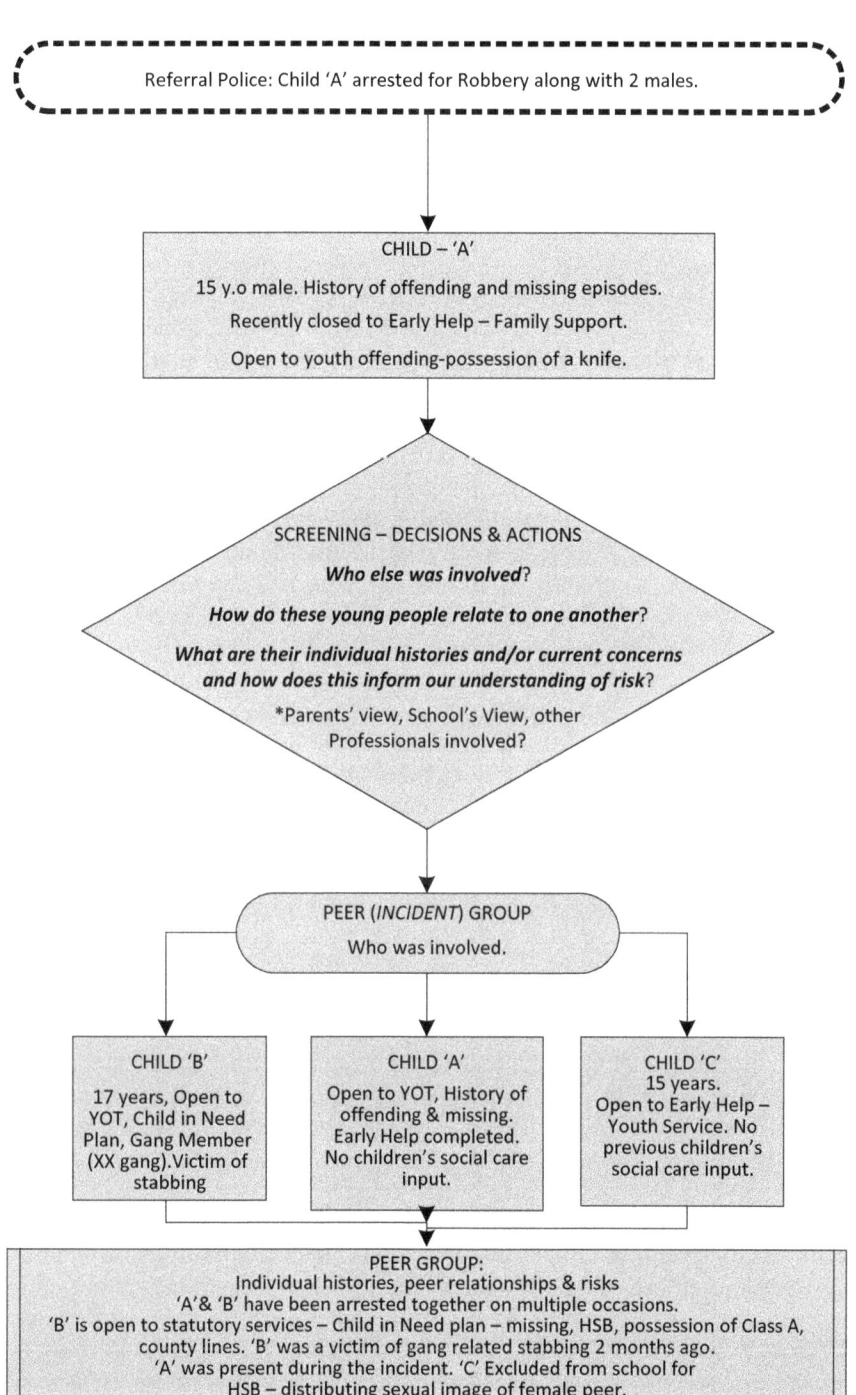

*Figure 9.1* Illustration of Contextual Analysis during Referrals

In reflecting on these changes, the practitioner who had developed and documented them stated that:

> But I think it fundamentally is a totally different outcome when you start looking at the dynamics within a peer group, the risks, the pull a peer group might have on a young person. And in this example, it totally changes the outcome, so where we didn't look at peers, we closed it to an Early Help service, and when we started looking at peers, we realised actually this is a very risky situation. So yeah it fundamentally changes the outcome because you have far more information about risk than you did if you didn't look at peers and peer relationships.
>
> And you are understanding the importance of that relationship on a young person, the power of that relationship on the young person. And I guess also looking from the young person's point of view, perhaps traditionally we're looking at things happening to young people and people protecting young people in a very linear traditional approach. In this approach we're saying this young person is participating in things and is a part of things by choice. And lots of these things are things that they enjoy and are positive, you know, being outside the home, being out late, things that we might perceive to be risky are actually for a young person they're not perceived as risky. It's the other stuff that's happening to them when they're in that situation that are the things we should be focusing on. So yeah, it fundamentally changes the outcome I think, which is a total eye-opener and experience I must say.
>
> And I think on the surface looks quite complex doesn't it, because you're now introducing a whole bunch of things to consider, you know, far more complex relationships, but if you invest the time now, and you think more holistically, contextually, you know more thorough, you have better outcomes in the long run, because you don't see repeat referrals for the same things, because you're investing all that time and energy in mapping and getting it right at that point. And potentially you're addressing the needs of lots of young people in one instance, rather than just individual young people in isolation of each other. So it's a lot of investment at first point, but I think it does lead to better outcomes and a greater understanding of what's happening for young people longer term.
>
> (Social work manager, screening service, test site)

Recording information about peers, schools, and locations at the 'front door' of children's services gives a contextual frame to concerns about children and families who may be assessed. It points social workers to the idea that in some cases the risks faced by the child sit beyond their front door – and the assessment process, therefore, will need to assess those factors in order to make an informed decision about the most appropriate form of support. For example, in one MASH I observed, social care, policing, and health practitioners discussed a referral they had received about a young man who was being criminally exploited to move and sell drugs. He had been physically assaulted previously, there were ongoing significant concerns for his physical safety and his emotional well-being. The referral had been made by the young man's father. The MASH recommended children's services accept the referral and undertake a full assessment due to the level of harm this young man faced. When agreeing this decision they explicitly noted that his parents were protective and this recommendation had been made given the level of risk faced to the young person in extra-familial contexts.

To progress referrals like this, much work has been undertaken in both test sites and via the Contextual Safeguarding practice network to contextualise the assessment of children and families impacted by extra-familial harm.

### *Assessment*

As noted in chapter 7, changes made to England's statutory child protection guidance in 2018 stated that during assessment social workers needed to consider the risks in, *and faced by*, a family from a child's perspective. While only three words, the insertion of 'and faced by' significantly shifts how a social work assessment is positioned and its focus of attention. It also provides a clear example of how narrow the assessment lens had been, from a policy perspective, prior to 2018.

Practitioners in test sites and the Contextual Safeguarding network have been grappling with how to convert these three words into a practical reality.

So Sara has been referred into children's services having disclosed to a sexual health nurse that she has been raped in a park and at a bus stop, as well as being sexually harassed at school. If responded to contextually, the referral process would have named these contexts as areas where Sara has experienced significant harm – a risk of which was thought to persist. What routes are there for to a social worker to integrate contexts into their assessment of Sara and her family? By routes I mean both the methods for gathering this information, and the mechanism for using it to form a conclusion and propose a plan.

Starting with methods, practitioners have developed activities under two main banners. The first is designing ways to talk with young people and parents about the contexts that impact their choices, sense of safety, and quality of relationships. The second has involved identifying activities that social workers and others can use to better understand the nature of the peer groups, schools, and public spaces that parents and young people may identify – and through this source options for creating change.

> Consider how the wider socio-political environment creates structural inequalities which impact on and limit the choices this young person and their family have within their environment (i.e. the way public spaces are designed, lack of opportunities an influence/agency, experiences of

discrimination etc.) (Hackney Contextual Safeguarding Project, 2019:20) *Exert from guidance on assessment and planning for children's social care*

Factors contributing to harm or vulnerability:
Familial

- Severe and/or complex relationship difficulties within home/family relationships leading to significant impairment of functioning and wellbeing.
- Missing or trafficked child/young person primarily due to 'push' factors which come from the home environment.

Extra-familial

- Child/young person appears to have been trafficked.
- Severe and/or complex relationship difficulties outside the home (i.e. peer group) leading to significant impairment of functioning and wellbeing.
- Missing or trafficked child/young person primarily due to 'pull' factors outside the home.
  (London Borough of Hackney, 2019:7) *Exert from well-being framework used in Hackney to support discussion about the levels of harm and identify the most appropriate response.*

These are just two exerts from tools developed in Hackney to assist social workers in contextualising their view of, and interactions with, young people and parents affected by extra-familial harm. They illustrate the intention of these tools to guide practitioners to consider contexts when assessing the needs of young people and parents: creating opportunities to think about the contexts/situations young people navigate each day – and how these might be informing their decisions and relationships. Such work has been supported by direct tools for use with young people and parents to talk about contexts and peer relationships outside a family home (Broughton, 2018; Nykaro, 2018). The tools suggest:

Start writing down the locations where the young person feels safe or unsafe and the reasons for this. Once you have completed the assessment of risk, working with the young person, start to develop a safety plan for them. This means helping them to consider who or what to do if they feel unsafe. For example, taking a location they have identified as 'red' you could ask them the following questions:

- What would they do if they feel unsafe?
- Is there anyone they know there who they could go to for help?
- What would they expect that person to do to help keep them safe?
- Do they have contact details accessible?

(Nykaro, 2018:3)

When (your young person is) in the community:

- What is XXX doing at the moment that you are happy with?
- Is there anything that you are concerned about?
- What might you do to help XXX to be safe?
- Who else can help and how?

(Broughton, 2018:1)

While such activities appear, in some respects to be quite simplistic – if not common sense – they are a critical underpinning to change ingrained practices. When one considers assessment frameworks, such as the child and family assessment, designed for social workers they are invariably framed around the home environment, the parent–child relationship and the individual responsibility/behaviour of the parent or children in question. While these tools don't prevent wider discussion of other contexts, when used in a system that is foundationally wedded to the field of the family, they also don't prompt or facilitate a broader exploration.

Practitioners around the country are also increasingly engaging young people in conversations about their peer, as well as familial, relationships. Family-mapping, sometimes referred to as creating 'genograms', is a long established method used in social work assessment. It allows a practitioner to build 'a graphic representation of a family tree that displays detailed data on relationships among individuals' (GenoPro, 2016). Mapping activities have proved to be a useful route for supporting young people to reflect on their peer relationships, and to assist practitioners in identifying protective and concerning elements of those relationships. Some of this work will be explored in the following chapter (particularly in relation to how practitioners have worked together to build plans around groups). But here it is important to also recognise how peer mapping can create opportunities for young people, and their families, to talk about safety in relation to friendships and peer influence.

A range of research and practice methods have been developed to support young people to map their friendships (i.e. Gundermann & Gest, 2018). Moving beyond exploring connections, peer mapping can be used to understand the 'strength' of young people's connections and the direction of influence between those connections: and this in turn should inform decision-making. For example if a young person identifies a relationship as being based on a strong connection practitioners might think twice about trying to break that friendship as part of an intervention. Even if there are concerns about the influence that these young people have on each other, knowing that the young person has no interest in ceasing those connections can be considered when weighing up the likely impact of attempts to fracture the relationship. Likewise, if a young person reports a connection is quite weak, and it is one that professionals (and the young person) view as positive it might suggest that support is needed to strengthen those ties – perhaps by identifying a positive activity that those young people can engage with together.

Peer mapping is a dual method – giving young people the opportunity to talk about contexts while offering practitioners an insight into the nature of those contexts themselves. Beyond peer mapping practitioners need to identify how to understand the school and neighbourhood contexts that young people and parents may talk about during assessment. In order to 'assess' the risks faced by a child and family practitioners need to identify ways to understand what is being described. In test sites we explored the idea of social workers visiting the location/area where young person experienced harm – as well as their family home – when it was safe to do so. When visiting it was important for practitioners to think about whether any elements of the place were a barrier to achieving safety, and identify opportunities to enhance safety in the future. For example- is there a local shopkeeper who is willing to provide a refuge to young person if they are feeling unsafe on that street as they walk to school?

Such questions don't solely apply to social workers. We have been informed of voluntary sector organisations for example who are also walking with young people around areas where they spend their time – and identifying potential community guardians or safe spaces they can approach should they feel vulnerable (Contextual Safeguarding Network and Redthread, 2019). Spending time in local areas gives practitioners the opportunity to identify protective as well as risk factors in contexts – and for that to inform a decision about the risks faced by the young person and/or family who are being assessed. Alternatively, if a young person is vulnerable to sexual bullying within an education provision, accessing information about the quality of sex and relationships education in the provision and ascertaining whether there have been similar concerns about other students in school will be critical to forming a contextual conclusion during an assessment of that young person. In both cases, this approach moves the assessment beyond a discussion of what the young person and/or their parent is doing to create safety, to explore what a wider network of social actors could offer for safeguarding the welfare of that young person.

An assessment, for example, could conclude that a young person and parent is doing all they can but that protective adults need to be identified on a young person's journey to school in order for the risk of a further robbery at knife point to be reduced. Likewise a young person can access therapeutic support to address the impact that sexual violence has had on their mental health and emotional well-being; but harmful attitudes held by peers at their school are relevant to any ongoing assessment of how vulnerable that young person is to further harm.

As such, techniques to actively consider contexts as forming an assessment of a young person's needs, vulnerability, and access to protection begins to shape the plans that are developed to increase safety in extra-familial contexts.

### *Planning and intervening*

One of the moments where we continue to see most anxiety during tests of Contextual Safeguarding is when assessments are complete and the time to plan and intervene comes. Practitioners are anxious – and rightly so. Many are extremely worried about young people. They have valid reason to believe that this young person could come to serious – if not fatal – harm, and/or they could do the same to someone else. They want to protect that young person. They also know that if they don't then there are consequences not only for that young person and their loved ones but also potentially for them and their colleagues. One might ask – are my team and I are setting practitioners up to fail by driving approaches to assessment that acknowledge risks that feel beyond both the target of child protection legislation and the reach of traditional social work practice? All of this sits behind the statement I often hear from individual practitioners tasked with adopting a Contextual Safeguarding approach; 'I know what the risks are, I just don't know what I can do about them'.

The primary flaw in the statement above is the word 'I'. In many cases there isn't much that an individual social worker can do about a contextual or social risk. At a minimum they would likely need to work with the young person and/or their parents as partners in responding to the concerns raised by the assessments. Beyond this is the need to potentially work with the peers, school, or neighbourhood settings identified as a concern in the assessment. And much of that requires partnerships with agencies and individuals based in, or with an influence over, those said contexts. Much of how this has been attempted will be explored in the following chapter. For the purposes of Level 1 Contextual Safeguarding, practitioners have been considering how to contextually deliver their direct work with children and families.

Planning is a critical stage in this process – setting the tone for focus of the interventions that follow. If at the planning stage practitioners focus solely on individualised dynamics of risk, their field of vision for where they intend interventions to reach also narrows. Test sites and network practitioners have tweaked existing meeting structures, introduced new ones, and designed alternative planning frameworks to facilitate more contextual plans for addressing extra-familial harm.

In many areas a critical question has been about the use of child protection conferences and plans for children at risk of extra-familial harm. A child protection conference is defined in statutory guidance as a meeting that:

> Brings together family members (and the child where appropriate), with the supporters, advocates and practitioners most involved with the child and family, to make decisions about the child's future safety, health and development. If concerns relate to an unborn child, consideration should be given as to whether to hold a child protection conference prior to the child's birth. (The purpose is to) to bring together and analyse, in an inter-agency setting, all relevant information and plan how best to safeguard and promote the welfare of the child. It is the responsibility of the conference to make recommendations on how organisations and agencies work together to safeguard the child in future.
>
> (HM Government, 2018:46)

As will be explored in far more detail in chapter 13, fundamental questions have arose during tests about the efficacy and suitability of child protection conferences for children who are at risk of harm in extra-familial contexts but who live in relative safe and protective families. Putting this query to one side for the moment, in cases where there is both harm within the family and beyond the child's front door, context is still relevant and a child protection (CP) conference may be used to develop and oversee a social worker's plan. In these cases further consideration has been given to when and how references to extra-familial contexts might be built into a CP conference. Inserting a question that asks parents to describe the context in which they are caring for their young person has been a helpful start. Its place has varied depending on the structure that an area uses for a CP conference. But ensuring that these broader challenges, and their interplay with parental decision-making, are acknowledged in a statutory meeting can provide some means of explaining why change within a family may have occurred or have been frustrated at different points in time.

Consider, for example, Sara's carers. If there had been a situation in which the young people who were thought to be sexually assaulting Sara had been successfully engaged in an intervention or disrupted in another way, then this wider contextual change might open up opportunities for healing family relationships that had been fractured previously by peer influence. If on the other hand an attempt to engage this group had failed, and/or there was information to suggest that they were becoming increasingly violent it would be unsurprising to hear that attempts by carers to instil some more boundaries for Sara and keep her away from the group might have failed. Sara was so fearful of this group that she often complied with their demands despite pleading from her parents. If contextual activities outlined above had occurred during the assessment process itself then they may have offered the information required to frame meetings where plans were agreed or reviewed. If a young person has completed a safety map for example this could be presented at the conference (with a young person's consent) to inform recommendations for any positive activities offered to that young person; particularly those located in a young person's red zones.

Moving beyond traditional meeting and planning structures, other areas have created alternative meetings. In one test site they are trialling young person-led meetings for some cases of extra-familial harm. For young people who are safe with their families but unsafe at school or in their neighbourhoods these meetings provide space for the young person to identify what their priorities might be for increasing their sense of safety and which adults they want to participate in that process. A parallel meeting is held amongst practitioners to form their view of the plan required to safeguard that young person, with the aim of bringing together both sets of recommendations and developing a safeguarding plan that everyone can share. Both meetings, and the plan itself, are overseen by a social worker – ensuring that the work remains framed as a child protection issue – despite the levers and partners for change varying from the norm. In addition to changing or introducing novel planning meetings, areas are amending wider panels that oversee the plans for 'cohorts' of young people affected by extra-familial harm – these will be explored in more detail in chapter 11.

Contextual assessment and planning supports the identification of contextual intervention. Talking with young people about their friends can also open up opportunities for social workers, and other practitioners, to engage with them – either formally or informally. I remember being contacted by a social worker who was a member of the practitioners' network. Having read materials on Contextual Safeguarding they had started to make a conscious effort to know (where possible) the names of the friends identified by the young people they were supporting. This proved critical when one young woman they had been working with went missing. Normally she would post on social media and be found within a day, but on this occasion she was missing for days and concerns for her welfare was escalating rapidly. There was no word on social media either. But this social worker had a plan. She had met with this young woman in a number of public places – and when she did she had met some of her friends. She had introduced herself to those friends and over time she engaged some in conversations and identified some who had the potential to be protective. They too knew her. Importantly she knew which ones were also being supported by other social workers and youth workers. So when all usual efforts proved fruitless she contacted a friend of the young woman. This friend remembered the worker and trusted her enough to let her know where the young woman might be. The young woman was found later that day. The social worker was convinced that if she hadn't known which friend to speak to they would have been none-the-wiser about where this young woman might be.

Voluntary sector members of our practice network have informed us of walking tours they have undertaken with young people they are supporting. They have used these to understand local areas from the perspective of the young person, as well as identify opportunities for intervention. They have identified local shops or businesses that they know to be protective, and sought the permission of young people to go into those shops and ask if a young person can come into the business if they feel unsafe when out and about. As such they are taking steps to build guardianship in local communities, and map the community assets available to increase a young person's sense of safety in public spaces where they feel vulnerable.

In many test sites and across our network, we have also seen the development of parent's groups as a route to supporting families – and sometimes building guardianship around peers groups – who are impacted by extra-familial harm. Parenting during the period of adolescent development can be hard. Caring for a young person during adolescence who is also affected by exploitation, relationship abuse, bullying and harassment at school, or street-based robbery is even tougher. When I meet parents they often comment on how isolated they are; and how individually responsible they feel for what has happened to their child. By bringing parents together to share the challenges of, and tips for, supporting young people, areas are attempting to address this issue. These groups give parents the space to recognise that they aren't on their own and that other parents also face similar struggles. In doing so they provide a setting in which something that has been experienced as a private deficit of an individual can be seen as a more social challenge faced by many. Some areas have gone a step further and brought together parents whose young people are connected – either through a shared incident, shared context, or through friendship. In one site, parents were invited to a meeting whose young people were spending time together in the community. These parents didn't know each other and were not in contact with each other. When their young people were together they were setting fires in the community, climbing up buildings, and causing criminal damage. Practitioners facilitated a meeting between the parents to support them to identify opportunities for working together, and to increase their collective oversight of the group. In another locality, following an incident of serious violence, all the parents of the young people who were connected to the incident in question were brought together within 24 hours to build a collective safety plan for supporting their children over the weekend and de-escalate risks of reprisals.

These attempts to provide collective to support to parents are, in part, a response to parents commenting to the Contextual Safeguarding team that they don't always know how to reach out to each other and can feel isolated when trying to care for a young person who is in difficulty. Creating groups has the potential to facilitate non-judgemental, peer support settings for parents but the extent to which this potential has/can be realised requires ongoing assessment. At this point in testing these groups appear to have variable levels of success – and the factors which are most important for their efficacy are currently under review. However, they serve as helpful examples of how to develop contextually informed support for children and families affected by extra-familial harm.

## The implications of Contextual Safeguarding at Level 1

Level 1 testing of Contextual Safeguarding shows great promise. Firstly, it suggests that when shining a light on peer relationships, school and neighbourhoods associated to extra-familial harm professionals act differently. They identify different concerns when young people are first brought to their attention; some young people are considered to be in need of further support that previously would have been closed to children's services. Some are thought to require support but not necessarily through a statutory plan, when the efforts of their parents are framed within the broader contexts in which their child is at risk of significant harm. Practitioners are able to build assessments that accurately identify where risk and opportunities for protection can be found across all contexts that are relevant during adolescence. And in so doing provide more contextual direction for plans, that in turn can

Table 9.1 System requirements Level 1 Contextual Safeguarding

| System expectations | Referral | Assessment | Planning | Intervention |
|---|---|---|---|---|
| **Target** | System logs location of harm, any peer associations to a child who has been referred into children's services | Assessments of children and families consider how peer, school and neighbourhood dynamics around them impact on parental capacity | When planning support, the weight of influence that different contexts have on a young person are considered to prioritise interventions | Interventions support a young person and family to understand contextual dynamics and recommend interventions to address them |
| **Legal Framework** | Referrals for children and families affected by extra-familial harm are received by children's services | Assessments for children and families affected by extra-familial harm are centred around child welfare/protection | Planning activity for cases of extra-familial harm have the oversight of children's services | Interventions are focused on safeguarding the welfare of children and families are the primary objective |
| **Partnerships** | All partners who have contact with young people in extra-familial spaces are alert to the signs of extra-familial harm and can make referrals, and provide contextual information during referrals | During assessments of children and families affected by extra-familial harm partner agencies provide information on contexts impacting risk as well as the individuals affected | Partners, including those who work in extra-familial contexts, are involved in planning support – including offering community guardianship or safe spaces | Interventions work with peers, parents, and young people as partners in safeguarding, and those with a reach into extra-familial contexts deliver interventions to increase safety around a young person |
| **Outcomes** | Contextual information is recorded at the point of referral against which to track contextual impact throughout the system response | Assessments record baseline, and latter changes to, contextual dynamics relevant to extra-familial harm to give an accurate account of safety | Plans are focused on creating sustained contextual safety for young people and families | The success of interventions is measured in regards to whether contexts have become safer – and not solely the individual who features in a plan. Their behaviour change is also measured in a contextually informed way |

facilitate interventions that utilise or engage with those contexts (in both a planned and reactive fashion). As all of these opportunities remain in test, the long-term outcomes of doing things different are unknown. Parents and young people who have participated in some of the activities outlined above have been favourable of them. Some have engaged with social workers more positively – and some for the first time. But as with any systems' change, the initial impacts have been on the system itself – how it functions, its culture, and what it offers. Only once that change is embedded will the onward impacts on children and families be truly understood – and the accounts from individual parents and young people will accumulate to provide a mass of evidence regarding impact.

As Table 9.1 illustrates, however, tests of Level 1 approaches to Safeguarding begin to create child protection systems and safeguarding partnerships that are better equipped to respond to, and prevent, extra-familial harm. What you might also notice is that work at this level only gets you so far. To fully embed a Contextual Safeguarding approach, areas have had to move beyond contextual work with children and families, to build systems, tools, and approaches that engage directly with peer group, school, and neighbourhood contexts themselves: also known as Level 2 Contextual Safeguarding. The following chapter documents these attempts, and what they suggest about the feasibility and value of changing the contexts in which young people have come to significant harm, as a key part of creating Contextual Safeguarding systems.

# 10  Believing that change can happen

Level 2 Contextual Safeguarding

When we do well at Level 1 Contextual Safeguarding, our eyes are opened to all manner of troubling truths. We start to see trends. We recognise the cumulative impact of individual incidents on groups and locations. Take Connor (chapter 2) as an example. I introduced him as the person who led a group assault on Malik. When he was younger he had been mugged on his local high street. The person who took his phone lifted the bottom of their baggy jumper to expose a large black handle protruding from their waistband; the sunlight bounced off the glint of silver metal that sat underneath it. A knife – he knew it instantly. He handed over the phone without question. This was one incident, affecting one person; how they thought about themselves and how they saw the world around them. However, he wasn't the only one. Most of the boys who assaulted Malik had been threatened with violence, or had their property stolen, in their local area. They held an implicit understanding – a shared victimisation that told them that this area, and not just them, was unsafe. Their collective accounts normalised harm and put in motion a set of social rules that were conducive with the assault they later inflicted on Malik. We step tentatively into these worlds when we do Level 1 Contextual Safeguarding – we see the collective, cumulative, contextual harm that can build in a set of relationships and/or shared space. And this view can send us running in the other direction. It is too big. One child we can work with – a whole group and the impact of a high street on their welfare – that's too much and potentially impenetrable. If we want to act on information that builds from Level 1 Contextual Safeguarding, we need a way of understanding and changing contexts themselves. By developing Level 2 Contextual Safeguarding, test site and network practitioners are showing us how such impact can be achieved.

In this chapter I will document the activities, processes, structures and cultures that have emerged when creating Level 2 Contextual Safeguarding work – and the impact that this is starting to have on the lives of children and families. A thread that runs through Level 2 work and in many respects distinguishes it from work done at Level 1 is that it is characterised by the design of new structures, processes, and activities – rather than amending/adding to those already in place. For example, at Level 1 test sites have added

questions or prompts to the child and family assessment which supports practitioners to frame parenting capacity and a child's needs with reference to the
extra-familial contexts in which harm may have occurred. However, at Level
2 test sites have created completely new assessment frameworks for peer
groups, schools, and neighbourhoods – and structures which support these
assessments to take place. In doing so they are exploring how much a child
protection system could and should do, broadening its potential reach and
questioning, or arguably clarifying, its purpose throughout.

To illustrate these changes I will adopt a similar structure in this chapter
to that used in the previous one and detail the advances made at the point of
referral, assessment, planning and intervention within children's social care.
Having done so I will detail how far that work has taken us in realising a full
implementation of the Contextual Safeguarding framework – before using
later chapters to reflect upon what this has meant for policy and partnerships in local areas, and what the implications of all of this has been for
the conceptual framework itself.

## The stages of Level 2 implementation

How can a child protection system, designed to identify, assess and work with
children and families, broaden its reach to peer groups, school and neighbourhood environments – and what does it need to achieve this? Our learning so far
has shown that the answer to both those questions is 'quite a lot'. The structure
which hold elements of the system together has required attention. The tools
used within that structure, the partnerships and relationships that bring those
tools to life, and practice cultures which enable them to thrive – have all
changed during the course of testing Contextual Safeguarding approaches.
Testing is ongoing at the point of writing this book.

### Referrals

The child protection system responds to what it sees. Once Level 1 Contextual Safeguarding work commenced peer groups, schools and neighbourhoods
organically became more visible, and this in turn has had an impact on what
is referred into the system for consideration. Some Level 1 amendments have
led directly to these changes.

For example, by recording connections between young people referred
into children's services separately, and recording the location where they
jointly came to, or instigated, harm, safeguarding hubs have been able to
identify contexts and groups of concern. In one case a young man, under
the age of 16, featured in multiple groups referred into children's services
over several months. If group recording had not been in place, he would
have rarely come to the attention of the person screening referrals. However,
because these processes were being trialled, he was identified when a referral
was screened, as someone who had been on the periphery on multiple

occasions. Follow-up work identified he was one of the most vulnerable young people in the group, but he wouldn't have been seen by professionals at all if it were not in reference to wider group.

New locations have also been identified. The introduction of safety mapping activities with young people in one local authority alerted social workers, who were members of our practice network, to an address where children were being sexually exploited: an address that had not surfaced through traditional 'hot spot' mapping or problem profiling that has been built solely on crime data.

These are just two illustrations of how contextualising direct work with children and families can in turn contextualise how harm is profiled and understood. They were not associations and contexts that were 'referred' into the child protection systems in question – the children were. Contexts were identified down the line through work with children who had been referred.

Building on these developments, some sites have begun to make structural changes so that a location or group can be referred into the child protection system as a concern in its own right. This has been required for two reasons. Firstly, there are some contexts in which young people are thought to be vulnerable to abuse, but where the names/identities of those young people are unknown. For example, members of the public, business owners and council workers (such as refuse collectors or housing officers) may be concerned about witnessing adults pulling up in cars and talking to young people outside a local takeaway shop. At this stage, there is no evidence of a crime having taken place and no individual young person who has been named. It is not clear how anyone could raise concerns about this situation in a straightforward manner and articulate that this is because they are concerned about the welfare of young people and not because they want to report a crime. At most this may result in a complaint about anti-social behaviour, but on the scale of more 'severe' forms of such behaviour it may not be prioritised in that sense. Being able to highlight concerns about the welfare of young people in general, enables communities and wider partners to take an active role in raising concerns and doing it early.

This is also important in the aftermath of incidents. Paramedics have told me how they sometimes feel that they are being called out to attend to scenes of violence or substance misuse amongst young people at the same locations repeatedly. They don't always see young people when they arrive (some will have run off), and even when they do they are not sure what, if anything happens, about the locations themselves.

Beyond a need to refer contexts where children are relatively anonymous, structural changes that facilitate context referrals have also created a route to recognise and respond to cumulative harm in an area. This recognition might occur through direct work with young people already being supported by a service (as noted above). However, it might also be identified by multiple reports made to teachers that young people have been late to school in the mornings as their phones have been stolen – a school might not think it reasonable to refer any of those individual children for further support but they may still want to flag their concerns about the bus route where all the robberies have taken place.

When a context or group is identified, children's services have had to make amendments to receive those 'referrals' so that they can be tracked through in the foreground of the child protection system – rather than solely sit in the background notes of children who are being impacted by them. The context itself becomes 'a case' – providing a structure to hold the attention of partners who are focused on and concerned with reducing risk and increasing safety in that context. This in no way would replace any informal work that already happens in localities to build connections and create protection. Rather, it seeks to further this work in cases where harm is thought to be significant so that efforts can be increased, and impact monitored, until young people are safer in that group or place. To achieve this organisations that make referrals as well as the children's services departments which receive those referrals have created resources/structures to support that process.

For the most part, multi-agency safeguarding hubs have been the location for testing how to receive referrals about contexts. In Hackney they developed a group recording system so they could start to accept referrals for groups of young people who came to harm, and/or instigated that harm, when together. These groups were defined around those incidents and information used in that regard (rather than implying that those groups were static and unchanging). Changes to referral forms have been created so partners can formally refer in a concern about a place. Most significant changes have occurred on children's services case management systems. These systems are used to record assessments and interventions used when supporting children and families. To embed Level 2 work new recording systems have been introduced to record assessments of and interventions with contexts. This record is initiated at the point of 'referral', where children's services create/open a file on a context on their case management system.

In most sites this work remains in test environments and at the time of publication is yet to go live across all systems in any local area. What tests demonstrate, however, is that case management systems can then be used to track the extent to which interventions in contexts are informing the safety and welfare of a number of young people – not all of whom are being supported via statutory social work plans. For example, consider a bus terminus where numerous young people have had their property stolen, two fights have broken out in the month prior and a young person has been seriously injured there when he was stabbed. In a Contextual Safeguarding approach not all of the children being impacted by harm at the bus terminus would need to be officially supported by a children's social worker. The young person who has been stabbed, and is at risk of significant harm, may have a social worker overseeing his plan. One or two others who have experienced robbery may be in receipt of early help support. There may even be young people at the bus stop where there are bubbling concerns that they are involved in robberies and have carried weapons, but who are also already in receipt of social work support as they are experiencing neglect in the family home, for example. There will be many others who are there but who are not known as individuals to children's services. By referring the transport hub (assessing it and developing a plan for it – see below), a process is started where the risk in that setting can be addressed and by proxy inform the safety of the range of young people listed above. The changes to Information and Communication Technology (ICT) systems have meant that those workers supporting young people affected by harm at the bus stop can also link their young person's record to the bus stop's record. As work is undertaken with the bus stop these workers can be notified and should ongoing assessment suggest that safety is increasing at the bus stop they may amend their assessments for individual young people to reflect this changing situation.

Outside of children's services we have been alerted to a range of agencies which have amended their paperwork so they can document and refer contextual concerns. The ambulance service, for example, has sent through exemplars of forms they have created so that paramedics can document and share information about locations where they think young people may be at risk of harm. Similar adaptations have been made in some hospital departments (Niamh Ni-Longain and Contextual Safeguarding Network, 2019) and other council services such as housing. As referenced in statutory child protection guidelines youth offending services are also identifying contexts where the young people they support appear to be vulnerable to harm – using their relatively contextual assessment process 'Asset Plus' to record contextual matters that impact a young person's risk of committing offences and/or coming to harm themselves.

By embedding Level 2 work across partnerships therefore, we are seeing formal and informal changes to actions, processes and systems, so that locations and groups can be identified as a safeguarding concern. But once these locations are identified and recognised as contexts of concern, there needs to be a way to prioritise them. It wouldn't be possible, or indeed proper, for children's services and wider statutory agencies to intervene with every locality or group where harm might have, or has, occurred. How do they know when it is time for a safeguarding response, overseen by children's services, to be initiated following robbery in the park or sexual harassment on the bus? To answer this question Level 2 Contextual Safeguarding has featured extensive work on assessment.

### Assessment

Once a peer group/relationship, school or public setting has been referred into the child protection system, a decision has to be made as to whether there is a safeguarding concern that warrants attention. In some cases the answer will be no. In other cases the answer may be no but there are some emerging concerns that are apparent and a conversation with community organisations, local businesses, and/or youth services for example to alert them may be enough to quell any further escalation. In other instances the answer might very well be yes, and with a relatively straight forward solution being evident. For example, there is a concern about a cupboard on a stairwell with a broken door that is being used to stash weapons. An immediate response to such a concern might be to fix the broken door and then monitor whether concerns begin to emerge elsewhere, or if the door is purposefully broken again, and so on. For other occasions the answer will be yes, and there is a need to understand why that safeguarding concern has emerged: what is the primary difficulty, is there any evidence of protection/strengths to build upon, and what does this mean for how agencies and communities respond. In short there is a need for the context, group, or situation to be assessed – before action can be agreed.

As was the case when thinking about assessments with children and families, two areas of work have emerged when seeking to assess peer relationships, schools, and localities. First is the method required to build the assessment in the first place, and second is the framework used to analyse the information gathered and reach a conclusion. These two activities have developed, and redeveloped, in a cyclical fashion. To begin with, practitioners and researchers had to think about what they would need to know about a context in order to assess the safety of children within it – that is, build a framework. Then they designed methods to complete those assessments. But in completing the assessments the frameworks themselves were refined. Attempts to apply the initial frameworks created demands for methods that could capture the information required to reach conclusions about contextual dynamics. Further trials of assessment methods have continued to inform assessment frameworks – and created opportunities for variation across localities. Areas have started to look at their own assessment frameworks and practice tools – for example, their Signs of Safety™ resources – and considered whether they could apply those to peer groups as well as families.

Let's consider peer relationships as an example of this process. When we first arrived in test sites, or undertook site visits to interest areas in our wider network, we regularly observed meetings that had been convened to discuss multiple young people who were all being exploited together – and whose risk of abuse, in this sense, was shared. Each young person would have their own practitioner – an early help worker, a social worker, a family support worker or youth justice officer and so on – and every one of these workers would attend the meeting. As a result, meetings could involve up to, and sometimes in excess of, 20 practitioners, each talking about their own individual young person, along with various teachers from their schools, police officers, anti-social behaviour officers and so on commenting on how they encountered the group when they were altogether. These meetings could run from 60 to 120 minutes. For the most part they consisted of multiple brief discussions about a list of individuals but rarely did these discussions result in an assessment of a group. They also sometimes featured the sharing of personal information about different young people and their families which wasn't necessarily relevant or required to build an assessment of need within the group (as a collective rather than a set of individuals). The primary method in these assessments was to draw information about each individual child and family into one meeting – but without a framework to structure what had been shared.

It has therefore been critical to identify what methods could be used to build a richer picture of a friendship group or set of peer relationships. Mapping of relationships (as referenced in the previous chapter) has been one way of doing this. By mapping connections between young people – from both their own perspectives and those of practitioners – social workers and their colleagues have been able to visualise the collective and how it functions. This has been particularly evident when practitioners have moved beyond mapping connections to understanding the value, strength, and influence of those connections. Working alongside practitioners in test sites, and with those who have sought advice over the network, me, Jenny and others members of the research team, including Katie Latimer who joined us for the Hackney work in 2019, have deepened how peer mapping is undertaken and utilised: identifying key questions to be considered during mapping exercises (Figure 10.1).

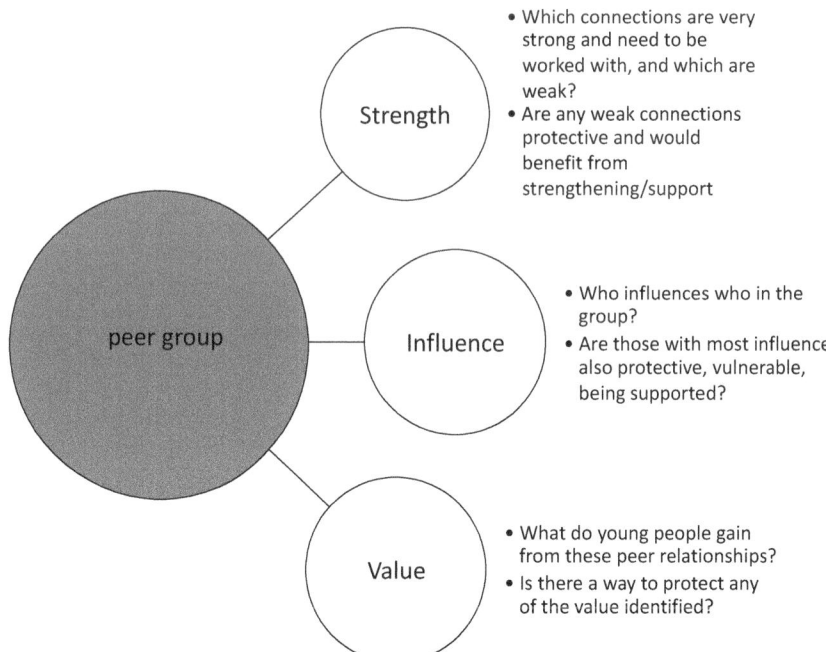

*Figure 10.1* Peer Assessment Considerations

Taking this approach has broadened the view of peer interventions (detailed later in this chapter) and created opportunities for 1:1 work and its impact to be seen in the light of friendship. By way of explanation: in supporting one young person (who plays a leadership role amongst their friends) to engage in positive activities, an impact can be had on their wider network. In this sense effective peer assessment creates opportunities for 1:1 work to have network/group impact.

Mapping has also proved an integral method in the assessment of school and neighbourhood locations. Practitioners have developed resources for young people to heat map areas in their schools or neighbourhood where they feel unsafe or protected when undertaking Level 2 Contextual Safeguarding assessments. Researchers have used techniques from situational crime prevention and whole-school approaches to help practitioners think through how to design and use mapping (Smallbone, et al., 2013; Taylor, et al., 2013). On some occasions, young people and practitioners have walked through localities together to physically point out and map areas of safety. In one test site a practitioner used mobile phone technology to 'drop pin' areas on their phone-map where young people identified locations of concern and/ or safety. Printed maps of schools and local spaces have been handed out to individual young people to colour code or write across (as referenced in the previous chapter). At public events large maps have also been placed on walls and flip charts and using post-it notes young people and other local residents have marked concerns or examples of safety on the maps.

Beyond mapping, school, neighbourhood, and peer assessments have also involved direct engagement with the people who spend time in those contexts. During child and family assessment efforts are made to speak to all the children living in a household and key adults connected to the family or who spend time in the family home. In larger locations – such as schools or public spaces – surveys have been tested as one route to gathering information from those who spend time in a context that is under assessment. On some occasions these surveys have been ICT or paper-based exercises – such as the surveying of parents (n=24) and students ($n$ = 131) that was trialled in our first schools' assessment in Hackney. On other occasions this was in-person surveying. Taking lessons from residents surveys trialled in the Australian 'Neighbourhoods Project' to take a contextual approach to peer-sexual abuse (Smallbone, et al., 2013), the research team designed ways that practitioners could survey residents in areas impacted by different forms of extra-familial harm. Social workers and youth workers pounded the pavements, knocked on doors, and consulted residents on both the welfare of young people locally and their capacity to provide guardianship. Businesses have also been surveyed in the same way, often surfacing examples of how they are trying to safeguard young people, or de-escalate concerns, independently of wider statutory networks:

> One chicken shop owner explained how he had negotiated with the local secondary school to allow students to enter his shop at lunchtime.

This was based on the understanding that he would liaise with the staff member responsible for lunchtime duty, whose phone number he was given. Previously students had been banned as a dispersal measure. The shop owner reported positive relations with local young people and said that on the rare occasions when tensions arise, he gives extra free chicken wings which costs him little but keeps his younger customers happy.

(Exert from business survey in pilot neighbourhood assessment)

A deputy manager in a branch of a supermarket gave an example of a 15-year-old boy running into the shop with three stab wounds and another of an unaccompanied 3-year-old. She said local young people knew her by name and trusted that she'd act to keep them safe, she suggested that the shop had bright lighting and was open 24-hours which she felt meant young people felt safe.

(Exert from business survey in pilot neighbourhood assessment)

Where appropriate, discussions with groups or individuals who spend time in contexts under assessment have also been used as a means of direct engagement, for example, group discussions with teachers in a school, or with students, presenting them with scenarios and exploring how the school currently responds. In these settings participants have been able to explain the protective capacity that they perceive within a context – something that has been critical to informing the conclusions of any context assessment.

Two other methods have been used to gather information during context assessments: observation and record checks. When assessing a child and family a social worker will visit the family home – observing interactions and the wider home environment. They will also speak to professionals in other agencies who have contact with the family, gathering their perspectives of safety, needs, or risks within the family setting. In the case of observation, researchers and practitioners have co-designed approaches to observe extra-familial contexts (Contextual Safeguarding Network, 2019) – producing animations and guidance documents to explain what they have found. During these observations practitioners have been looking for examples of actual or potential guardianship/protection in the context, and any examples of vulnerability (poor visibility for example) and risk (locations where young people are being approached/groomed by adults). They are also observing the quality of interactions between young people and adults in those contexts – and the extent to which these are positive and protective – or have the potential to be so. Observation templates have been developed to support practitioners in recording their findings – documents which can then be appended to a final assessment.

Many agencies and individuals have information about contexts which could inform an assessment. This is information that they already hold – rather than that gathered specifically for an assessment (for example during surveys or interviews). During tests, practitioners and senior leaders have had to ascertain what information is held by different agencies, how this information can be accessed and in what ways it can be used. For example, waste management agencies record the rubbish they collect – including, for example, evidence of drug use or sexual activity in public places. At present this data is used to profile anti-social behaviour in local areas, but is not drawn upon during safeguarding assessments.

Beyond datasets, agencies and individuals might hold information about a context in 'real time' (which hasn't been included in a dataset yet) or that is too qualitative to ever be recorded in that way. Consider schools for example. When assessing a school in which a sexual assault has occurred, a practitioner might want to know: have there been previous allegations of sexual violence between students at the school; what is the quality of sex and relationships education at the school; does the school engage with external agencies to provide specialist or independent support/advice to students; how many students have been excluded from the school in the past year; and so on. Answers to these questions will not necessarily be held on computer data-sets. Nonetheless, a range of professional may hold some answers to those questions – and so during assessments practitioners have had to identify ways to gather this 'softer' information to enrich the assessment process.

Policies and procedures that services design, and operate to, give one indication of how they manage safeguarding concerns. Schools, youth clubs, transport providers, leisure centres, cinemas and so one will have health and safety policies, policies for logging and reporting concerning behaviour and so on. How these concerns are framed – for example, whether the language of safeguarding is used – is one way of sensing the capacity a service has to safeguard young people within their setting from extra-familial harm. The extent to which their policies recognise their own practices as contributing to safety – and therefore thinking about responses that go beyond making referrals to children's services – also indicate where the service places responsibility for safeguarding and their expectations in terms of response.

Most services also have systems to log concerns. I have spent time in transport coordination centres and learnt about how bus drivers complete incident logs at the end of their journeys. Most schools utilise some form of behaviour incident log to record incidents that have occurred and how they have responded. Where these records are in place, the language used to record incidents gives a sense of how safeguarding concerns are viewed and interpreted by staff. If logs record the action taken by staff in a response to an incident they also illustrate whether responses were able to increase safety in the immediate moments after an incident occurred. With both policies and logs there will be many limitations – neither can offer a complete picture of agency practices – but they give a snapshot of the actions of views taken by adults within a range of settings and therefore can contribute to building a broader assessment of a location, schools, or group.

Level 2 context assessments yielded vast amounts of information when put to the test. The next challenge for us all was to revisit the frameworks for organising this information and forming an assessment. When we first started testing context assessments we had devised an assessment sheet – directing practitioners to record behaviours, strengths, risks and vulnerabilities for each context featured in the assessment (Table 10.1).

The assessment sheet had initially been designed to facilitate Level 1 Contextual Safeguarding work and was first conceived when seeking to contextualise meetings about young people who displayed harmful sexual behaviours in the first tranche of local area work in 2013–2016. In this sense it was intended as framework for organising summary information about the contexts surrounding a young person and drawing the attention of practitioners towards the context in which a young person was most vulnerable.

*Table 10.1* Context assessment data collection resource

| *Child/Context* XXXINSERTXXX | *Vulnerabilities* | *Risks* | *Strengths* |
| --- | --- | --- | --- |
| Individuals | | | |
| Families | | | |
| Peers | | | |
| School | | | |
| Neighbourhood | | | |

From the perspective of completing an assessment of a context however, this table had limited value. Firstly, context assessments needed to be built around a context (peer group, school, or location) where there were concerned – not a young person affected by them. Secondly, the table required practitioners to record information about every potential context around a child when in the case of a context assessment only one or a few of those contexts might be relevant. In some respects the table remained helpful for organising information to assess peer groups, and what was happening in the school and neighbourhoods in which they spent their time. This was particularly true for the activity of 'context weighting': identifying which context presented the most concern, and therefore where practitioners needed to focus their attention. An example of this was an assessment of a peer group who had shared sexual images of other students via a social media platform. The assessment of the group concluded that the context of concern was actually the school in which they spent their time, and that school cultures, policy and staff training needed to be the focus of the intervention process:

> This assessment considers that social media applications are part of the 'environment' of the young person and interplay exists between these and the harmful behaviours of peers who use them, especially through the facilitation of posting indecent images.

However, the context of priority in this assessment has been identified as the school. This assessment finds that whilst harmful attitudes and behaviours are prevalent amongst the peer group (as informed by wider societal norms), these are manifested across – and perpetuated by – the context of peer relationships at the school. There is an opportunity for schools to intervene in harmful peer group dynamics in order to prevent reinforcement of harmful attitudes.

Family was identified as the main source of support for peer group members, and this assessment recommends maximising on this as part of the intervention plan.

(PG2 assessment, social worker weighting assessment)

However, beyond context weighting this initial framework didn't facilitate the level of analysis required to formulate an assessment of a context that was analytical and not solely descriptive. Practitioners who were chairing the meetings where context assessments were being discussed were struggling to hold everyone's focus on the context itself – and not the individuals affected in the context – and requested a clearer analytical framework and structure for organising the meeting.

And so commenced a series of activities to build frameworks that better supported context assessments. Jenny was integral to this process, as was the method of embedded research. I was frustrated. I initially struggled to understand why the initial assessment table was proving limited when implemented at Level 2. Jenny, who was sat alongside social workers each day, understood the challenge far better than I did and set about trying to resolve it with two members of the practice team. Information had been gathered to assess a peer group. Jenny was sat next to the social worker leading the assessment trying to capture what she was doing to analyse the information she had gathered and reflect this back via a practice resource. The social worker went back to the guidelines for assessing children and families and stated – 'I feel like we need something like this'. What she was asking for was a clearer guide for the process of collecting, assessing, and understanding the information gathered. In looking at the guidelines for assessing children and families, and reflecting on what the social worker had been doing, the 'peer group assessment triangle' (Figure 10.2) was born.

The triangle reflected both the framework for assessing children and families, and the questions asked during the assessment itself. The social worker had been trying to explore the dynamic of the group, the guardianship around them (in this case the teachers and other adults in the school where they came together), and the wider environment in which the group spent its time (in this case the school). Considering strengths, risks, and vulnerabilities in the peer group, school and families associated to the assessment informed the questions the social workers asked, but the triangle provided a framework to organise that information towards a plan.

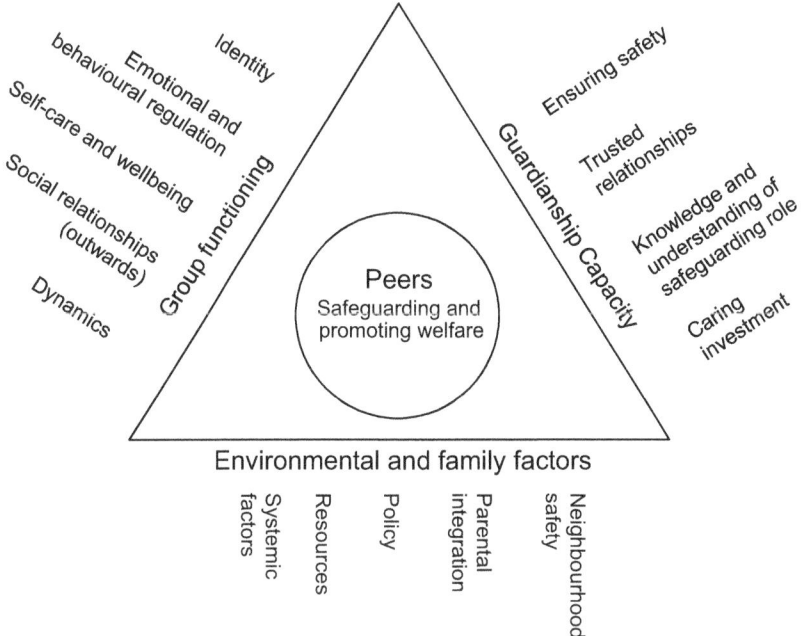

*Figure 10.2* Peer Assessment Triangle

This was a pivotal moment in the application of Contextual Safeguarding and provided the foundations upon which we built school and neighbourhood assessment frameworks (Figures 10.3 and 10.4; Contextual Safeguarding Network, 2019).

Context assessment triangles (Figures 10.3 and 10.4) have been used in a range of local areas across England. We have been notified of sites initiating assessments of high streets, housing complexes, sparse locations around and behind skate parks, streets around youth hubs and clubs where young people have been assaulted – and schools, including alternative education provisions.

This diverse development of approaches to framing and undertaking assessments continues to shape how we understand and communicate techniques for putting Contextual Safeguarding into practice. Regardless of the approach, all three triangles provide consistent points of reference for initial, as well as detailed, assessments of contexts. As they are tested over the coming years, they will undoubtably be revised. At this stage, however, they provide a central articulation of what Level 2 Contextual Safeguarding is all about and a practical roadmap for discussing a sum of a context instead of its individual parts and players.

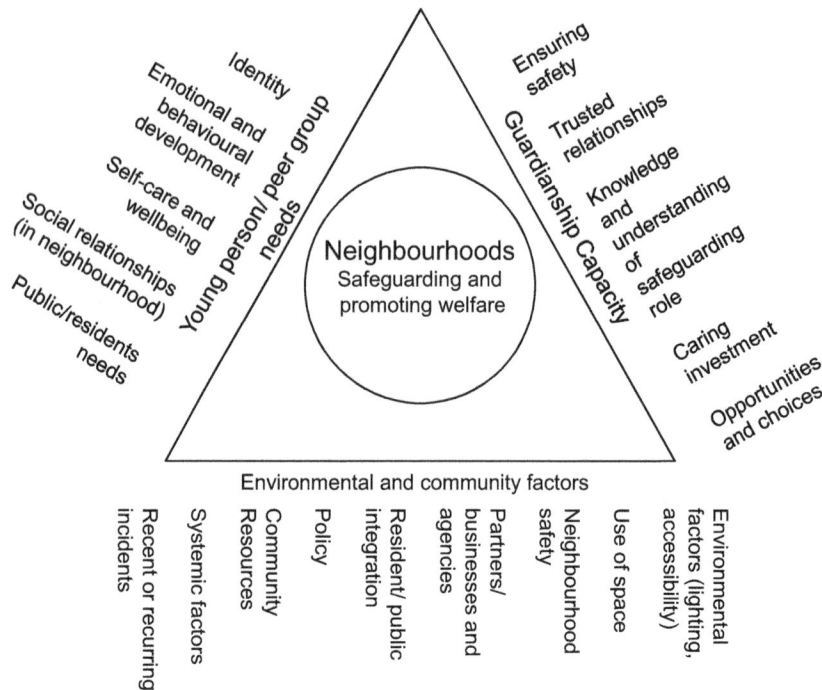

*Figure 10.3* Neighbourhood Assessment Triangle

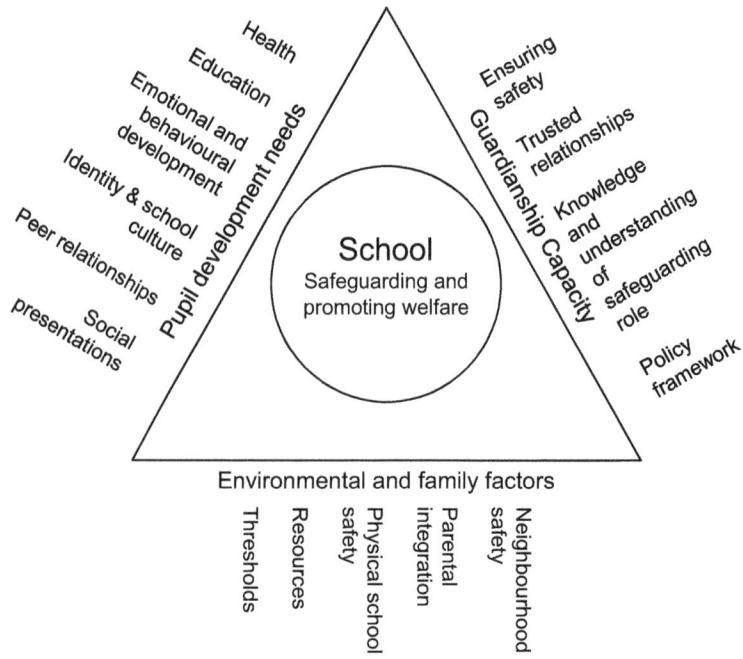

*Figure 10.4* School Assessment Triangle

### *Planning and intervention*

A young man had been stabbed. So had two others – on separate occasions but in the same location. A home had been shot at. This young man and his family had been assessed by children's services and were being provided support via a voluntary social work plan. But this plan did not impact the context in which he, and other young people, remained vulnerable. And so a neighbourhood assessment was initiated. It drew on many of the methods outlined above – residents and business surveys, mapping with young people, observations, information gathering about the location from others etc. The information was organised into an assessment of the neighbourhood location and identified what needed to change for safety to increase. It was time to act.

There were two key steps required to turn context assessments into change for children and families. The first was to agree an approach to developing plans, and the second was the implementation of the agreed plan.

In terms of planning, a range of meetings have been developed in local areas. Some have been called Contextual Safeguarding review meetings, others have called them Context Protection Conferences, others have called them Community Conferences and so on. Some of these meetings have been chaired by child protection conference chairs, others by safeguarding advisors or senior managers (heads of service) within children's social care. Most recently, some are being co-chaired between community safety and children's services, or school safeguarding leads and children's services.

The effectiveness of the various meeting structures remains under review, but there are already common features emerging across them. The first is that they provide a forum for agreeing *a plan for the context* in question – not for individuals who are vulnerable in that context (a matter already provided for in general social work practice and Level 1 Contextual Safeguarding work). The second is that they are attended by a range of organisations and individuals who wouldn't have previously been involved in safeguarding meeting – local business owners, residents associations, town planners, park wardens and gardeners, waste management staff, and so on.

These two common factors have required new information sharing and meeting agreements so that non-traditional safeguarding partners can be included in conversations. They have also raised questions about the commissioning and availability of local services. For example, assessments of schools have resulted in the offer of bystander intervention session for students and staff to address sexual harassment – but not all local areas have commissioned this type of work. Facilitating new partnerships has been integral to the development of relevant and realistic plans. For example, if an assessment identifies a need for increased community guardianship in a local area, but those who could act as guardians for example, resident and business owners, aren't represented in those meetings, then agreed actions become unachievable.

The impact of Level 2 changes at the point of referral and assessment is clearly demonstrated when one looks at the interventions agreed to address concerns. Concerns about drug dealing and drug use amongst young people around a library resulted in relationship building work between library staff and young people, and peer group support for up to 30 young people who were choosing to spend time at the library after school. Reports of sexual image-sharing amongst a friendship group have led to the updating of school policies, staff training on disclosure and bystander intervention activities with whole year groups. And complaints about risks of adults grooming young people who were hanging out in their local park have resulted in training for park gardeners to support improved relationships between them and young people in the park. Facilitating these positive relationships works towards the park being a place where the welfare of young people is at the forefront of people's minds: adults have their eyes out for young people; young people know who these adults are; and this in turn creates a hostile environment for those seeking to approach and groom young people in the park. The impact of this work remains under review but in the case of the library for example, a practitioner informed me that

> Looking at responding to young people in this situation through a contextual safeguarding lens allowed all key partners to work together and understand their role in supporting and safeguarding young people in this space. This response led to a decrease in anti-social behaviour and helped to form a stronger relationship between the young people and the library staff, ultimately, creating a safer space for young people to socialise. This in turn has had a longer impact on safeguarding young people engaging in this space as the library staff are more confident in engaging with young people and identifying and raising safeguarding concerns.

## System-wide attention on systemic harm

Where we have witnessed Level 2 Contextual Safeguarding in action we have also seen the Contextual Safeguarding framework come to life. In order to refer, assess, and intervene with contexts to safeguard young people all four pillars of the framework have been initiated (Table 10.2).

Cumulatively all Level 2 work is underpinned, and motivated, by a belief that (a) these contextual factors are not an inevitable part of life to be survived/navigated and (b) it is possible to affect change in peer groups, schools, and neighbourhoods. Throughout the project of implementing Level 1 Contextual Safeguarding we have encountered attitudes of resignation – what is the point of flagging contextual issues when we can't do anything about them? Level 2 work requires, and enables, a challenge to that position and its creation signals that practitioners believe that change is possible. To embed this ethos

Table 10.2 System requirements Level 2 Contextual Safeguarding

| System requirements | Referral | Assessment | Planning | Intervention |
|---|---|---|---|---|
| Target | The system can receive and screen referrals for peer groups, schools and locations where young people are thought to be at risk of harm | The system can assess peer group, schools and locations where young people are thought to be at risk of harm | The system can coordinate plans to reduce risk, and increase safety, in contexts where young people are at risk of harm | The system can coordinate/commission/instigate interventions designed to increase safety in contexts that compromise young people's welfare |
| Legal framework | Extra-familial contexts are referred into systems designed to protect children (not solely those concerned with community safety, crime prevention or policing) | The welfare of children and young people are at the heart of system assessments of extra-familial contexts rather than solely measuring the likelihood of crime or anti-social behaviour | Plans are convened under frameworks designed to coordinate support for children and families – with a shared focus on safeguarding the welfare of young people across the partners who are involved | Interventions are focused on creating sustained pathways for safety in contexts or with groups where there have been concerns about child welfare-building guardianship capacity and securing safety in environments where young people spend their time |
| Partnerships | Partner agencies are alert to contexts where young people are at risk of harm, and are supported to notify children's services of these concerns | During assessments partner agencies provide information and access to data that can be used to build a picture of harm and safety in contexts | Partners who have a reach into extra-familial contexts are involved in building plans to increase safety in those contexts | Partners who have a reach into extra-familial contexts deliver, or oversee, interventions that increase the safety of young people and reduce the risks they face |
| Outcomes | At the point of referral contextual concerns are documented so as to create a baseline against which impact of intervention can latterly be measured | Assessment provides partners with a route to identifying the elements of the context most in need of attention (guardianship, group dynamic, wider environmental factors) as a means of tracing impact | Plans are used to agree priority actions against the factors in the context that most require attention and set the ambitions for intervention (this is the change we expect to see as a result of the plan) | Interventions are aimed at having contextual impact – and this is what is recorded when plans are reviewed. Interventions that impact individual young people, but in which contextual risks persists, will be insufficient in the system. |

throughout a children's services department, and across local partnerships, the activities outlined thus far needed to feature in the policies and procedures that governed local practice. The following chapter highlights some key changes made to local policy and procedures to date: changes that have been required to move from 'testing' this approach to it becoming business as usual.

# 11  Policy frameworks and strategic partnerships

Imagine we didn't have a child protection system in England. Instead, we had a response to children who were neglected in their families. And then we had a separate response for children who were sexually abused in their families. This sat separately from responses to children who were being physically abused at home – distinct again from how a local area protected children who were being emotionally abused at home. Even when we knew that some children who were being physically abused were being emotionally abused, practitioners met separately to discuss each issue rather than collectively. They didn't consider the cumulative impact of harm in a home or on all the family members within it; they firstly developed a plan for the eldest child. And then later that day they developed a plan to support the youngest child. They developed each plan without reference to, or knowledge of, the other. And so on. It sounds preposterous. It sounds like an approach of missed chances and siloed thinking. It sounds like a waste of money, time and resources. It also sounds like how extra-familial harm has often been addressed in England over recent decades.

In the absence of a child protection system that could reach into peer groups, schools and neighbourhood contexts where young people were harmed (chapter 3), local areas and government departments created responses to separate issues that might emerge in those contexts. Each 'issue'– sexual exploitation, youth violence, criminal exploitation, bullying, teenage relationship abuse – has been viewed largely independently of the others and responded to accordingly, but rarely anchored to a broader child protection system geared to address extra-familial harm.

In developing Contextual Safeguarding systems, local areas have needed to explore what that broader system might look like. After all a Contextual Safeguarding framework is not applied separately to each issue impacting the welfare of young people – quite the opposite. It is one part to developing a coordinated response to all forms of extra-familial harm; and therefore would characterise one overarching response to contexts in which harm had occurred across a system. Practitioners in test sites have first met to talk about a park where young people are vulnerable to harm. Such a meeting has replaced previously separate conversations about young people at risk of sexual exploitation that has been happening near the park toilets; those vulnerable to drug dealing that's been spotted near the gates; and young people who have been involved in fights that have broken out as students travelled through the park after school. Following the two-level approach to Contextual Safeguarding, outlined in the previous two chapters, practitioners have built an integrated response to these distinct issues by:

- Recording the location of the park for each child who experiences harm there and is referred into the system – providing parents and young people the space to talk about the park and what has been happening there during the process of assessment; flagging the park as a potential location for intervention and supporting the young person to identify 'green people' in the park that they can go to if they feel unsafe (Level 1 Contextual Safeguarding).
- Referring the park into the system – drawing together the cumulative evidence of harm that has amassed across individual referrals; assessing the park through observation, business and resident engagement, and trawls of data from waste management, community safety and others about the park; holding a community conference to discuss the findings of the assessment and agree a plan for increase guardianship and safety in the park – including disrupting adults who may be grooming young people into abusive behaviours (Level 2 Contextual Safeguarding).

In order to work in this way, senior leaders, legal teams, and service managers in local areas have had to review and rework the policy and meeting structures that both produced and sustained siloed working.

In this chapter I will document the successes and challenges of building this integrated policy and meeting framework for responding to extra-familial harm. I will also outline the overarching issues that we have been trying to address through such integration, reflecting on where work is still required to move from integrated approaches to holistic impact.

## Integrated policy and meeting frameworks that address extra-familial harm

All current test sites, and all local areas who have worked with us before them, have (a) recognised the pitfalls of multiple issue-specific meetings and (b) been intent on developing more integrated structures. The desire to do this has been shared by network members, who engaged with a learning project on this topic in 2017. Even back when we were first considering holistic responses to peer-on-peer abuse in 2013–2016, the integration of meetings and policy frameworks was viewed as critical to progress (chapter 5). So why in 2019 does this still feel like such a challenging summit to reach – the path to which appears laden with setbacks? One way to explore this question is to document the ways that integration has been pursued.

*Integrated strategies*

Back when George and I were reviewing local responses to peer-on-peer abuse in 2013, we had *a lot* of documents to review. From strategies that addressed 'violence against women and girls' through to those focused on 'youth violence', 'sexual exploitation', 'knife crime', 'bullying', 'school exclusions', and so on – we waded through a mountain of paperwork. And through that myriad of pages emerged a critical missing link: a shared vision, or narrative, that detailed how each area safeguarded young people.

Increasingly local leaders have recognised a need for greater integration. For starters, ever decreasing budgets have driven a need to avoid duplication. However, as the evidence base on the issues in question have improved, a case has been built for coordinating responses to issues that often occur in the same places and that may affect the same young people. Local areas, however, have taken varying approaches to achieve strategic integration.

Some have developed strategies that are integrated around issues. 'Exploitation' strategies have been published by some areas (Devon County Council, 2018; Gloucestershire Safeguarding Children Board, 2018; North Lincolnshire Children's Multi-agency Resilience and Safeguarding Board, 2018): a move informed, in part, by the increased identification of young people who have been exploited into drug dealing as well as sexual activity. In other areas professionals have integrated strategies to safeguard children who are being exploited (sexually or otherwise) and children who are missing from home – based on a recognition that many children who are being exploited are missing when this happens. Services commissioned to support people who are missing from home therefore must be accessible to those who have been exploited – and the strategy upon which such commissioning decisions are made must too be integrated.

Others have sought to integrate their strategic approach to populations of young people who might be affected by a range of extra-familial harms. For example, 'Vulnerable Adolescents' strategies or 'Safeguarding Adolescents' strategies have been published in some local areas (Greenwich Safeguarding Children's Partnership, 2019; Leeds LSCB, 2017; McElligott, 2018). These documents seek to reframe how extra-familial harm is responded to locally by setting it in the context of all harms (including those within families) that might be experienced during adolescence, and details how areas will respond effectively and in some cases preventatively:

> Many of the existing safeguarding services and structures were designed to address familial risk, while young people's needs and experiences may be very different.
>
> As children mature, risk may also come from their own behaviours and that of their peers as well as schools, neighbourhoods and the wider environment. We also know that the transition to adulthood is a particularly

challenging and vulnerable time and that needs do not end when a young person turns eighteen.

An awareness and response from a wide range of partners addressing these different contexts and issues is required when working to safeguard adolescents. We need to ensure that we promote resilience and young people's ability to respond to changing challenges. Our role is not only to protect, but also to prepare young people for adulthood.

(Greenwich Safeguarding Children's Partnership, 2019:5)

In some cases local leaders have foregrounded the uniqueness of adolescence as their rationale for developing these strategies – arguing that systems designed to safeguard much younger children from abuse fail to work with the opportunities that adolescence presents. In other cases they have argued that a range of issues impact the same cohorts of young people, and therefore it is critical to offer one response to them rather than siloed responses dependent on the issue identified on any given day.

### Integrated meetings

Tasked with turning the words in strategic documents into a practical reality are often the 'strategic' and 'operational' boards which sit underneath them. Back in 2013 George and I observed even more meetings than documents we reviewed – each sexual exploitation strategy also had a sexual exploitation strategic group, and then an operational group and sometimes even sub-groups of those groups; and the same was in place for each of the other sector-specific strategic documents an area had developed.

As strategies have integrated so too have the meetings that sit underneath them. Issue-specific meetings to oversee local responses to missing, sexual exploitation, youth violence, and so on have merged. In their place have appeared 'Multi-Agency Child Exploitation' panels and strategic groups. The panels are focused on reviewing operational responses to cases of young people identified as being affected by exploitation and identifying any themes that cut across those cases. The latter group reviews thematic issues, and agrees responses to them where appropriate, as well as oversees issues such as workforce development, profiling, and the commissioning of services. Likewise, safeguarding adolescents or vulnerable adolescents panels have formed to discuss and review plans for all young people currently experiencing harm in local areas, and/or strategic groups meet to agree approaches to commissioning/ training for work that safeguard adolescents.

### Integrated profiles and mapping

Attempts to integrate meetings have been facilitated in many areas by investment in analysts (as discussed in chapter 5). Analysts have been tasked with pooling information on the different issues impacting young people in a given area and providing an integrated profile of harm. Initially this has taken the form of an integrated profile of people. For example:

> We had 30 children in the area who we believed to be experiencing sexual exploitation; and a further 26 who we knew were going missing from home. When we combined these lists we found that 17 of our missing children also featured on the list of the 30 who were being sexually exploited.

Moving beyond this, analysts have identified locations in which multiple forms of harm have been identified. For example:

> There were concerns about a local take-away shop a 'hotspot' for children who were being groomed into drug dealing – it is also a location where there have been two stabbing in the past six months, and multiple reports of robbery.

From a strategic perspective, this type of profiling has supported partnerships to identify whether there are specific locations and schools where risks of extra-familial harm are clustered, or if the issue is more spread across a larger geographical area. It also provides an evidence base upon which to commission interventions – if profiling identifies exploitation associated to transport hubs, then intervention in that context seems sensible. If profiling suggests an issue between peers in schools is more dominant, this in turn might shift the commissioning requirement. Operationally, analytical input has enabled practitioners to better understand and discuss connections between the young people they are individually supporting and convene meetings around these connections and patterns, rather than run a series of discussions about each young person individually. Analytical support to build and develop complex maps of peer relationships prior to meetings has offered one mechanism for ensuring conversations are about the group (and their connections) rather than each individual (component part) of that network.

### Integrated teams

At their most practical, integration has occurred within teams. Ten years ago, teams had been built around issues. Co-located sexual exploitation teams, for example, were resourced in many parts of England and Wales – bringing together social care, policing, health, and voluntary agencies which could offer a multi-disciplinary and coordinated response to the issue. As other forms of extra-familial harm have surfaced, the scope of these teams has broadened, becoming 'exploitation teams' for example (Berelowitz, et al., 2013; Firmin, et al., 2019b). Other children's services departments have created an 'adolescent service' or 'adolescent team' – bringing together its youth services, youth offending teams, and social care staff focused on adolescence to provide a more integrated offer from early intervention through to specialist support.

As with exploitation teams, some adolescent teams are multi-disciplinary and also feature youth workers, police and health colleagues – in other localities they are made up solely of children's social care staff.

### Integrated for what?

Much of the integration detailed above has, and would have, occurred independently of the development of Contextual Safeguarding. It has been driven by a combination of limited resources and an evidence base that recognises the interconnected forms of adolescent safety and extra-familial harm. However, in all areas that are adopting a Contextual Safeguarding approach, this streamlining of systems, strategies, and partnerships has played a central role. In this sense you can pursue integration without adopting a Contextual Safeguarding approach, but you can't adopt a Contextual Safeguarding approach without some level of integration.

And yet having said this, the broadening or merging of policies, panels, profiles, and practice doesn't appear to have resulted in the coordinated response painted so far. As indicated at the start of this chapter, hurdles on the road to integration remain evident. Take an integrated meeting for example. Instead of holding separate meetings on sexual exploitation, criminal exploitation, missing children, and serious youth violence, an area decides to hold one meeting on 'safeguarding adolescents'. There are some benefits to this. Practitioners only have to attend one meeting instead of four. Furthermore, links between young people (who would have been discussed at separate meetings) are identified and discussed. However, for the most part practitioners in this meeting still spend vast amounts of time talking through lists of young people, and feeling at a loss about how best to respond. Bringing together the lists of young people, and having some analytical support to understand those connections, hasn't yielded a coordinated response to the safeguarding issues at hand. Likewise, developing one strategic document that makes a series of commitments to respond to the different issues impacting young people doesn't in itself address the challenges that those issues collectively pose to services.

Sitting back and thinking about this in test sites, and amongst network members, I better understood the blockage. Somewhere along the path to service improvement, the idea of integrated responses has been conflated with holistic ones. When George and I set out, we were looking for 'holistic' responses but initial steps to get there in local areas had been the pursuit of integration – the challenge being that once integration was achieved the extent to which this enabled holistic practices was not always understood. As meetings and strategies were integrated, they were largely brought together around either issues affecting young people or cohorts of young people affected by similar issues. However, it isn't clear that these steps have ensured coordinated responses to the challenges that these extra-familial issues, and the stage of adolescent development, present to traditional child protection services. Therefore, you can group together meetings about different issues impacting young people: but unless you can understand the common denominators shared across these issues and target those through a coordinated response, the holistic impact is lost. One factor shared across the different forms of harm in question and/or the age of adolescence is the extra-familial dynamics of risk and protection. As such integration should facilitate a shared response to extra-familial contexts in which harm occurs (regardless of the type of issue that presents that harm). This would achieve a holistic response – and it is this element that has often been lacking in the pursuit for integration.

## Issues that holistic frameworks target

The need to reach into extra-familial contexts, however, is only one of a number of shared system challenges that have emerged when trying to implement a Contextual Safeguarding approach. Looking across the research evidence base on the nature of extra-familial harm, coupled with the learning from policy and structural developments in test sites, and reported by network members, a number of key factors emerge as being central to building holistic frameworks for contextual practice.

### *Adolescent agency*

First and foremost, a holistic approach to adolescent safeguarding needs to work with the increasing desire for autonomy displayed by young people during this developmental stage (Blakemore, 2018; Coleman, 2011; Hanson & Holmes, 2015). As documented at the outset of this book, child protection systems have too readily problematised young people's decision-making – or located risk, instead of opportunities, in young people's appetite was self-determination. For young people, and their peers, to be viewed as potential partners in safeguarding (Warrington, 2013) any holistic response would need a consistent approach to adolescent agency. And yet in meetings, integrated or not, I still hear young people being described as 'out of control', 'putting themselves at risk', 'making risky choices', and 'not engaging' in the services offered to them.

In some respects integrating approaches have started to disrupt this narrative. For example, young people are rarely described as 'choosing' to be sexually exploited in strategic documents. However, 'youth crime' or 'youth violence' strategies have persistently referred to young people 'continuing to choose to associate with gangs or engage in criminal behaviour'. Pulling these strategic documents together makes that inconsistency more evident: creating an opening to challenge 'victim-blaming' across the piece.

However, integrating meetings or teams around issues has not automatically resolved this challenge in the round. Practitioners still require techniques, activities, and practice frameworks that see young people's decision-making as something they can work with. Contextual Safeguarding offers one way to do this. If we recognise that young people make choices within a given set of circumstances, a Contextual Safeguarding approach asks us to identify any-thing about that circumstance that we could change, which would in turn create new choices for a young person to make. Therefore rather than focus-ing on the young person's decision, we consider the decisions available and whether these can be increased, or constraints surrounding choices can be alleviated, through interventions. Contextual Safeguarding both enables and requires this approach across strategies, meetings, and teams for the Contextual Safeguarding framework to be embedded through systems.

### *Locality based and dynamic harm*

Extra-familial harm is by its nature often associated to locations beyond the family home (chapter 2) and in this sense can be unpredictable. It escalates in contexts that go beyond a social worker's field of vision. It escalates in ways that practitioners, parents, and communities can fail to understand. It pushes against the somewhat static nature of risk assessments, problem profiles, and monthly meeting cycles. It requires agility. As such, integrating profiles is one thing, but if they are only discussed once a month they will be of little use in deploying an effective response. Furthermore, if profiles are integrated but focus on people and individual demographics, rather than location, group, and time-based factors, they won't necessarily capture the elements of extra-familial harm that are interwoven. For example, two different issues might be impacting two different groups of young people, and in that sense require little integration. But the two groups may both be impacted on the same high street, or at a similar time of day and so on.

As areas have started to adopt a Contextual Safeguarding approach, they have critically assessed their analytical capacity, and the extent to which their assessment of risk and protection is fit for the purposes of understanding extra-familial harm. Using activities, such as safety mapping, that bring young people into the conversation (rather than relying on historic data) can offer a more current picture of risk and safety. Building these conversations in with young people across different partner agencies, and as a matter of course, has the potential to shift what people think to notice, record, or even flag during assessments.

We have also seen areas move to daily, weekly, or bi-weekly morning meet-ings to plan around issues of extra-familial harm, and to build reference to contexts into the system in ways that enable short notice strategy discussions. For example, after critical incidents systems would often be geared towards identifying all children connected to a family, but could they do the same for a location and/or peer group? In some test sites we have seen practitioners coordinate around groups of young people following murders or other serious incidents. In these cases they have been able to quickly identify all the young people in the peer network who might be affected, notify parents, risk assess with them and convene meetings to bring parents together within 24 hours (chapter 10).

This level of intelligence and agility is required across responses to extra-familial harm – and simply integrating meetings and profiles doesn't get us there. Instead, those running safeguarding partnerships have had to ask whether the strategic assessments and structures they have integrated are geared towards the contextual and dynamic nature of extra-familial harm – and re-design accordingly.

### Peer influence

As eluded to in Parts 1 and 2 of this book, any response to extra-familial harm needs to recognise and work with peer relationships. Young people may disclose being sexually exploited to their friends, all carry knives together and take part in bullying collectively, but integrating responses to these issues doesn't, on its own, ensure a response to peer relationships themselves (Allnock, 2019; Ashurst & McAlinden, 2015; Barter, 2009; Catch 22, 2013; Finkelhor, et al., In Press; Gardner & Steinberg, 2005; Pawlby, et al., 1997; Warr, 2002).

As detailed in the two previous chapters, understanding, and working with, peer relationships is central to a Contextual Safeguarding approach. The integration of meetings and problem profiles, and even teams, has facilitated the identification of peer relationships associated to extra-familial harm. What integration alone fails to achieve, however, is a roadmap for effectively responding to these relationships. To achieve this next step workforce training, the commissioning of services, and the development of ICT systems all need to geared more heavily towards peer relationships. For example, does the local strategy commit to commissioning interventions that work with peer groups as well as individuals? Has the workforce, particularly in social care, been supported to identify opportunities for group work amongst young people during assessments – does it know how to assess friendships as well as family relationships? And can the ICT systems used in social care to track responses to young people experiencing different forms of extra-familial harm also track their connections?

A holistic response to extra-familial harm would engage with peer relationships regardless of the specific form of harm (serious youth violence, sexual exploitation) in question – a move to integrate responses hasn't necessarily achieved this.

### Grooming, coercion, and debt-bondage

Can we undo what keeps a young person locked in an abusive situation?

Some will have been groomed – manipulated, persuaded and tricked – into believing that the abuse they are experiencing is to their benefit (Hudeck, 2018; Pearce, 2013). They may see the person/s who is harming them as their friend/s and/or partner. They may have come to believe that the companionship, money, clothing, alcohol or acceptance they get for carrying drugs, being sexually abused, or threatening others is worth the pain that might come with it.

They may have been coerced into the situation they are in – through perceived or actual risks (Pearce, 2013; Pitts, 2013). They might have been told that if they don't get in the car that is waiting for them someone will post the video they have of them being raped all over the internet. They may believe that if they don't print those train tickets and drop the drugs off at the agreed house, someone will burn down theirs. They may have been told that someone will be waiting for them at the school gates, ready to settle a dispute one way or the other. They may have seen the knives in their school friends backpacks and think they need to fill theirs the same way. They may have had their phone stolen twice already and know their parents can't afford for it to get 'lost' a third time.

They may have started off owing someone £10 for some weed they smoked at a house party. This might now be £50 with interest. And then they agreed to sell some drugs to pay that off, but had those drugs stolen from them and the debt has doubled again. And they can't stop selling now until the debt has been paid: who knows when that will be.

They may think that this is as good as it is going to get for them. If the response we offer is the wrong one they could be right.

The risks that come with extra-familial harm are complex and at times can be severe. It isn't always easy to know if there is anything that can be done to extricate a young person safely from some of the situations that they are in. Integrating responses doesn't magically resolve these challenges. Neither does Contextual Safeguarding. In fact, there is no silver bullet for impacting the risk posed to some young people.

But there are lessons that have been learnt from the past. Adults who have groomed children into sexual exploitation have been disrupted – which of the techniques that we employed for that would also apply to criminal exploitation (Home Office, 2019)? Effective responses to bullying have developed over decades – how much of that is relevant to sexual harassment in schools (Cowie, 2011; Lloyd, 2018)? To develop a holistic response to extra-familial harm we could use the opportunities that come with integration to share successes developed in response to one issue and consider their replicability to others (Firmin, et al., 2019b). Likewise, the partnerships involved in those responses could affect change for other forms of harm that previously had been out of their domain.

By coordinating around contexts where multiple forms of harm may be coalescing we have the opportunity to begin to build a holistic response to coercion, grooming and debt-bondage. But this will only form one element of an effective approach to this issue. Ultimately services need to ask themselves – what is our response/s to grooming – to coercion – to debt bondage? Regardless of the issue that was involved, how do we respond when we see this? Developing an answer to this question takes areas one step closer towards achieving the holistic impact to which integrated approaches strive.

### *Parental isolation and community guardianship*

In addition to friendship, family and community relationships are integral to safeguarding the welfare of young people (Catch 22, 2013; Ellis & Dietz, 2017; Ewell Foster, et al., 2017; Jack & Gill, 2010; PACE, 2020; Scott & McNeish, 2017) – a matter evident during the testing of Contextual Safeguarding at both Level 1 and Level 2 (chapters 9 and 10). In regards to parents, what emerged was a consistent need to address the isolation of parents whose children were being impacted by extra-familial harm. Whether that was giving parents the opportunity to discuss any concerns about their child's friends during an initial assessment, or to meet with the parents of their child's peers during interventions, developing professional and community networks around parents seemed key.

All work with parents sought to identify what factors were undermining their capacity to protect their child – and what factors were beyond their reach. When factors appeared beyond their reach – such as the threat of mobile phone theft on local buses – attention then turned to broader members of the community who had a presence in the contexts where a parent did not. What was our collective capacity in any extra-familial context to increase safety or disrupt risk? Identifying and skilling up existing community members to take on a guardianship role – or putting guardians into localities (such as detached youth workers) when there weren't any available – was central to Level 2 work.

This type of engagement builds upon previous attempts to involve communities in responses to serious youth violence or sexual exploitation. With the latter, training has been delivered to taxi drivers, security staff, and so on to spot the signs of sexual exploitation (D'Arcy & Thomas, 2016) – however, the same has not been done for criminal exploitation. Community marches have been organised against the impact knife crime, but the same has not happened in response to young people's experiences of sexual harassment or robbery on public transport. Integrating responses to harm could in some way mobilise communities in a more consistent fashion and engage them in activities to tackle different forms of extra-familial harm. Community guardianship provides a broader framework in which to hold many of those activities. It also elevates community engagement to be one concerned with the creation of safe spaces rather than solely the identification of, or protest about, unsafe individuals. This builds upon traditions of community development work (i.e. Jack & Gill, 2010) and locates it as a central pillar of holistic response to extra-familial harm.

The need to address parental isolation and build community guardianship has emerged across test sites. We cannot meet that need solely through integrating responses to extra-familial harm. After all, we too often continue to look to parents to prevent the exploitation of their children when most of us would struggle to take on a criminal gang, organised crime network, or group of young people persistently harassing our child on our own. If the response to different forms of extra-familial harm is to offer parents classes on boundary setting but not to connect them to other parents, then, despite being an integrated offer, the intervention wouldn't address a holistic challenge faced when responding to extra-familial harm.

As such when partnerships develop a strategy for tackling extra-familial harm community guardianship would need to feature. And when interventions are commissioned to support families affected by these issues, services that can bring families together and build parent support networks would need to be considered. In taking an integrated approach to building parental and community capacity, areas would start to shape holistic response to extra-familial harm.

## From integrated to holistic – the strategic framework that enables a Contextual Safeguarding approach

In testing Contextual Safeguarding we have started to understand what is required from broader strategies and partnerships that would sustain and embed the approach. Contextual Safeguarding has developed at a time in which local areas are integrating responses to different forms of extra-familial harm – and in many test sites Contextual Safeguarding work has intersected with these efforts. What has become apparent in that process is that integration on its own is insufficient for sustaining a Contextual Safeguarding approach. Rather, strategies, meeting structures, profiles, and teams that hold the approach need to address the challenges that emerge when trying to respond to extra-familial harm using traditional safeguarding systems.

A child protection system that can respond to extra-familial harm therefore is one that can: work with adolescent agency; disrupt parental isolation; build community capacity to safeguard; understand the significance of young people's friendships; combat the impact of grooming, coercion, and debt bondage; and display the agility to respond to locality-based and dynamic risk (Figure 11.1). Sitting underneath this overarching system would be topic-specialism. For example, the nature of sexual abuse is not the same as criminal exploitation – and neither is their impact. Understanding the issue of 'consent' and public discourses regarding sexuality are critical to responding to sexual harm. Resolving how you safeguard a young person who has been found in possession of firearms, and has inflicted physical harm on others, but has been groomed to do so is central to responding to criminal exploitation. But if we grapple with those challenges in a system that takes a holistic approach to working with adolescent agency, for example, rather than doing it for one issue and not the other, we are part way there. We begin to rectify the legacy of not having a system with extra-familial harm in mind and begin to foster the integrated and holistic environment required for a Contextual Safeguarding approach to grow.

Over this chapter, and the previous three, I have detailed the steps taken to develop a Contextual Safeguarding approach in practice – the people involved, the tools they used, and the strategic environment required to sustain and

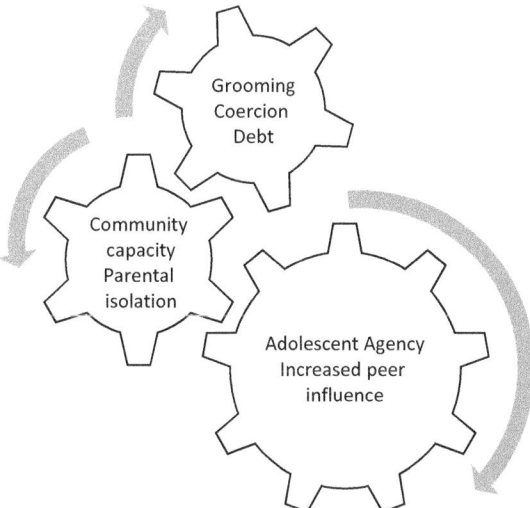

*Figure 11.1* Systemic Needs of a Holistic System

embed what has been achieved. I thought I knew what a Contextual Safe-guarding approach would look like when I first wrote the four-domain frame-work. While those four domains still apply, my understanding of what they say about child protection and safeguarding systems has deepened; and through this process so too have my thoughts on the overarching implications of the approach. The following chapter, the final in this part of the book, will detail the values that have come to the fore when testing Contextual Safeguarding, and how this continues to shape how my team and I think about its potential for the future.

# 12 Values and impact

## Deepening the Contextual Safeguarding framework

I like to think I am known for my brilliant brownie baking skills. Birthdays, weddings, graduations – whatever the celebration you can guarantee – I'll offer to bake and deliver a tower of chocolatey deliciousness to the festivities. As much as I enjoy bathing in the compliments that follow, if I am being honest they are by far the easiest baked good to perfect. The recipe is simple. The baking time is quick. A wooden spoon, bowl, bain-marie, and weighing scales are all the equipment you need. I generally keep this to myself. But one day my dear friend Brie sent me a message from her hometown in Canada asking for the recipe. I jotted it down in step-by-step straight-forward instructions, sent them through to her and thought nothing much of it for the rest of the day. The next morning I woke up to a picture message on my phone. It was Brie, in front of her oven, the brownie mixture dripping over the sides of the baking dish and all over the inside base of the oven. It had been a total baking disaster.

I was confused. How could something with so few steps, and only minimal ingredients, turn out so differently to all of my previous attempts. Sure I have baked enough to know that cakes turn out a little differently depending on the type of oven you use for example. But this level of divergence from the norm couldn't be explained that way. When I spoke to Brie later that day two more significant differences in her approach to baking became apparent. The first was the flour she used. The type of flour I was describing was simply not available where she lived in Canada – so Brie tried something else, and that something else resulted in a completely different outcome. Secondly, Brie is an excellent cook – she is creative, she likes to mix things up, she doesn't always follow the recipe. While that might work when knocking-up a soup, curry or gravy, it isn't quite the same with a cake. Brie confessed she 'interpreted' rather than followed the recipe; she hadn't quite understood that in this case the measurements were relatively integral to ensuring success. There were areas where you could get creative: you could use square tin or round tin; choose whichever brand of dark chocolate you so desired, cut them into squares, rectangles, or hearts. But the measurement of the ingredi-ents, and the type of flour one used, was pretty essential to achieving a baking triumph. My brownies may come out slightly differently in different ovens – they are contextually informed. They may also taste a little different depending on the chocolate I use and how much of a 'pinch' of salt I sprinkle in for that extra kick – they will be shaped by the nature of the players/ingredients involved. But they will always be brownies – and they will never explode over the inside of my oven – so long as I weigh my ingredients and use the correct type of flour.

The more we test and develop Contextual Safeguarding the more I realise that the Contextual Safeguarding framework is very similar to my approach to baking brownies. When applied in different contexts the practical results will also vary. Some areas will have a large youth work service to draw upon as they develop their approach, for others this opportunity will be minimal. However, there are some things that will need to remain true however the framework is used – that is, how the recipes is followed – if a mess is to be avoided.

This is a fine line to tread. At this point in testing it feels to me, and the rest of the team, that Contextual Safeguarding will always be an approach to safeguarding rather than a model of practice. In this sense it must be contextually driven and not too manualised or prescriptive. We also know, from testing to date, that allowing for flexibility yields a greater understanding of the approach and its' potential. The vast majority of what I have written in previous chapters in Part 3 of this book was not conceived before testing commenced. If we had focused too heavily on a manualised approach to the work, we may never have realised Level 1 and Level 2 ways of working – and all the learning that has come with them.

And yet we through work in test sites and via our network members we have learnt two important lessons about the risks of this stance. Firstly, that there are some underpinning principles to doing Contextual Safeguarding that must be understood if we are to avoid unintended and potentially unethical consequences when implementation is attempted. This deepens how we understand Contextual Safeguarding. And secondly, that if you apply the framework to its fullest there are a number of reflexively reinforcing impacts and requirements that come to the fore, whatever the context. This sharpens how we understand Contextual Safeguarding and assures its use aligns to its intentions.

In this chapter I will detail and reflect upon these two points of learning to close this part of the book. In doing so I round up what we know about Contextual Safeguarding to date before I use Part 4 of the book to signal what we might need to know next.

## Unwritten and underpinning – the values of Contextual Safeguarding

As has been detailed in many parts of this book, young people have been approached and groomed into exploitation in take-away shops. Sara was raped in the toilet of a take away shop. So when I found out that the UK government had launched a campaign that targeted chicken shops as a way of tackling serious youth violence I was initially excited. These are a context where young people encounter harm – it makes sense to target these places for intervention as well as the young people abused in (or nearby) them. And then I started to get emails. People asking me if I had something to do with the campaign. Is this what I had meant by Contextual Safeguarding? Was this the Contextual Safeguarding framework in action? And these questions were not ones of intrigue – they were laced with concern.

Within five minutes of looking up the campaign I could understand why. The interventions weren't targeting chicken shops at all. Instead, the campaign targeted individual young people who were in chicken shops. And furthermore, it sought to achieve this through stories written on the inside of chicken boxes about other young people who had 'chosen' music lessons or sport over weapon carrying. The message being you can be marginalised; you can live in a violent context; you can be approached by exploitative adults while eating chicken with your friends; and you can still choose to do something else. It was in essence an individualised response to a contextual issue. It was the complete opposite of Contextual Safeguarding.

This was one of many occasions in 2019 that I was confronted with a reason to elevate and explicitly state the values that underpin the Contextual Safeguarding framework. Members of the team, particularly those who joined us with fresh eyes in 2018–2019 such as Lauren Wroe, Katie Latimer, Joanne Walker and Rachael Owens, also raised this issue with me; as had developers in the test sites and on the practice network. The question was – if you develop a system that targets contexts, through the lens of child protection and child welfare, with a broad range of partners, to achieve contextual impact – will you always be doing Contextual Safeguarding? It is worth noting that the chicken shop campaign didn't achieve this – it targeted young people in the chicken shop and didn't seek to change the contexts themselves: it felt short on Domains 1 and 4 of the framework. And yet, the answer to whether the four domains of the framework is enough has felt increasingly uncertain without stating three previously unwritten values that characterise our approach to delivery.

### *Unwritten values*

The Contextual Safeguarding framework is built not just on the idea that context matters – but that context matters to human behaviour. True to its Bourdieusian roots, it sets out to target contexts because the human behaviours we are concerned about are informed by the rules at play within them. Therefore in adopting the approach we don't ignore individual decision-making – rather we seek to understand the drivers of human agency and in doing so work with it. Much of the work at Level 1 of Contextual Safeguarding is to engage individuals in discussions about contexts: supporting parents and young people to reflect on the influence that contexts have on their decisions, as well as identify how their decisions shape contexts. The latter point is equally applicable to Level 2 work where adults and young people are asked to identify the role they could play in creating safer parks, high streets, schools and so on. World views that abstract human behaviour from environment are like oil to the water of Contextual Safeguarding – they will never mix. But so too would approaches that neglect the role of personal responsibility, for one's own welfare and for the welfare of others. This may seem obvious to some readers of the Contextual Safeguarding framework, but testing has shown us that there remains a legacy in which extra-familial harm is conceptualised as the consequence of 'poor decisions' – rather than decisions made in a set of poor/constrained situations. The chicken box campaign, as with many other examples, clearly illustrated that. A belief that context matters to agency and vice versa – and that this matters to safeguarding children's welfare – is the first unwritten value that drives a Contextual Safeguarding approach.

Not all contexts are equal    and neither is how we experience them. Public spaces that have been assessed in test sites are not dangerous places for everyone who spends time in them. The streets that students have identified as unsafe when walking to and from school are the same pavements pounded by commuters who are rarely concerned with being stabbed on their journey to the office. The trains I sit on to visit practitioners around the country have been used to traffic children miles away from their parents to sell the drugs they have been groomed to carry. The sexual harassment reported by some young women in their youth clubs and school corridors is not a concern shared by other students and staff who occupy those same spaces. Racism, sexism, homophobia, and a general disdain for, or fear of, 'young people' play out in the contexts where they encounter harm. While not stated as a domain of the Contextual Safeguarding framework, an ethical application of the approach must recognise inequality, therefore, as both a cause and consequence of contextual harm.

Consider how we identify contexts of concern. As detailed in previous chapters, neighbourhood or location assessments have been initiated in test sites. The locations under assessment have not always been identified as 'hot spots' when we have reviewed reported crime data. Young people have not always reported their experiences of crime, or have articulated that they feel unsafe in a local area via traditional reporting mechanisms. As such, when location concerns have emerged so too have debates about whether an area is 'unsafe'. During one location assessment for example, tens of parents shared that their children had experienced robbery – a matter disputed by the police who had only received four such complaints. Sitting underneath such disagreements are various inequalities. Firstly is the matter of some young people not reporting the crimes they experience as they (a) don't believe that adults can always protect them and (b) don't think they will be believed (Anderson, et al., 2017; Bevan, 2014; Lammy, 2017; ONS, 2019; Rypi, et al., 2019). Added to this dynamic is the likelihood that some people who report crimes or make complaints about anti-social behaviour, may occupy a place where they (a) don't question whether they will be believed and (b) feel like something can, and must be, done to address their concerns. If we require crime data to drive our contextual practices we will remain blind to the concerns raised by young people in welfare-based assessments, interactions with teachers, youth workers, and so on.

These same inequalities create opportunities for contexts to remain harmful. If we fail to target the locations where young people feel vulnerable but don't report crimes, these locations continue to be ones in which adults can approach and groom our children undeterred. If we fail to challenge broader discourses that blame young people or see them as anti-social and problematic, then we maintain a status quo where they can be abused in plain sight: no one will see them as vulnerable at the bus stop or on the high street, no one will feel able to intervene if they are concerned. If we continue to blame parents, particularly mothers, who live in marginalised, neglected areas for not being able to safeguard their children from abuse on public transport and in schools, we further isolate them and undermine their parental capacity – rather than include them and bolster the care and concern they have for their children. The reality of inequality, and its relationship to contextual harm therefore, is a second unwritten value that drives the application of the Contextual Safeguarding framework.

And finally, the Contextual Safeguarding framework requires hope. For some this may be at odds with the 'pessimism' (Lawler, 2004) attributed to Bourdieu's worldview. If social rules are informed by human behaviour and inform it in a reflexive fashion, how do we rewrite them? If you accept that contextual change is impossible, then the Contextual Safeguarding framework becomes unworkable. It is premised on the idea that the rules of social contexts can change and that through this process so too can human behaviour – and furthermore that the human behaviour can be part of this rewriting process. However, it is also premised on an acknowledgement that this type of change is not always easy. That changing the rules of contexts may require multi-pronged activity: some of which can come in form of quick wins (such as trimming down hedges in a park to remove opportunities for drug dealing in hidden places) and some are longer-term goals (such as building relationships between park staff, young people, and parents of younger children to foster community guardianship in a public space and create an environment that is hostile to grooming).

The long term goals can feel unreachable – particularly in systems that are predicated on the idea that success lies in individual case working to de-escalate risk as quickly as possible in order to 'close' the case. The long road to impact can breed the pessimism for which Bourdieu has been critiqued. However, when testing the Contextual Safeguarding framework practitioners have grappled with whether change feels impossible or just a long way off. In the case of the former, Contextual Safeguarding will be undermined. We have witnessed this in action. Assessments of housing estates where 'drug dealing has always happened so there is no point trying to change it' scupper development. The response from those testing the approach has, and needs to be, 'why is that acceptable'? Just because somewhere or some group feel consistently associated with harm, it doesn't mean that such harm must be tolerated. If a child was being abused by a parent, we wouldn't suggest they just stay in their room, or try to leave the house early each morning for school, to avoid the person abusing them. We wouldn't ask them to make better choices to navigate the abusive situation they are in (Lloyd, 2019). So why would we ask that of children and families who are navigating harmful contexts? A Contextual Safeguarding framework is informed by a position that contextual harm is no more acceptable, tolerable, or inevitable than harm within families: a position which makes up the third and final unwritten value of the approach.

### *The lens through which a Contextual Safeguarding framework is viewed*

As well as identifying three unwritten values that sit behind the Contextual Safeguarding framework, work in test sites has required us to share the lens through which we view it, and particularly Domain 2. In doing so we have brought the vision of the system we are seeking to create into sharper focus.

Back in 2016 I included Domain 2 in the Contextual Safeguarding framework for two reasons.

The first was to maintain a position that recognised extra-familial harm as abuse. Child protection systems have developed to safeguard children from abuse – extra-familial harm is abuse and therefore is a child protection issue. This clarity of position was important. The Contextual Safeguarding framework was introduced into an inconsistent policy and research landscape that positioned some forms of extra-familial harm as safeguarding issues first (sexual exploitation) and others as crime and disorder issues first (such as serious youth violence) (Parts 1 and 2). The Contextual Safeguarding framework recognised that despite its ill fit with the parameters of traditional child protection practice and policy, these issues all posed a risk of significant harm to the welfare of children and the system designed to protect them from that harm needed to mobilise in response.

The second was that where contextual practices had emerged in the field of extra-familial harm they were largely built on traditions of situational crime prevention and place-based policing. 'Disruption' was the cornerstone of much of this – increasing police presence in 'hotspot' locations; serving dispersal notices on young people who were congregating in areas thought to be unsafe and so on. While there was no desire to exclude policing work from a Contextual Safeguarding approach, it was critical to see it as part of – rather than the sole route to – achieving contextual change. In this sense the welfare of young people would sit at the heart of decision-making and would inform criminal justice actions. For starters – some measures like dispersing young people targeted them and not the contexts in which they were vulnerable. A Contextual Safeguarding framework would encourage policing options which pursued adults who were exploiting children; for example using offences such as drugs possession or lack of car insurance to stifle their ability to freely move around and access children unnoticed (when those behaviours of most concern could not be proven), rather than the children themselves. A wider partnership of community members, youth workers, parents and others might offer support through positive activities or guardianship to the group of young people who would previously have been subject to dispersal. Likewise, while increasing police presence in an area may make some people feel safer – there is not always evidence that it has the desired effect for the young people who have been vulnerable in that area; and furthermore that attempts to constrain or control young people to increase safety in a location can have the opposite effect (Guerette & Bowers, 2009; Klein, 2012; Wortley, 1998). Finally, once the police leave an area, the level of supervision decreases. Domain 2 allows for interventions to be driven around the sustained safeguarding of young people in area – for example, identifying individuals or companies who are already there and supporting them to provide permanent guardianship of an area.

Through Domain 2 I positioned the Contextual Safeguarding framework within a lens of child protection to situate extra-familial harm as abuse and contextual interventions as welfare driven. In short, the drivers were to push against the criminalisation of the issues and the young people affected by them. Less consideration had been given to the potential shortfalls of a child protection framework and risks that these could undermine a Contextual Safeguarding approach. Mounting critiques of Western child protection system, coupled with emerging blockages in test sites, brought this oversight to the fore.

All is not well, or contextual, in the world of child protection. In many countries child protection systems are increasingly geared towards the fixing of people rather than the situations those people are in (chapters 3 and 4). Calls to revive the social justice in social work have emerged in light of the unjust outcomes the system has produced. Consider a system that holds a woman responsible, for example, for staying with an abusive partner and uses this as the reason for taking their children into care – instead of the actions of the partner, and the broader situation they may also be in, being the primary concern (Ferguson, et al., 2019). Such perverse outcomes and system limitations have been increasingly rehearsed by social work scholars and were documented in earlier chapters in the book. By viewing Domain 2 alongside the other three elements of the Contextual Safeguarding framework, we hoped to mitigate some of this – for example, Domain 1 requires that the system targets the social conditions of abuse, rather than individualising it. But there are other limitations to child protection systems that aren't immediately resolved through the other three domains in the Contextual Safeguarding framework – and the two most pressing of these are the adoption of a 'deficit' approach to harm reduction and systems approaches that could compromise rather than protect the rights of children.

From being positioned to receive referrals about abuse, through to assessing the level of risk, and basing success measures around an absence of risk, child protection systems have been geared towards deficits. What is it about you – the parent – that means your child is at risk of abuse? What would you need to do better for us to be less concerned about this? Which children are unsafe, how unsafe are they, how worried should we be? From the moment we commenced testing it was evident that the same lens could be applied to peer groups, schools and neighbourhoods: we have assessed this young person and their friends present the greatest risk of harm; we have problem profiled our area and identified this high street as a red zone – and so on. With this deficit lens comes blaming, labelling and marginalisation. Communities, already feeling the effects of reduced community resources or increased school exclusions, are labelled as places where young people are at risk of abuse. Young people who have grouped together to try and stay safe when travelling to and from school – and who have armed themselves with knives in the process – are viewed singularly as having risky or problematic associations. Going down this road severely limits the potential of a Contextual Safeguarding framework. It simply moves from labelling children to labelling their friends, schools or communities and in the process achieves a superficial recognition of context and reinforces the inequalities that Contextual Safeguarding seeks to address.

When reflecting on testing to date a deficit approach to Contextual Safeguarding is evident. Localities are problem profiled more readily than they are safety profiled. Practitioners are mapping and assessing friendship groups where they have concerns more frequently than in cases where they believe a young person's friends are protective. They are developing plans to reduce risk in local areas rather than increase safety (albeit these aren't mutually exclusive). The Contextual Safeguarding team and I have been part of these processes, as a desire to incorporate the Contextual Safeguarding framework into local child protection systems has sometimes come at the cost of adopting the negative, as well as positive, elements of existing practice (explored further in chapter 15).

And yet when adopting a Contextual Safeguarding approach we have also witnessed some practitioners disrupt this trajectory. The starkest example of this came when finalising the assessment of a school. A practitioner commented that it wouldn't be appropriate to suggest that the school leaders were being ineffective in their safeguarding role: that this would be blaming of them, and fail to consider the other contextual factors at play when a violent incident occurred between students. The point was a valid one. It also flew in the face of the tone taken with many parents of young people who were at risk of extra-familial harm, who had been blamed for the risks their children faced. Adopting a position of blame was unhelpful across the piece – and yet it felt easier to challenge this on behalf of a teacher than on behalf of a parent.

As a result, the Contextual Safeguarding team have questioned how we have been applying the Contextual Safeguarding framework to date, and whether we too have promoted the extension of deficit models across different contexts, or facilitated a more strengths-based approach to safeguarding in extra-familial contexts. Active engagement in the field of strength-based social work (Graybeal, 2001; Williams, 2019) and working with localities who are trying to embed that culture into all child protection practice continues to inform that learning. In adopting this view it becomes quite easy to visualise a move to safety profiling: understanding where an area's green zones are and having goals to increase these rather than to solely decrease the ones in red. Likewise, engaging with young people's peer relationships as a matter of course should create opportunities for safeguarding professionals to recognise their contribution to well-being (explored more below). There is no reason why a Contextual Safeguarding approach wouldn't be strengths-based, and in many respects this direction of travel is far better aligned to the hopeful values that inform it. However, we have come to realise that saying Contextual Safeguarding is aligned to child protection approaches is not enough to ensure that this happens. Articulating that the framework be viewed through a strengths-based lens is critical for avoiding an individualised and blaming interpretation of the approach.

The same too can be said of children's rights. Domain 2 positioned Contextual Safeguarding as offering a response to abuse and pushed that extra-familial harm be seen as such. In this regard I lent on the belief that children have rights – one of which is to be protected from all forms of abuse and exploitation: these rights do not change if a child is abused on a high street instead of their family home. However, as broader work on responses to child sexual exploitation has indicated, there are other rights to be considered when we strive to safeguard the welfare of young people. In prioritising abuse over all other matters we risk constraining the rights of children to be part of decisions that affect them (Ellis, 2018; Lefevre, et al., 2018; Warrington, 2013; Wroe, 2019) – trampling over their desire for autonomy with our desire to take control. Likewise, when practitioners have concerns about the risk a group of young people collectively share we have witnessed attempts to keep them apart. And furthermore, when concerns about a young person's safety in their local area escalate, they can be moved away from their friends, communities, and sometimes their families against their will – in a bid to secure their physical protection (Firmin, 2019; Shuker, 2013).

While a Contextual Safeguarding approach is positioned to safeguard children from abuse, the lens of Children's Rights more broadly helps us recognise the wider set of issues that would need to be considered in tandem with this to avoid an oppressive application of the Contextual Safeguarding framework. In some areas for example professionals have challenged the idea of peer mapping – suggesting it moves towards the surveillance of young people. We have been at pains to stress that increasing surveillance of young people is not aligned to the principles of a Contextual Safeguarding approach. We are concerned instead to create contexts, and social conditions, in which young people can safely associate; peer mapping can help us identify opportunities to do this. Furthermore, we readily encourage practitioners to involve young people in mapping exercises – giving them the opportunity to inform decision-making and ensuring professionals build a complete picture about the value they place on their peer relationships. Similarly, we would be encouraging professionals to identify how to increase safety in a park so young people can continue to spend time outdoors, together, rather than using dispersal powers to dissuade young people from socialising there.

It is only through testing the approach via our network and in formal test sites that we have understood the need to require the Contextual Safeguarding framework to be viewed through a strength-based and children's rights lens. In the absence of this the overarching goals of the framework, and its unwritten values, can be lost; and what it requires of child protection systems can be underestimated.

## A collective approach – the requirement and impact of Contextual Safeguarding

Identifying the unwritten values of the Contextual Safeguarding framework, and the lens through which it should be viewed, advances how the approach is understood. The four domains of the framework, plus the values and viewing lens are all key ingredients to cooking up a Contextual Safeguarding approach. In addition, however, learning from network members and test sites has started to illuminate what might emerge when those ingredients are put to use – regardless of local variations. Whether sites use panels or community meetings, take referrals in a discrete team or across services, there are some outputs that they all seem to share. Understanding the practice features that emerge from the approach across localities clarifies what system leaders and practitioners might expect should they implement the framework to its fullest.

### *Expanding capacity to safeguard*

A Contextual Safeguarding approach questions the capacity of a broad range of people/organisations to safeguard young people. The person/s in question will be determined by the context in question. Historically, the question of capacity to safeguard has been reserved for a child's parent and provides the grounds upon for state intervention, both in England and internationally (chapter 13). If a parent does not have the capacity to meet a child's needs and/or protect them from harm the state has a duty to do so. But in the case of extra-familial harm a parent's capacity will often be limited and far more limited than those who manage or have a presence in the context/s in which the harm has occurred. If a young person has been stabbed on journey to school, those using the approach would ask who on the journey, if anyone, has the capacity to safeguard that young person. Is it the bus drivers, other bus users, transport police, detached youth workers, shopkeepers, rubbish collectors – and so on? Who is making a difference, who could make a difference, and what would an increased collective capacity to safeguard mean for that child and family?

### Safeguarding being everybody's business

As noted in chapter 3, an increasing awareness of the contextual dynamics of extra-familial harm already generated engagement with businesses and individuals who have a reach into, or oversight of, those places. Outside of a Contextual Safeguarding framework this engagement has mainly focused on training taxi drivers, security and hotel staff being alert to the signs of exploitation and reporting any concerns to children's services. In the case of hotels and shops some test-purchase work has also been undertaken (Home Office, 2019). This has been geared to identify if staff in hotels would book rooms for adults accompanied by young people who weren't related to them for one afternoon or a night – with no luggage – for example, or sell knives to young people who looked under-18. This work goes a step further, and starts to identify actions these agencies could take to disrupt abuse in progress: moving beyond referring concerns to acting on them. For example, the hotel might refuse the room booking, disrupting the process of committing an assault on their property; they might refuse to sell a knife and thereby prevent a serious offence occurring. In one of the original cases, I reviewed a number of young people bought knives from local shops on their lunch break and later that day killed another young person in a planned fight; these micro-disruptions could be effective.

When engaging broader partnerships in the assessment of, and plans for, extra-familial contexts, those using a Contextual Safeguarding framework have extended this work and in doing so reframed what it means for safeguarding to be 'everybody's business'. Assessment of, and intervention with, contexts has involved professionals, adults, and organisations who spend time in those places. Their views have informed the assessment of safety in those areas; they have been involved in meetings to agree intervention plans that result from those assessments; they have played a role in delivering the interventions agreed on those plans. Throughout this process safeguarding being everybody's business has been about a range of partners working together to create safe spaces – not solely working together to spot abuse. Collaboration has been pivotal to this work. Social workers have not told bus drivers, residents or teachers what they could do to safeguard the welfare of young people. Instead they have asked them what they think they could do to affect change in a given context; and through problem-solving they have reached shared solutions.

### Recognising peer relationships as significant

A critical partner in this endeavour has been young people's peers. Every test site, and various network members, has significantly increased their use of peer mapping as part of assessment work. The challenges and opportunities that have come with this are detailed in chapter 10, but cumulatively they are evidence of an increasing belief that the significance of friendship and peer influence is such that it must be considered when safeguarding the welfare of a young person. The different routes to assessing and engaging with peer relationships across test sites are further testament to this. Practitioners invested in advancing their practice have critically engaged with the mapping process, sought to involve young people and parents in this, and used peer assessments as a foundation for working with peer relationships. It is this latter point which has emerged as both an impact and requirement of the Contextual Safeguarding framework.

To do Contextual Safeguarding practitioners, and their managers, are having to explore options for: working with peer groups, rather than only one individual from a peer group; maintaining peer relationships that they may have previously sought to disrupt; and investing in approaches to intervention that increase guardianship around peer groups – rather than requiring young people's friendships to change in contexts which remain persistently unsafe. From bringing together parents of connected peers, to reinvesting in detached youth work, I remain surprised at the investment that has gone into this area of practice. A senior manager phoned me over the summer to discuss their proposed next steps for adopting a Contextual Safeguarding approach. Within the first five minutes of speaking to me they explained that they have been using Contextual Safeguarding resources – particularly peer assessment and mapping tools – and as a result had pushed for and secured money for four new detached youth worker posts. They didn't feel that Contextual Safeguarding was possible without that investment, and trialling elements of the approach had led them to that conclusion. The variation in approaches to peer group support and intervention continues to be documented across sites – and much of this is determined by the organisations, partnerships, and roles already available in sites. But regardless of the type of support that can be offered, there is a general recognition that a way of working with peer relationships is required to implement the approach.

### *The risks, strengths and vulnerabilities of places, groups, and people*

The assessment frameworks for schools, peer groups and neighbourhoods developed in Level 2 testing of Contextual Safeguarding applied the language of strength, risk, and vulnerability beyond people and levelled them at places. While the assessment triangles assisted practitioners in organising the information gathered, or monitoring the impact of plans, these resources were built on a broader understanding that risks or strengths could be held collectively in groups or in places.

The more we developed training on the Contextual Safeguarding framework, the more this needed to be articulated. Without the language to contextually describe the risks of abuse or the opportunities for protection, test site practitioners and training participants would often revert to an individualised account of the harm in question. Additionally, they often conflated risks and vulnerabilities – and struggled to conceive of strengths.

Consider a transport hub. For the most part this transport hub is not one in which abuse is a concern. However, at 4:00 pm each day students from various schools converge on the bus stop. This is not a risk. Most days students pass through the hub without incident. However, studies into situational crime prevention and problem-orientated policing (Burton, 2008; Newton, et al., 2014), and the work of analysts in test sites (Firmin & Abbott, 2018; Firmin & Hancock, 2018), have suggested that this could present a vulnerability of harm occurring. Convergence does multiple things. It firstly provides anonymity. If tens of young people are all in the same place, wearing the same school uniform, it is hard to see who threw the first punch in a fight. Convergence also brings together young people who don't know each other into a shared space, and it would only take one young person to take issue with another for tensions to flare. Convergence also means increased numbers and opportunities for anyone looking to groom a young person. An adult would only need to offer a certain number of young people a free bag of chips for example before one says yes and a relationship is initiated. As a result, it may make sense to safeguard the context at 4:00 pm each day and increase supervision. This already happens in a number of areas. My local transport hub regularly has police officers stationed at it in the after-school window. However, I often wonder why it has to be the police. Why could it not be youth workers – or youth workers and young people working alongside each other? In a Contextual Safeguarding framework this would be preferable – and positions concerns as one of child welfare and safeguarding rather than crime and disorder. For other adults in the vicinity it gives the message that these are our young people, and we are working with them to achieve safety in this locality – not policing young people who pose a risk to everyone else.

This is different to there being an active risk identified in the transport hub. Professionals have been made aware that some young people have been approached and groomed at the bus stop. Others feel unsafe there and have started to carry weapons on the school journey as a result. Such a scenario may require the active engagement of key players at the bus stop in an assessment of what is happening, and a coordinated plan to be developed to increase safety. This might involve police action against adults who have approached young people; increased visibility of youth workers in the area; awareness-raising with parents about concerns and so on. The assessment would need to inform the plan, and the plan overseen as one concerned with safeguarding the welfare of young people.

The nuance of contextual safety, risk, and vulnerability continues to be documented in test sites to give an indication of what might constitute each and what might warrant further investigation; and attempts have been made to create exemplar tables that illustrate what might constitute a contextual, as opposed to individual, vulnerability, or risk. The fact that this level of detail has been required to assist in the testing of the approach is telling. One might assume that by stating the system needs to target contexts in which abuse occurs, Domain 1 of the Contextual Safeguarding framework gives enough indication of what is required of the safeguarding system. However, to uproot the foundations of individualised practice, a language has been required to describe risks, safety, and vulnerabilities contextually. An inability to do so frustrates attempts to do Level 2 Contextual Safeguarding work, and risks interventions with contexts being seen as work with individuals who are in those contexts – rather than the contexts themselves: taking us right back to chicken boxes and the young people who eat out of them – rather than the shops and streets in which those young people are based.

## Values, principles, and requirements: below the waterline of the Contextual Safeguarding framework

Once Brie tried to bake my brownies, I realised that my basic list of ingredients was not enough. I needed to be clearer about when she needed to follow the recipe, why this mattered, and when she could be more flexible. Brie needed to measure the flour – and use the right kind – but the brand of chocolate or amount of salt (if any) that she used were totally down to her. Ultimately the outcome would also reflect the baking tin she used and the type of oven she baked in – and that was all fine as well. But a broad framework, that left too many requirements unsaid or implied, resulted in an inedible mess.

Attempts to test the Contextual Safeguarding framework have also been messy – much in part to what we assumed in 2016. At that stage it would have been impossible for us to realise (a) what unwritten elements of the framework would require emphasis; (b) what lens would be required so that the framework was viewed and applied as intended; and (c) what practice requirements would consistently emerge from application of the framework. Three years on and we are much clearer on all of these points.

Figure 12.1 illustrates where our thinking has got to. The core framework remains unchanged, but the values that sat before it, the lens through which it is viewed (the principles of the approach), and outcomes of application have, now come to the surface. The Contextual Safeguarding framework was built on three values, which in many respects preceded the design of the framework but have been articulated latterly. The need to adopt a strengths-based and children's rights approach to application however was not in mind when the Contextual Safeguarding framework was first published. The importance of this lens has materialised in 2019, as have the practice features which have emerged during the framework's application: both amongst network members and in test sites.

The Contextual Safeguarding framework I have presented here is arguably more prescriptive than it was in 2016, but the idea that it is an approach and not a model of practice holds true. In chapters 9 and 10, I detailed the varying ways in which the Contextual Safeguarding framework has been interpreted in practice – and these variations can all be accommodated by the values, lens, and practice outputs documented in this chapter. So whether local areas run community meetings or context conferences; involve residents associations, or

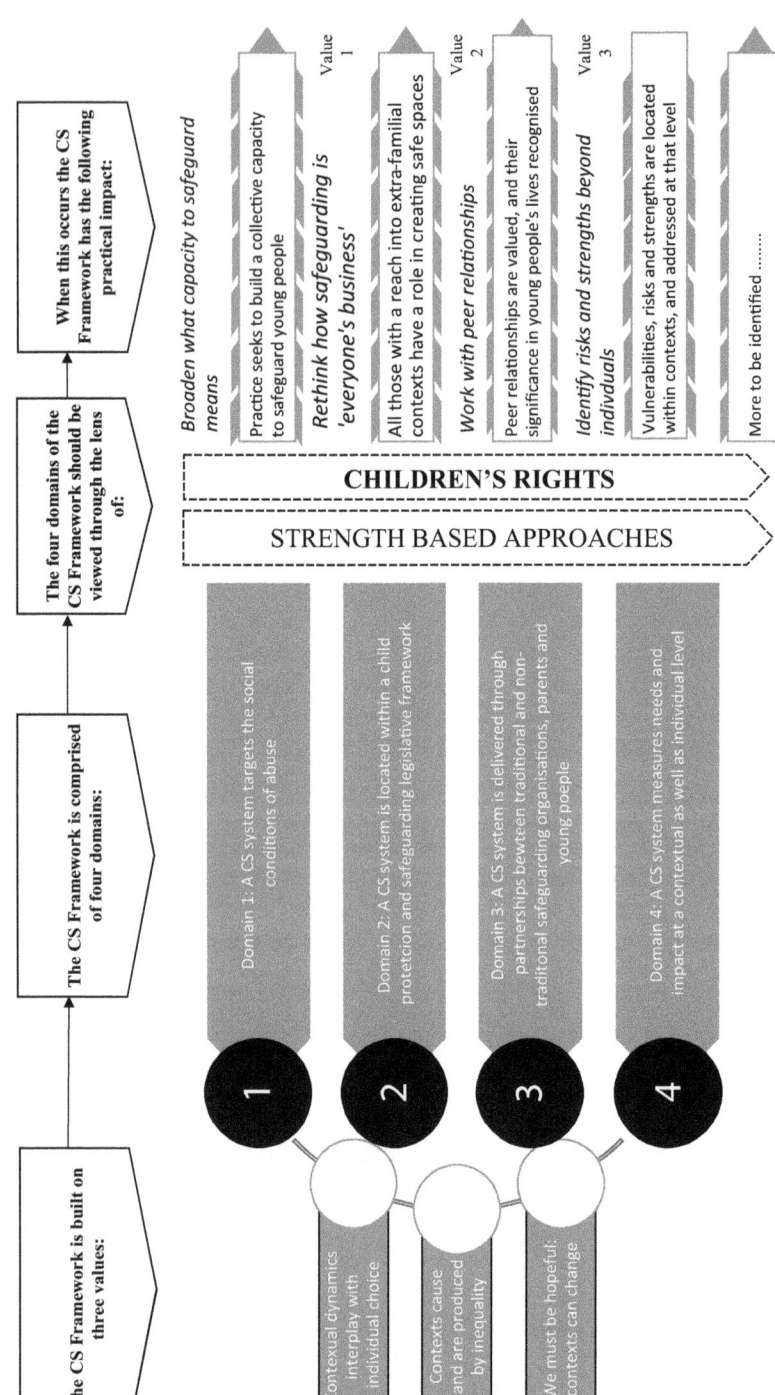

The CS Framework is built on three values:

The CS Framework is comprised of four domains:

The four domains of the CS Framework should be viewed through the lens of:

When this occurs the CS Framework has the following practical impact:

*Broaden what capacity to safeguard means*

Practice seeks to build a collective capacity to safeguard young people

Value 1

*Rethink how safeguarding is 'everyone's business'*

All those with a reach into extra-familial contexts have a role in creating safe spaces

Value 2

*Work with peer relationships*

Peer relationships are valued, and their significance in young people's lives recognised

Value 3

*Identify risks and strengths beyond individuals*

Vulnerabilities, risks and strengths are located within contexts, and addressed at that level

More to be identified ........

**CHILDREN'S RIGHTS**

STRENGTH BASED APPROACHES

Domain 1: A CS system targets the social conditions of abuse

Domain 2: A CS system is located within a child protection and safeguarding legislative framework

Domain 3: A CS system is delivered through partnerships beetween traditional and non-traditonal safeguarding organisations, parents and young people

Domain 4: A CS system measures needs and impact at a contextual as well as individual level

1

2

3

4

Contextual dynamics interplay with individual choice

Contexts cause and are produced by inequality

We must be hopeful: contexts can change

*Figure 12.1* Updated Contextual Safeguarding Framework

community groups; integrate exploitation teams or build adolescent safeguarding panels is matter for them. Once current testing is complete, further unifying practice features may emerge. In doing so it is likely that the chronological depiction of the framework in Figure 12.1 will graduate to a more integrated version presented in Figure 12.2. In this latter version the values that sat behind the first iterations of the framework, and the lens through which it is has been viewed retrospectively, all form a central value basis for the approach. The four domains of the framework and the practice features are what such a system produces (which were the previous requirements) are then developed around it.

By deepening the Contextual Safeguarding framework, its associations with broader theoretical frameworks have also become more explicit. While social fields (social rules) and individual agency (capital and habitus) remain at its heart, it is clear to see how the values and requirements of the framework align it to broader systemic approaches to social work, social justice, public health, and situational approaches to abuse prevention and violence reduction. In different ways it speaks to these debates and resolves some of the tensions associated with them (that were explored in chapter 4). Contextual Safeguarding avoids the labelling of populations by working with a recognised interplay between individual agency and contextual dynamics of harm and acknowledges the latter as production, and consequence of inequality. It also enables a practical route to engaging with the impact of systems, and grounds social work practice in key community, peer and family relationships that both

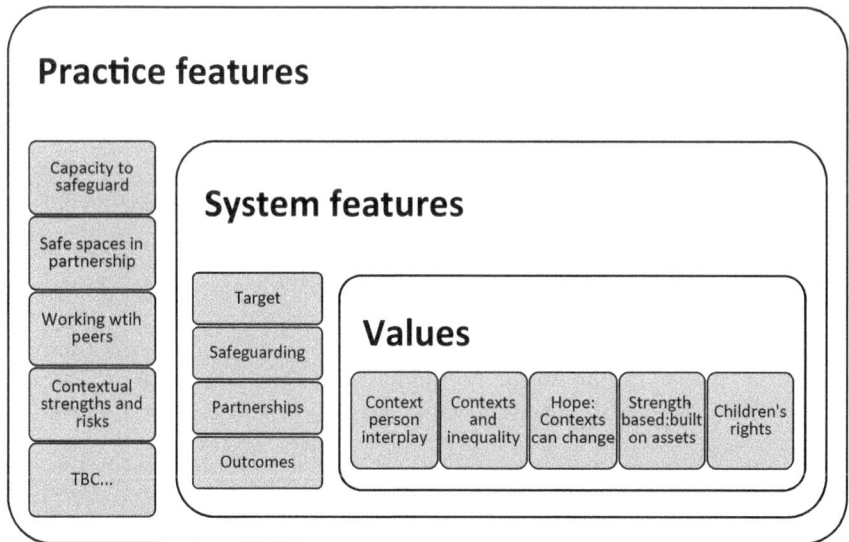

*Figure 12.2* Contextual Safeguarding Framework – An Ambition

inform young people's decision-making and shape the contexts in which they encounter harm.

At this stage the question of what a Contextual Safeguarding approach means in practice continues to be answered, and debated, by local partners. Out of these debates we may identify further practice features of the system, but at this stage the jury is out. And yet, the framework proposed in this chapter, and underpinned by the previous chapters in the book, ask much broader questions about what child protection means, the role of the state in safeguarding children from extra-familial harm, and the place of social work within this.

It is these larger questions that will shape the next and final part of this book.

# Part 4

# Looking back and planning forward

A pit stop on the path to Contextual Safeguarding

# 13 Reaching my threshold

The grounds for state, and social work, intervention

At this stage in testing Contextual Safeguarding I have come to understand the implications of pursuing this type of systems change as a relative outsider. I am not a trained social worker nor did I embark on a career in social work research. Starting out a philosophy student, and then engaged in the study of social policy, I was principally concerned with how governments, communities, and families responded to, and were affected by, violence between young people. It was the violence that I explored first – understanding the response to that violence came later.

As a somewhat outsider, I like many other lay people I know, made a number of assumptions about child protection systems, social work, and state intervention. I assumed that when a child was abused the state would intervene; I didn't for one second think that the threshold for such intervention would hinge on whether the person who abused that child was connected to their family or not. I also believed that children's services, and social workers more specifically, sat at the heart of that system in many countries around the world – and that they would therefore often be involved in protecting young people who had been abused. For me social workers played a key role in protecting children from abuse – all children – regardless of who abused them.

The idea that there was a threshold for such support – and that the threshold would be determined by anything other than the level of harm a child faced and/or the needs they had– never occurred to me. I was naïve to the many things: the pressures such systems faced; their relatively young stage of development; their legislative frameworks; and their intentions. Case reviews provided me with my first window into the realities of the system in England – shattering my assumptions and raising questions about the sufficiency of state protections for young people. It was those questions that provided the foundations for the Contextual Safeguarding framework; and one way in which they have continued to be explored is in relation to the matter of 'threshold'.

In testing that framework my team and I have gradually realised that unpicking, questioning, and shining a light on the meanings of 'threshold' and its use in decision-making is key to sustaining Contextual Safeguarding systems. Buried in that one word is a whole heap of assumptions, values, and anxiety. Seeking agreement on what types of harm, affecting which young people and in which location would warrant a state response – and more specifically a child protection response – has brought this heap of challenges to the fore.

As soon as we realised how central the idea of threshold would be to testing and embedding Contextual Safeguarding, we set about exploring the idea in three ways. The first was to dip-sample case records in test sites (method detailed in chapter 9) – exploring decision-making of social workers following initial assessments of young people referred into the system due to extra-familial harm. We examined the reasons provided for either progressing a young person for a social work plan (either voluntary or statutory) or closing them to children's social care and on some occasions referring them to an external or 'early help' agency (Lloyd & Firmin, 2020). This helped us understand, and on some occasions supported a site to change its approach to, direct work with children and families in regards to Level 1 Contextual Safeguarding. The second was to commence the design and testing of thresholds for contexts beyond families where a state intervention may be required to safeguard the well-being of young people (chapter 10). And the third was to raise questions about thresholds in training and masterclass sessions we were being asked to run for social work practitioners, researchers and students around England in 2019 – helping us to reflect on the ideas that were forming in test sites. This work has had a cumulative impact on how we now understand what a Contextual Safeguarding approach asks of a child protection system, and the questions such an approach raises for individuals, organisations, and states concerned with protecting young people from abuse and safeguarding their well-being.

Grappling with the challenge of threshold in test sites has surfaced questions about how England, the UK, and states around the world, should organise their response to extra-familial abuse. The idea of threshold, after all, has emerged as a tool for determining the grounds upon which states should intervene to address child abuse, and therefore sets the parameters for state intervention into the lives of children and their families. By questioning the definition of threshold, and its application, we have unintentionally started to question the rules of child protection systems and social work practice itself.

In this chapter I will present and explore these questions – drawing upon debates that have emerged in test sites, and framing them in relation to studies of international child protection systems. From exploring the inconsistent application of 'thresholds' for accessing support in children's services departments in England, through to trying to articulate a 'threshold' for state intervention into a context rather than a family, I will demonstrate the many levels at which Contextual Safeguarding hinges upon a shared, and expanded, understanding of 'thresholds' for child protection systems. Throughout this process I will reflect on what this could mean for future child protection and social work research and practice agendas – and how many others may need to confront and question assumptions they have made about child protection systems, abuse and state responsibility if Contextual Safeguarding is to be sustained.

## Parenting or abuse: what is child protection actually about?

When training professionals, or supporting senior leaders to design a plan for adopting a Contextual Safeguarding approach, I ask them about the likely pathways to support for four different children referred into children's social care (Table 13.1).

Initial responses to these scenarios, for the most part, acknowledge that the risk to life of both Child A and Child C is likely to be the same; and yet most practitioners also acknowledge that Child A would likely receive a more urgent social care response than Child C, and would definitely be allocated a social worker. This is about as far as agreement reaches.

In some areas practitioners believe that Child C would also be allocated a social worker – on a voluntary plan due to the protective behaviour of their parents, but in recognition of the level of harm they face. From 2018 to 2019, following the insertion of Contextual Safeguarding into England's statutory guidelines we are witnessing an increasing number of areas we visit who state that they take a similar approach. If the harm is significant, regardless of whether it was instigated by a parent or carer or someone connected to the family, a social worker will be allocated.

However, conversations with individual practitioners and senior leaders, as well as data from dip-sampling activities paint a more variable picture; one that is informed by matters such as service capacity, parental engagement, and

*Table 13.1* Four 'threshold' scenarios for familial and extra-familial contexts

| Child | Level of harm/risk in community | Parenting and safety at home |
|---|---|---|
| A | **Experiencing significant harm** <br> Was targeted and stabbed in their local park | **Significant concerns** <br> Believed to be domestic abuse in the family home and minimal boundary setting |
| B | **In need of support** <br> Has been found carrying a knife in a local park and say they do so for protection | **Significant concerns** <br> Believed to be domestic abuse in the family home and minimal boundary setting |
| C | **Experiencing significant harm** <br> Was targeted and stabbed in their local park | **No concerns** <br> Parents shocked and concerned about what has happened and taking all steps that they can to keep their child safe |
| D | **In need of support** <br> Has been found carrying a knife in a local park and say they do so for protection | **No concerns** <br> Parents shocked and concerned about what has happened and taking all steps that they can to keep their child safe |

professional discretion. Dip-sampling of 159 extra-familial cases in our test sites in 2019 evidenced (chapter 8) illustrated varying responses to young people who were at risk of abuse in their communities or schools, but safe at home. As the three exerts below illustrate, some practitioners were placing children on statutory social work plans due to the risks they faced, even when parents were protective; others referenced protective parenting as a reason to close cases. And then some, trying to find a middle road, were working with families on voluntary social work plans to acknowledge both the child's vulnerability and the family's efforts to protect them.

> D is believed to be at continuing risk of significant physical harm due to his behaviour and association with possible gang related activity within the community. As the risks posed to 1 are outside the family home it is crucial that when analysing the risk a contextual safeguarding approach is taken to do this … it is evident that D has been provided with a stable upbringing by parents who love and care for him. There is no evidence that there are any significant issues at home for D which would indicate there is another pull factor for D's behaviour which may be linked to criminal exploitation.… As D has stated that there will be further retaliation in relation to the most recent incident it is my professional opinion that D is at continuing risk of significant harm and therefore an Initial Child Protection conference should be held.
>
> (Dip-sampling exert, Test Site C, child defined as reaching a threshold for statutory social work oversight)

> Step down (from statutory oversight) to assess H's risk in the community, safety plan with parents and school around the risks for H with regards to unsafe places, possible drug use and lack of school attendance (due to risks of gang-association).
>
> (Dip-sampling exert, Test Site F, child defined as not reaching a threshold for statutory social work oversight, referred to early help)

> As part of on-going safety planning with A and her mother Push and Pull factors need to be identified and ensure that A has safe places and spaces which she can go to, to prevent further criminal activity or peer pressure to engage in risky behaviours.
>
> (Dip-sampling exert, Test Site B, child defined as not reaching a threshold for social work oversight via a voluntary plan, for concerns related to sexual exploitation and anti-social behaviour)

> Both parents have shown appropriate concern in relation to L's stabbing; offending and escalating behaviour … It appears with L's stabbing and his involvement in criminal activity makes him at continued risk of his own health and safety. It is evident that whilst [mother] must take

responsibility for her son in areas where she can (i.e. calling the police), she also requires support in implementing appropriate boundaries to deter L alleged gang involvement and to minimise risk as much as is possible to reduce instability within the family. It is also apparent that intervention is required to ensure that L is not attracted to gang culture and become involved in criminal activity in the next few years as he gets older. Both parents, L and his older siblings were asked if they required further support and intervention from children's services and it was agreed that he should be referred to [youth service] will be helpful in building the parent's confidence and strategies in managing and understanding L' risky behaviour. It was agreed that there is not further role for Children Social Care.

(Dip-sampling exert, Test Site A, child defined as not reaching a threshold for statutory social work oversight)

### What sits behind this variation?

During some visits with network or test site practitioners, concerns have been raised about the capacity of social workers to hold cases of extra-familial harm; cases that they may have previously closed when families were found to be protective. Social work managers have raised concerns about 'opening the floodgates' if children who are severely injured in community settings, or sexually abused by peers, are all allocated social workers via children's social care; they don't have the capacity to take this on. What's more, even if they did, some believe that social workers wouldn't have much to offer by way of interventions as their plans would focus on parenting; and in such cases there are no concerns in that regard. Hence the phrase 'there is no clear role for social care at this time' features in the records of many a closure decision we have reviewed.

Such a justification is telling. It suggests that the role of social workers, and the child protection systems in which they work, is to address parenting concerns (and risks posed by parents) as opposed to addressing abuse (in all its forms). Such a conclusion has become even more apparent in relation to the pathway for Children B and D in Table 13.1. In discussions with professionals, there is a routine acknowledgement that Child B may receive a more expedited response than Child C from children's social care even though when there is a more apparent risk to life to Child C than Child B. Further to this, it is more likely that Child B will be placed on a statutory child protection plan, whereas Child C will be supported via a voluntary 'child in need' plan due to the actions of their parents. In essence decision-making is driven by a concern about parenting rather than levels of (extra-familial) abuse being experienced by the child of those parents.

However, when the different pathways, of Child B and Child C, are explained to me, practitioners also reference engagement as key rationale point. Child C's parents are doing all they can to keep their child safe and a statutory child protection plan could isolate them from services. Such plans are described as focusing solely on parenting, and in this case there are no concerns in that arena, and as such parents may feel blamed for issues that are beyond their control. A child in need plan is viewed as a route to acknowledge the protective capacity of parents and work with them as partners in safeguarding their child. An approach much aligned to a more family support orientation of child protection system (Gilbert, et al., 2011). Some also make note of the greater flexibility that comes with the time frames for a child in need plan, which gives social workers the space to get to know a young person and family without a need to complete a statutory enquiry with a specific amount of days and so on.

There are many merits to taking this position: a desire to not overly interfere in the life of a protective family, to recognise the strengths that the parents bring, and to create the conditions for building a relationship with the young person. In reflecting on this pathway, I am not questioning these merits or suggesting this course of action to be inappropriate. It is important to note, however, that the factors which lead to divergent decisions are the level of concerns about parenting first – and secondly what will leverage best engagement – not the level of risk the child faces. I continue to question to what extent this rationale is understood by partner agencies which refer concerns for young people into children's social care and don't understand why they feel these cases haven't 'reached a threshold' for a statutory social work intervention despite evident danger (ITV News, 2018).

In terms of partnerships and engagement a further nuance has emerged in discussion with practitioners about the use of statutory versus voluntary social work plans. For some social workers, placing a young person on a child protection plan is a means of ensuring partnership buy-in and cooperation with interventions and support, which they believe may not always be offered for young people in voluntary plans. As a result, in some cases even when parents are protective, if they and social workers are sufficiently concerned about a child's safety a child protection plan may be used to ensure partnership cooperation in delivering interventions. Engagement again, but this time informed by a concern about the level of harm, drives the decision-making process in these cases. It must be noted that dip-sampling rarely surfaced this scenario, but it has not been an uncommon reflection during practice observations, workshops, and training sessions.

And so what of Child D? For the most part both dip-sampling and other informal means of discussion/reflection suggested that they and their family would be closed to children's social care. In some instances they may be referred to a voluntary organisation to take part in positive activities or education sessions about the consequences of weapon carrying. Not because they faced fewer risks in his community than Child B (who would likely be on a statutory social work plan, or at least on a voluntary social work plan), but because they were less concerns about how safe they were at home. While the support offered to Child D may or may not be beneficial at increasing their sense of safety, such support is offered without the oversight of social workers, and therefore the state lead for child protection services. They had not reached a threshold for the state to play a role in keeping them safe – or having oversight over a plan intended to make them safer than they had been previously.

And so we are faced with a question – what are child protection systems for? I had always thought they were how state's organised their responses to child abuse. But our ongoing examination of 'thresholds' for accessing state support from the child protection system suggests that where the abuse is located – and the role of parenting in that regard – inform whether the state is viewed as having a legitimate role to play in increasing safety. Is child protection therefore about parenting first, abuse second? In some respects the inclusion of Contextual Safeguarding in statutory guidance in England and the direction of travel in test sites to place some of these young people on voluntary social work plans suggests the answer to this may be in transition. But the fact that there is a transition at all, suggests that at some point previously, the answer to that question had been yes – and that for some young people and families it still will be. But why does understanding and debating this matter for developing a Contextual Safeguarding approach – or for the welfare of young people more broadly?

## A quadrant deprioritisation

A Contextual Safeguarding approach is primarily concerned with offering a child-welfare, and when required statutory child protection, response to children abused in extra-familial contexts and relationships. The variable responses to Children A, B, C, and D outlined above illustrates how existing systems and frameworks can deprioritise children who are unsafe in extra-familial, as opposed to familial, settings; and as such might be structurally incompatible with the pursuit of Contextual Safeguarding approaches. Resolving this therefore is central to the Contextual Safeguarding project – without a resolution it is difficult to envisage how the objective of a child welfare response to extra-familial abuse can be realised. Testing of the approach has identified a quadrant of additional factors that inform decision-making related to the idea of 'threshold' at different points of a child's journey through England's child protection system. These are nestled within and interact with the broader legislative and policy framework, outlined above, that links state intervention with parenting as well as abuse.

Firstly, the system struggles to apply a threshold focused on the level of risk/harm for a child who will turn 18 in four months' time, for example, as opposed to those who are younger. He rarely comes home despite the best efforts of his parents to get him there. The professional network scratch their heads. Of what value, they ask, would a statutory or voluntary social work plan be for him? By the time the assessment is completed and the plan formulated he may be days away from being too old to fit the parameters of the child protection system currently reviewing his case. What's more, he continues to vote with his feet, refuses to engage with services, no one has even managed to see him. He doesn't turn up to college either so a trip to try and visit him there has been futile. Everyone in the professional network is concerned. Everyone believes that he is being criminally exploited: trafficked around the country to distribute drugs. He has already been subjected to a brutal, and sustained, physical attack that resulted in a stay in hospital. He is at risk of significant harm. He is being threatened. He lives in fear. But he is nearing an age where he is no longer legally considered a child, and therefore the system available to protect children has no statutory grounds to intervene. Social workers close his case. Not because they believe him to be safe. And not because his parents are protective. But because he is too old for them to reach him.

Then there is the system's struggle to support a child who is like Child C and Child D. She is safe at home. The sexual assault and ongoing harassment that she experiences at school are not attributable to how she is being parented. And furthermore, she has never been sexually abused at home or within her family network. The social workers confirmed that she was safe and protected at home when they visited her there. They spoke with her alone, they spoke to her parents, and her two younger siblings. They assessed their interaction as a family, could see that everyone's basic needs were being met. She was a child who had been sexually abused by peers, and remained at risk of sexual abuse – but only within that peer network and educational environment where they spent time. The peer network was not assessed, and neither was the capacity of the school to keep her safe. Only the capacity of her parents was under scrutiny – and within the confines of what they could do legally (i.e. not keep her at home and away from school which would have been illegal) they were doing all they could do to keep her safe. Social workers close her case. Not because they believe her to be safe. And not because her parents are protective. But because the place where she is being abused is beyond their reach.

Thirdly there is the child who is 15 years old and is abused by someone who is 14 years old. He initially disclosed to his parents that a boy in the year below him at school had groped him on the bus and threatened to tell 'everyone' that they had been having sex if he didn't do what he said in the future. After months of emotional outbursts and many refusals to travel to school he told his parents what had happened. But when they reported their concerns to the school, and then on to the police, their son retracted his statement. He was afraid of the reprisals he might face. Without his statement there was little in the way of evidence to proceed with a criminal investigation and so the police closed his case. Once the police did this, the social workers who had been reviewing the case were at a loss. How could they engage the 14-year old in an assessment, and work, around a sexual offence that had not been proven? They had no other concerns about either family in the case. If this 15 year old had made an allegation about an adult, they may have taken some steps to prevent ongoing contact between the adult and the child, using a Child Abduction Warning Notice[1] (CAWN) for example. But with the allegation being against a 14-year old the professional network struggle to identify what they can do to de-escalate risks. Social workers close his case. Not because they believe him to be safe. And not because his parents are protective. But because they can't see a way to offer a welfare-based assessment/intervention for a peer-on-peer case of abuse that doesn't feature a criminal charge.

And finally there is the system response to seven children who have all been approached by an unknown adult outside a fast food restaurant. Or the nine who have had mobile phones stolen in the same park. Or the group of six friends who were all contacted by an adult who was attempting to groom them via a gaming network. Each was referred separately into children's services. Some were closed when the referral was being screened as this experience, alone, didn't signify a risk of significant harm. Some children were completely unknown so the referral couldn't be accepted: business owners, members of the public, etc., had witnessed interactions that caused them concern but without a named child no action could be taken to progress the referral being made. Some were accepted – the harm was a concern, and the child was named – but an initial assessment of them and their family suggested that all was well at home. Individually, none of these children reached a threshold for the state's child protection system to intervene – either voluntarily or on a statutory footing. The risk they shared as a group, or the cumulative impact of multiple incidents of harm in the same place, was lost in the process of referral and initial assessment. In reality the fast food restaurant was being used as an access point to approach and coerce young people in to drug-dealing lines. The park was becoming a locality in which violence was expected, and there was a belief that adults couldn't keep young people safe when they spent time there. And the gaming platform was being used by adults to groom, sexual abuse, and extort money from young people – who as a group began to normalise the experience and keep it to themselves as their parents became concerned. But the locations or groups were not something the system could respond to. At best, social workers and the wider professional network could advise young people to stop going to the fast food restaurant, park or gaming platform; and they could ask their parents to communicate the same message. Social workers close all these referrals. Not because they believe these children to be safe. And not because their parents are protective. But because the system they work in can't engage with the contexts and group dynamics that compromise their safety.

In these four ways we have seen child protection systems deprioritise referrals for children at risk of extra-familial harm. Suggestions that some of these cases might warrant a child welfare or child protection response have sometimes been met with fears that:

> *Every child in XXX will be open to us if we include drug dealing in the neighbourhood as a reason for support.*

It would be remiss of me not to acknowledge that putting a response in place for some of these children may increase demand on an already overstretched system. However, the answer to safeguarding many of these children may not sit in each of them individually 'meeting a threshold' for direct, 1:1 social work intervention. It may be that the situation they face collectively or the context in which they spend their time does. Introducing debates, therefore, about when a situation, place or group might require state assessment, support and/or intervention has been the final way in which we have grappled with 'thresholds' on the road to implementing Contextual Safeguarding.

## The grounds for intervening with places and not people

A Contextual Safeguarding framework requires that systems can target the contexts in which abuse occurs (chapter 6). Not every bus stop where child has a phone stolen however, nor every park where they are sexually harassed, could fall within scope of a welfare assessment and intervention. Firstly, this would overwhelm services and be impossible to resource. But secondly, and more importantly, it would be 'overkill'. There are professionals, community members, young people and parents amongst others who manage public and school environments, and who resolve group tensions, in the absence of state intervention. In the same way that child protection frameworks of many countries caution against unnecessary state intervention in family life (Gilbert, et al., 2011; Merkel-Holguin, et al., 2019) – one would also do the same in extra-familial contexts. Threshold documents are one resource used by multi-agency partnerships to agree the grounds for state intervention in family life, and the nature of the support/intervention required, to meet the needs of individuals. As such, during testing we sought to develop a similar resource to guide decision-making for contexts.

One way to explore whether state intervention in a context is required is to examine the nature of the harm occurring within it. Informed by Hackett's 2011 continuum used to characterise harmful sexual behaviours, we identified two intersecting mechanisms for characterising harm: its frequency and its severity. So one instance of mobile phone theft at a transport hub (relatively low severity) may not warrant a safeguarding assessment and intervention, but a young person being targeted and stabbed might (relatively high severity). However, multiple mobile phone thefts in a locality (high frequency) might suggest that those who are there are struggling to keep it safe for young people and that young people may begin to feel unsafe there or believe that adults don't have the capacity to keep them safe. The cumulative harm resulting from multiple incidents may suggest a safeguarding assessment and intervention is required.

Harm alone however, isn't sufficient to characterise a place. One has to balance this harm against the protective capacity of a context/group. Testing of Contextual Safeguarding systems has identified two levers for creating protection in extra-familial contexts. The first is the role played by adults in that context. So even if a child has been stabbed in a transport hub, are the adults who run and use that transport hub confident in responding and organising themselves to increase a sense of safety for young people in the aftermath – or do they need to support to enhance their protective capacity? Second is the protection afforded by the structures, partnerships and policies in place to support adults and young people in contexts to increase and/or sustain attempts at protection. For example, in a school or youth club setting are there clear processes for managing disclosures that young people make? Does the school or youth club have effective partnerships in place with other agencies (including local businesses for example) which could support them in building community guardianship in the environment that surrounds their buildings for example.

Initial screening decisions of contextual concerns into a child protection system will be principally driven by the identified level of harm (severity and frequency), but the need for ongoing state intervention will more likely be informed by the behaviour of adults and the structures in, or around, the context/group in question. State intervention rests on whether a safeguarding partnership has a role to play in addressing the behaviour of adults or improving structural factors that could increase safety in the context. If adults and young people in localities are already willing, able and resourced to take such action, statutory coordination should be unlikely.

This conceptual approach to understanding thresholds for contexts was first translated into a document by the London Borough of Hackney. The Context Threshold Guide detailed how behaviours that, if they occurred in an extra-familial context, might require a statutory intervention to increase safety; whereas the role of adults and/or structures in that place may mitigate these initial concerns and to such a standard that a need for support may be offered on a voluntarily basis. Professional discretion, and dialogue with the communities involved in any given case, would help to resolve the most appropriate course of action. In many cases it is likely that further support might be offered to increase the protective capacity of adults in the space on a voluntary basis – enabling, rather than intervening with, a community. At this stage of writing however this document is yet to be used in 2019–2022 test sites. Future testing in multiple locations will provide further indication of whether the aspirations of the use of 'thresholds' in a Contextual Safeguarding system, can be realised in practice.

## Legal, aligned but insufficient – where do we go from here?

Understanding the threshold for state intervention in cases of child abuse sits at the heart of many child protection systems around the world. Much of this is informed by a desire to reduce state intervention in family life and therefore only to intervene where there is an evidenced need for support. In many countries including the United States, Canada and Australia, the definition of harm/abuse that would warrant state intervention specifically names 'parents' or 'caregivers' as being those who cause the harm (see chapters 3, 14, and 16). Without parental involvement it isn't clear that child protection systems have any remit to intervene. In some respects England's child protection system has developed along the same lines. The definition of abuse doesn't name parents; however, the points of escalation through a child protection system do (chapter 3). As such we find we have systems that are built on a definition of abuse that implicitly or explicitly relate to parenting. Examination of decision-making in England suggests that this can result in systems which intervene on the grounds of parenting, and not on the grounds of abuse. This is not solely a matter of semantics – these are children's lives. The system presumes parenting relates to abuse. When this isn't the case the parent, rather than abuse, factor can drive responses – denying children, and their parents, state protection from significant harm.

Adopting a Contextual Safeguarding framework further forces this issue. It provides a lens through which we can see the state stepping back from families affected by extra-familial harm because: the child is nearing the legal end of childhood; the child is not at risk in the family home; the child has been abused by someone younger than them; or the contextual dynamics of the harm children face (particularly its cumulative or shared nature) is overlooked. Examining decision-making in cases of extra-familial harm, therefore, illuminates a two-tiered nest of threshold application that has little to do with abuse and much to do parenting and family contexts (Figure 13.1).

In this light, our work to date suggests that child protection systems require thresholds for state intervention that go beyond the nature of parenting and the home environment. Such an approach also needs to cease a conflation of the definitions for abuse and parenting. Such conflation has resulted in state responses to extra-familial abuse that are legally compliant and yet insufficient for safeguarding the welfare of young people.

A Contextual Safeguarding approach however is not one that can do away with thresholds – or some equivalent idea to identify need and limit unnecessary intervention into families and communities - altogether. While they are relevant from the perspective of system capacity, they can also guide a proportionate use of state intervention into the lives of communities, schools, friendship groups, as well as families. The ongoing debate about the grounds for public institutions to disrupt the private lives of families (Merkel-Holguin, et al., 2019; Parton, 2014) will also feature in a Contextual Safeguarding system. The rights of individuals to have friends, to organise in communities and so on require protection (Lefevre, et al., 2018; Williams, 2018; Wroe, 2019). If anything, I would hope that a Contextual Safeguarding approach would protect those rights – by providing framework in which the state can support the creation/protection of safer extra-familial spaces. Contextual thresholds therefore acknowledge the protective role of adults in school and community contexts – as well as around peer groups – and guide that these be supported rather than enforced upon.

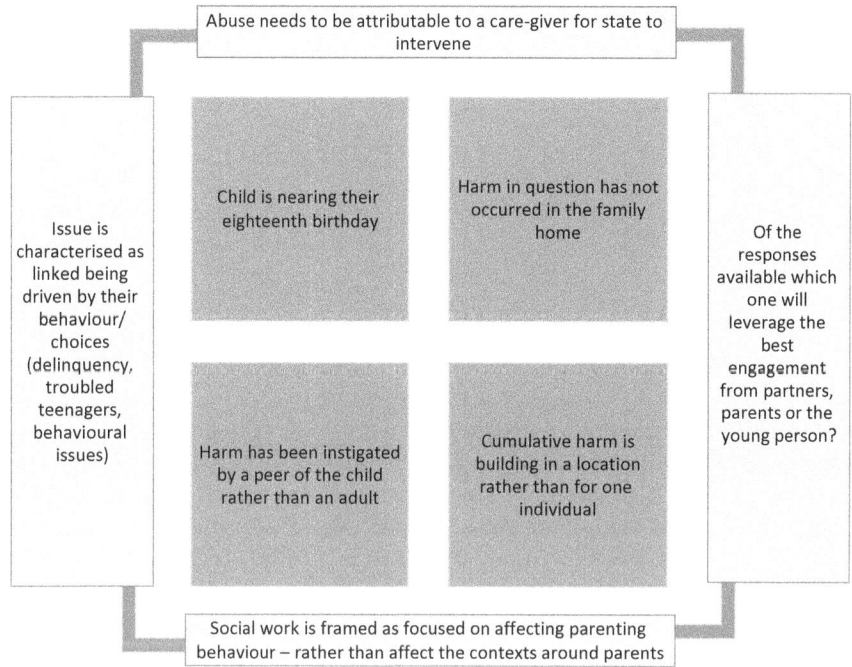

*Figure 13.1* Nested Rationale for Thresholds Applied to Extra-Familial Abuse in England

The proof, as they say, will be in the pudding, and ongoing testing will illustrate whether contextual thresholds are used to safeguard and support, or police and survey, communities.

Unpicking and redesigning thresholds for state intervention, however, is not an isolated action. How thresholds are understood and applied speak to, and are informed by, how child protection systems more broadly are perceived and utilised. By questioning thresholds for state intervention with extra-familial abuse we are also questioning the rules that underpin child protection systems, and the responsibility of those professionals who work within that system. One such profession is that of social work – a matter to which I dedicate the next chapter.

## Note

1 According to the College of Policing is a Child Abduction Warning notice is sent 'to inform a person who has associated with children or a child that, should they continue to do so, they may commit an offence. A CAWN may be issued where: no criminal offences are committed; the person is associating with children for whom they hold no parental responsibility; it is a necessary and proportionate response to safeguard children or a child

# 14 Formulating the 'social work' offer in a Contextual Safeguarding system

Debates in the previous chapter question the parameters of child protection systems and whether Contextual Safeguarding sits within or beyond them. At the heart of this debate are social workers whose practice is informed by those parameters. If Contextual Safeguarding broadens the intentions of the child protection system, does it also extend the responsibilities of social workers? If Contextual Safeguarding is viewed as encroaching on a crime and community safety agenda, then does it require social workers to be become police officers and anti-social behaviour wardens? For me, Contextual Safeguarding reframes what social workers already do, and in some respects realigns social work with its value base and social justice ethos: rather than extending the social work remit or job description. In some respects the evidence presented in this book takes social work back to a community and social justice base (Bailey & Brake, 1975; Featherstone, et al., 2018; Fenton, 2016; Ferguson & Woodward, 2009; Rogowoski, 2012; Wood & Tully, 2006), albeit with more contemporary forms of abuse in mind, rather than towards a new frontier.

In this chapter I will explain how I have reached this conclusion, and the elements of it that requires further consideration as Contextual Safeguarding is scaled and diffused across and beyond England, Wales and Scotland. Reflecting on social work theory more broadly, and traditions of social work historically, I will identify an alignment between social work principles and the Contextual Safeguarding framework. Drawing on evidence from test sites and network members, I will illustrate how social workers have been critical in both the design and testing of Contextual Safeguarding. It is through these contributions that I, and others in the team, have been able to articulate social workers' roles in the delivery of a Contextual Safeguarding approach: roles that include advocacy on behalf of children and families, brokering relationships to safeguard children and families, and coordinating plans that prevent future harm and/or increase protection. Despite these points of clarity there have been, and remain, challenges to the positon that social workers have the skills or influence to effect change in extra-familial contexts. In grappling with these arguments I re-engage with those developed in the previous chapter, shining a light on the child protection system in which the profession operates and the extent to which its structures limit the potential of social workers to safeguard young people. To develop this point further I will reflect on two techniques that have been used to structure/organise social work practice and demonstrate how these could be used to instigate change in extra-familial, as well as familial, contexts. In doing so I outline ways for social workers to play a central role in the ongoing development of Contextual Safeguarding while also pointing out what more we need to understand and sustain that role as we move from testing to 'business as usual' delivery within safeguarding systems.

## The social justice of social work

In 2014 the International Federation of Social Work (IFSW) defined social work as:

> … a practice-based profession and an academic discipline that promotes social change and development, social cohesion, and the empowerment and liberation of people. Principles of social justice, human rights, collective responsibility and respect for diversities are central to social work. Underpinned by theories of social work, social sciences, humanities and indigenous knowledge, social work engages people and structures to address life challenges and enhance wellbeing. The above definition may be amplified at national and/or regional levels.
>
> (IFSW, 2014)

In referencing this position the British Association of Social Worker's (BASW) Code of Ethics, published in the same year reflected that:

> Social work in its various forms addresses the multiple, complex transactions between people and their environments. Its mission is to enable all people to develop their full potential, enrich their lives, and prevent dysfunction. Professional social work is focused on problem solving and change. As such, social workers are change agents in society and in the lives of the individuals, families and communities they serve. Social work is an interrelated system of values, theory and practice.
>
> (BASW, 2014)

In many respects the Contextual Safeguarding framework aligns to both definitions. The IFSW position in particular notes the values of human rights, social justice, and collective responsibility that have informed the design of, as well as generate practice requirements for, Contextual Safeguarding systems. Furthermore, practice, in both definitions, seeks to bring about social change, solve problems and engage people in that process as agents of change. The IFSW reference 'structure' and BASW reference 'environments' as interacting with the lives and livelihoods of people/communities.

But much is also left to interpretation and herein lies the rub. When such values either encounter individualised systems or even a broader spectrum

of approaches to child protection that locate abuse solely within family rela-
tionships/settings a lack of attention to context can emerge. Fenton (2016),
Woodward and Mackay (2012) and Ferguson (2013) amongst others have
noted the tension of seeking to engage social workers with the structural
dynamics of harm, within social work systems that lean towards fixing
people rather than situations (Bailey & Brake, 1975)

By framing the social work mission as one that 'enables people', the BASW
definition provides room for a practice framework focused on supporting
people to do better. As Fenton (2016) noted, when this is interpreted as
empowerment, rather than advocacy, enablement can slip into responsibilise
and individualise. It is not limited to this however. One could enable people by
increasing their contextual safety as has been documented in previous chapters
of the book. Advocating for such safety, brokering relationships, and coordinating plans to achieve this could all also be defined as social work activities.
But the conclusion one draws is largely informed by other theories about the
role of the state, personal responsibility, and the potential to change environments – none of which can be taken for granted.

The scope for variation is seen in the divergent methods of social work
practice that have developed in England, other European and Nordic countries,
Australia, the United States, and Canada in the 20th and 21st centuries. As
noted in earlier chapters of this book, all such systems have squarely focused on
protecting children from abuse associated to parents or care-givers. Despite this
consistency, the approach each country has taken to designing and developing
their system has varied. In 2011 Gilbert and colleagues identified three[1] 'orientations' for how states organise their responses to child abuse: family support,
child protection, and child focus. They noted across all three orientations the
increased use of risk assessment tools and systemic approaches which acknowledged the complex and contemporary issues with which child and family
services were grappling. Generally speaking, 'family support' approaches utilised
these via building support for families, identifying and meeting the needs of parents and carers, so they in turn could meet the needs of their children. 'Child
protection' approaches focused on assessing/investigating risks, as opposed to
needs, and holding parents to account for behaviour change as a route to
preventing abuse. The emergent 'child focus' orientation sees the child independently of the family and is concerned with enhancing child well-being more generally, such as the creation of 'child friendly' cities. Gilbert, et al. (2011) note that
broader cultural factors within countries may bring one of these orientations to
the fore, but that in many countries more than one can be identified. They also
note that countries which more generally have embraced a desire to enhance
individual responsibility (Gilbert, et al., 2011) may also interpret any of these
three orientations in a particular way.

Interacting with these wider narratives about the intention, scope and
design of child protection systems is decades of debate about social justice
in social work. From examples of community and patch-based social work,
to the development of both 'systemic' and 'structural approaches' to social

work practice, there have been multiple attempts, over five decades, to locate social work at the meeting point of contexts and individuals (Featherstone, et al., 2018; Fenton, 2016; Ferguson & Woodward, 2009; Wood & Tully, 2006). Such traditions have grappled with the introduction of case management approaches to social work (Bailey & Brake, 1975), the language of 'risk' (Parton, 2014), and agendas that have individualised success and safety (Featherstone, et al., 2018). Rather than it being seen as an either/or, many scholars and practitioners have sought to resolve these tensions by developing contextual approaches within case management structures; Bailey and Brake argued, for example, that they were not against case work, per se, just case work that reinforced, rather than challenged, inequalities (1975). Some have suggested this change from within be achieved via micro-assertions of context within otherwise individualised systems – such as considering the language social workers use to describe the harm they see (Rogowoski, 2012). Others have queried whether statutory social work can ever really have the space to be critical (Gray & Webb, 2013), and in this regard whether attempts at systemic practice within case management systems will ever be able to change the material conditions of people's lives (Ferguson & Woodward, 2009 ).

Locating Contextual Safeguarding within this broader development of child protection systems is important for understanding the drivers for those who either engage with, or push against, the approach. Contextual Safeguarding will sit more or less comfortably within family support, child protection, or child focused approaches for different reasons and likewise will realise the ambitions of radical or community social work for some and not for others. Some will suggest that what is proposed in this book is beyond social work, some beyond a child protection remit, some both. The extent to which this is social work business, is the focus of this chapter, what this means for child protection systems more broadly will be discussed thereafter.

## The centrality of social work in Contextual Safeguarding testing

In many respects Contextual Safeguarding can be viewed as completely aligned to social work traditions, principles, and practices – particularly those held within traditions of social justice in social work. And in as many other ways it can viewed as misaligned and out of scope, particularly in regards to systems that are built on definitions of abuse that solely relate to families. It is unsurprising, therefore, that we have encountered both viewpoints when involving social workers in the development of the Contextual Safeguarding Framework. On one day we can be told – 'this isn't what I was trained to do; how would I do this and all of my core work; I wouldn't know what to look for or who to speak to'. On another day we might be reminded that – 'we use to work like this all the time; this was patch social work; this is community social work by another name', and so on.

In testing Contextual Safeguarding we have had to balance both of these truths. Capturing how social workers (in test sites and via our network) have identified, assessed, and sought to change contexts has provided one route to illustrating this balancing act. We have used the evidence to build case studies which articulate the various roles that social workers play in designing and testing contextual approaches. Social workers have been our companions on this journey which has built on existing expertise as well as problem-solved or repackaged-practice to address apparent barriers in expertise or reach. The detail of much of this work was documented in Part 3 of this book. Thematic analysis of this detail points to three overarching activities that appear integral to a Contextual Safeguarding system and are ones that social workers are well positioned to deliver.

### Advocacy

> Whilst it would appear that to accommodate M3 and put him in care could keep him safe, evidence shows that this is unlikely that this would have the desired approach and could actually place M2 at more risk because at present he does return home each night according to mum. If M2 were to abscond from care, the risk from others to M2 would increase.(Assessment exert from test site)

Taken from an assessment of a child and family impacted by criminal exploitation in his local neighbourhood, this quote illustrates the importance of advocacy when adopting a Contextual Safeguarding approach. For this social worker, a recognition of peer influence on this young person's decision-making, and the protective nature of his family, resulted in the recommendation against taking the young person into care. To do so would have undermined what his parent has been able to do – he came home each night – and should one of the young people have been moved away they would have both been likely to go missing together. The conclusion they formulated therefore advocated for change beyond the family on behalf of this child's parents as well as him. They were petrified that one day their son wouldn't make it back home. They didn't have the economic capital to move away from the area where their son was vulnerable to abuse. They also didn't have family or friendship networks beyond the local area, and so moving away would have compromised the social capital that they could currently draw upon. They knew they needed the help of other agencies to de-escalate the situation they were in. They didn't have the cultural capital to (a) understand the rules of streets in which their child had been assaulted or (b) engage with the professional networks that needed to be leveraged to keep him safe. It fell then to the social worker, who did have the social and cultural capital to mobilise a response, to do so.

If this case had been closed to children's services because this child's parents were protective and concerned for him who would have fought their corner? Of course advocacy and community groups may have been able to step in. But ultimately, the ability to advocate for interventions to continue to target the groups who threatened their welfare in the community required statutory oversight. All of the advocacy skills a social worker might have used to access housing for mother and her children following domestic abuse, or to push for an educational needs assessment of a child who was struggling in school, were equally applicable in this case.

The severity of concern was also important. This social worker and their colleagues were not advocating that children's services be involved in every case of young people being influenced by peers or not listening to their parents – they did so on this occasion as such behaviours were associated to a risk of significant harm. This position is a contentious one, some sites may be concerned that to respond in this way on each occasion possible would overwhelm social care systems. For the purposes of this chapter however, this example illustrates the need for advocacy on behalf of children impacted by extra-familial, as well as familial, harm. Further to this, the social worker in this case was working alongside parents, illustrating their capacity to be protective and identifying what others could do to bolster this. As such, in addition to advocacy this type of work required social workers to broker relationships between children, families and wider services – as well as between services – to affect contextual change.

### Brokering

To broker is to arrange or negotiate (an agreement) (OED, 2019). The success of a Contextual Safeguarding system is dependent upon whether the partnership involved can agree an approach to creating safety in any given context. This partnership is broad – given the contexts in question. When assessing the situation of a young man whose home had been shot at, for example, a number of new relationships needed to be formed and the steps they would take collectively needed to be agreed. Following an assessment of him and his family, an assessment of the housing estate he lived on was initiated – a process documented in chapter 10. During this assessment the presence of social workers (alongside youth workers) brokered relationships on the grounds of child welfare, as opposed to community safety or crime reduction. Waste management services, Public Realm (who oversee traffic control amongst other things), residents, councillors, parents, and young people were all engaged in that assessment, but few had relationships with each other. To achieve change in that location, relationships needed to be built; what those relationships produced needed to be agreed.

In cases such as these, we saw brokering in two ways.

Gathering information to build an assessment required social workers to negotiate the involvement of individuals/organisations who didn't view safeguarding as their primary duty. They engaged residents in discussions about the welfare of children who weren't related to, or known by, them. They spent time with local business owners who were impacted by violence in the community but felt largely unable to effectively address it. They explained to council departments responsible for rubbish collection and facilities management that the information they hold, and tasks they undertake, could be relevant to the welfare of young people. All of these conversations were a matter of negotiation as social workers sought agreement on shared grounds. All partners had to share the goal to increase child safety. They all had to agree that they had a role to play in realising this. They also had to believe they could fulfil that role. During the information-gathering process social workers were pivotal in laying the groundwork for later agreeing and delivering a plan of action.

Planning was the other area in which we witnessed brokerage in action. When first testing Contextual Safeguarding in Hackney, social workers who chaired child protection conferences about children and families also chaired meetings held following context assessments of schools and locations. The meetings they chaired were convened to agree a plan for addressing the concerns, and maximising the potential, identified during the assessment. As was the case during assessment, social workers kept all participants focused on a common goal. Given the child protection framework through which meetings were convened this goal was the prevention of abuse and promotion of child safety. Participants in these meetings commented to researchers that the culture and ethos of such meetings differed from those they had attended about community safety or crime reduction. A shopkeeper, for example, stated that he had attended community safety meetings before and wouldn't do so again, but that this meeting felt driven by a commitment to the welfare of young people and that was 'something he could sign up to'. The tone, as well as the act of brokerage, emerged therefore as a benefit that came from social work involvement in the Contextual Safeguarding approach. In many respects, examples such as this crystallised the intention of Domain 2 of the original Contextual Safeguarding framework. As Contextual Safeguarding is tested in other areas the chairing arrangements for these meetings are shifting – and in some areas community safety colleagues are chairing meetings following neighbourhood assessments. It remains to be seen whether this impacts upon the tone of the brokering role – and therefore the engagement of partners (and whether this cost is worth the potential challenges that the Hackney approach encountered which are detailed later in this chapter). However, those developing alternative chairing arrangements have put measures in place, including training from safeguarding leads and having a social worker present at those meetings, to build welfare-based cultures into their tone and structure.

Having advocated on behalf of children and families, and brokered relationships and plans to increase their safety, social workers testing Contextual Safeguarding have also endeavoured to coordinate partners and activities to effect contextual change.

### *Coordination*

Contextual Safeguarding is not the only approach in which you see attempts to intervene with contexts. In any local area a range of organisations and sectors, from youth services to schools through to policing, town planning and community safety will play a role in shaping peer groups/associations, educational environments, and public spaces. While this presents great opportunities for leveraging action and change, it also creates the potential for duplication of effort or crossed purposes.

Consider a group of friends who are all being sexually exploited together, and by a group of their peers. There may be many people who are concerned about the welfare of young people involved. Some may have social workers already due to the level of harm they have experienced and/or instigated. Some may also have been arrested, may be going to school, might access local youth services, may have attended sexual health clinics, or presented with injuries at hospital. Friendship groups like this exist in sites that are testing Contextual Safeguarding. Because they are known by so many professionals, but in different ways, there is a potential that multiple agencies would all be trying to do the same thing. For example, sexual health services may have provided some of these young people with advice on consent and safe relationships. Others in the group may have been told something similar by pastoral staff in their school. Others still may have attended a session on consent at their local youth club. Some may have been arrested for sexual offences but not charged due to insufficient evidence, during which time they were warned of the seriousness of the allegations they faced. And social workers may have undertaken direct work with some on the nature of their current relationships and the extent to which they are safe.

In some respects hearing a consistent message from multiple sources is a positive thing – it can reinforce an idea. However, in this example it isn't clear if the messages are consistent, and furthermore if they are having any impact. The amount of effort that goes into a friendship group like this is significant, but without coordination will not necessarily amount to an impactful sum of its parts. It may be that the message only needs to be shared in a certain number of settings, and other agencies could have come at the issue from a different angle, utilising skill sets that were unique to them. For example, a youth club may have the opportunity to work with the group as a whole (or a subset of them) given that they all attend the provision together; a social worker who is only in contact with one of those young people might not be in a position to do the same. When a member of the group is arrested for an offence or taken to hospital due to injuries the respective police officer and medical professionals are in contact with them at a point of heightened vulnerability and potential fear. This won't necessarily be the case in more static or sterile settings such as a voluntary sexual health appointment or in a lesson of hypothetical scenarios at school. Likewise some partners in this group have statutory powers to intervene in the lives of children and families – other engage with them solely on voluntary grounds.

Maximising the potential of the professional/adult network around a group or context requires coordination. The interventions needed to achieve change may sit outside of a social work role. But before any interventions can be delivered, particularly in cases of complex and/or significant harm, coordination is required so they are used to best effect. As with the case of meeting structures, areas are exploring different options for who would fulfil a coordinating role. In test sites this role has been largely fulfilled by social work professionals. The value of social work oversight in this regard is twofold.

As was the case with brokering and advocating, social workers have coordinated plans around a common goal of safeguarding children. This has gone beyond a culture, principle, or intention. As is the case with child protection processes around families, the social work role has been leveraged to communicate the severity of some cases to a wider partnership and the fact that they require collective action to prevent or de-escalate the risk of abuse. Holding the best interests of children at the heart of this intention has proved important when balancing safeguarding with a community safety agenda, that has at times viewed children solely as a cause of harm rather than both victimised by, and instigating harm in, contexts of concern.

To coordinate plans social workers have grappled with complexities, weighted information and prioritised steps based on what they have found. To galvanise professionals around a plan, its rationale needed to be clear to all involved. Social work experience of assessing the welfare needs of children and families – and weighing up the information gathered – has been utilised when both designing and reviewing plans. Triangulating information, considering whether they are being told something that is true or something that needs to be true, using techniques of relationship mapping, observation, and engagement have all featured in this endeavour. Stepping above a stream of information to identify the central threads isn't always easy. When 25 practitioners have met to discuss one group of 12 young people who are all being criminally exploited together it is easy to get lost in each individual story and miss the bigger picture. In order to coordinate a partnership social workers have had to look beyond each individual and mobilise professionals around plan for group or context – in the same way, they might do for a family with multiple children and extended relatives.

Advocacy, brokerage, and coordination therefore have characterised the social work offer in the testing of Contextual Safeguarding; building on skills, perspectives, and positions, they draw upon to safeguard children in their families. And yet, much of what I have outlined above is reported to sit beyond the parameters of traditional 'social work'. In order to make a case for Domain 2 in the Contextual Safeguarding framework, this tension warrants consideration.

## The lanes of social work: staying or straying

To say that Contextual Safeguarding was standard 2019 social work practice would simply be untrue. Despite the many synergies between contextual practices and traditional social work roles/skills outlined above, there are three key areas where testing has required something additional from the social care workforce: the types of activities they had to undertake; the nature of the relationships they had to form; and the analytical frameworks they needed to use to assess and plan for contextual harm. Each of these has tested the agility of both individual practitioners and the systems in which they worked – and in many ways continue to do so.

Starting with activities, in some respects relationship mapping, record-checking, observation, direct engagement with young people's guardians and young people themselves are already common to social work practice. They are used by social workers to build a picture of a child's life, the protective factors within and around it and the opportunities to build on those further to miti-gate the risks of abuse. But for the most part social work practice in England in 2019 has undertaken these activities through a lens that is far narrower than the Contextual Safeguarding Framework requires. Relationship mapping has largely been confined to families: Contextual Safeguarding requires mapping peer relationships, the relationships of parents and other guardians that sit around those peers, or the network of professionals and/or other community guardians with a reach into those relationships. Not only does this require new knowledge, but successful mapping is built upon an understanding of adoles-cent development and the nature of peer relationships; a knowledge base that is wedded to family dynamics provides insufficient grounding for such an exer-cise. Likewise, observations have largely been conducted on the interaction between parents and children, or in the family home to build a sense of family dynamics. Far less observation is conducted of the school settings where young people spend their days, the parks, or bus stops they pass through each even-ing, or the stairwells they climb before they reach their front door. For social workers to increase their time in those settings is one thing, but to know what they are looking for (evidence of guardianship, a population's needs, and envir-onmental factors that meet or shape those needs) is another matter.

The relationships that make those activities feasible have also broadened. Social workers may be used to speaking to a local GP, health visitor or teacher when building a picture of a young person's life and that of their fam-ilies. They don't have the same relationships with the person who runs dry cleaners, drives the buses, coordinates the residents association or cleans the high street. This dynamic is particularly driven by a case management, 1:1 case work system; as opposed to community or patch-based social work methods of community social work from decades past.[2] Building, or reclaim-ing, those relationships has been one test, but more significant has been what is required by the nature of those relationships. Contextual Safeguarding requires that those relationships are coordinated not only to share information but to effect change in peer groups, schools, and public spaces. Having com-pleted assessments of schools, peer groups or locations social workers then had to propose plans of action – plans upon which other agencies needed to act.

When developing plans to increase safety within families, social workers feel they have a mandate. They also have routes to escalate if risk continues, safety doesn't increase, or they struggle to engage parents in work that they believe is essential to safeguard the welfare of a child. The ethics of some of these approaches continues to be debated amongst social work scholars (i.e. Featherstone, et al., 2018) – and this book does not suggest that all is well there either. However, the reactions of some practitioners during the testing of Contextual Safeguarding suggest the field of parenting is where social workers believe they can effect change. The fact that many of them have had the job title of a child and family social worker to some extent reaffirms this position. But that is only one reading of the term 'child and family social work'. If one considers the role of advocacy (explored earlier in this chapter) as also being key, then it could be the case that child and family social workers have a role in safeguarding the welfare of children and families and that this in turn gives them a far broader mandate with any agency which might impact that welfare, rather than solely with the family itself. When testing Contextual Safeguarding many social workers have adopted this alternative view. Their plans have included actions for professionals in public agencies such as policing, community safety and housing, as well as colleagues in private and voluntary organisations, such as local shopkeepers or residents groups. In some respects they have no 'mandate' to do so. They have relied on the good will of those agencies and individuals who have turned up to meetings and agreed to be trained as community guardians or fix the lighting in a particular stairwell. They have lent on their mandate to safeguard the welfare of children and to coordinate plans which achieve this; but there has been no legal or policy requirement for others to recognise many of the actions they have recommended (chapter 16).

In light of this limitation, it is somewhat unsurprising that some social workers have focused on work with families, even after assessments have identified the need to increase safety in extra-familial contexts. This has been particularly characteristic of cases where good-will and relationships haven't been enough to deliver on a plan. In one local authority I was told about a young man who had been groomed into selling drugs and was also at risk of exclusion. The social work assessment concluded that the biggest risk of escalation sat with the exclusion. If this young man was moved out of mainstream education and placed into an alternative provision, his risk would increase. The provision itself was already educating a number of young people who had been exploited; exclusion would have increased his time with this group. In addition, with alternative provision also came a reduced timetable. This would leave many hours each day where this young man had nowhere to be: increasing the opportunity for others to access and exploit him. The social worker was clear in their assessment; partners needed to do all they could to keep him in mainstream education. The school excluded him despite the findings of the assessment. The social worker felt they had no mandate to challenge this. As risk to the young man increased in his community and amongst his peers, the social worker retreated back to a focus intervention on the young man and his family – feeling unable to affect change in any other context that impacted his welfare.

While not uncommon in test sites, situations such as the one above does not fully explain all cases where social workers have continued to focus on families despite the most pressing needs affecting a child's welfare being evident beyond the family home. As detailed in the previous chapter the lens through which the social work profession has come to view families, and particularly parents (especially mothers), has also proved a challenge to Contextual Safeguarding. In 2019 child and family social work is primarily wedded to the assessment of, and intervention with, children and families. To break this limitation social workers have needed two things: frameworks that assist them in assessing and intervening with other social contexts and relationships, and; opportunities to work in this way as a matter of course.

As they say practice makes perfect. Or as Bourdieu noted, people need to be given the chance to embody the rules that are being proposed (1990) – to practice in an alternative social field.

> You need only think of the impulsive choice made by the tennis player who runs up to the net, to understand that it has nothing to in common with the learned construction that the coach, after analysis, draws up in order to explain it and deduce communicable lessons from it. The conditions of rational calculation are practically never given in practice.
>
> (Bourdieu, 1990:11)

Understanding that context matters in cases of extra-familial harm has not been sufficient to embed a contextual approach to practice. For some professionals this requires an uprooting of many assumptions upon which their previous practice had been based. Therefore, co-creative approaches to turn the Contextual Safeguarding Framework in to practical resources, and providing social workers with multiple opportunities to test these resources, have been central to understanding the feasibility of Contextual Safeguarding and ensure ongoing take-up (chapter 15).

The activities social workers undertake to deliver a location assessment, the relationships they form in the process, and the lens they adopt to understand their role throughout, all require consideration at best, and in some cases revision, for Contextual Safeguarding to take hold. These elements of the approach (activities, relationships and how social workers view their role) challenge the perceived, and in some ways actual, parameters of a social worker's mandate. The implications of this for the policy and legislative frameworks that govern child protection systems will be discussed in detail in chapter 16. For now, I turn to one approach common to child and family social work in 2019 to illustrate how Contextual Safeguarding both is and is not applicable to existing social work methods.

## The Contextual Safeguarding framework and social work methods: a case study

As has been noted already, relationships sit at the heart of social work practice, as well as being central to Contextual Safeguarding. Revived interest in

'Relationship-based' social work from the 1990's onwards (Ruch, 2005; Trevithick, 2003) is one such example of this. While to some extent all social work practice involves human interaction and so is in a sense relational, Ruch describes the idea of relationship-based practice as one in which:

> emphasis (is) placed on the professional relationship as the medium through which the practitioner can engage with the complexity of an individual's internal and external worlds and intervene. The practitioner–client relationship is recognized to be an important source of information for the practitioner to understand how best to help, and simultaneously this relationship is the means by which any help or intervention is offered.
>
> (Ruch, 2005:113)

Through this characterisation Ruch helpfully articulates how relationships enable practice: they act as route to understanding the contexts/situations/worlds a person is navigating – and also provide a gateway to finding solutions. Emphasising such an approach pushes against procedure or process-driven support, which neglects the opportunities to identify solutions through relationships rather than 'interventions' or don't recognise the intervening power of a relationship itself.

The power of relationships, especially ones between young people and trusted adults, somewhat dominated the 2018 policy response to serious youth violence (Lewing, et al., 2018). The Home Office set up the 'Trusted Relationships' fund in response to concerns about serious youth violence and criminal exploitation (Home Office, 2018). More generally, within local authority children's services young people are allocated a 'lead professional or practitioner' who they trust and who can advocate on their behalf (East Riding Yorkshire Council, 2019; London Borough of Merton, 2019; Tameside Metropolitan Borough, 2019). This all makes sense. Professionals, families, and young people have all identified that relationships matter in response to extra-familial harm (Cossar, et al., 2013; Gilligan, 2016; Lefevre, et al., 2017; PACE, 2020; Scott & McNeish, 2017; Turner, et al., 2019)

It has been interesting to see how this position has sometimes been interpreted by professionals in local areas who are trying to develop a Contextual Safeguarding approach. For some, they have stated that relationships, and not contexts, are what matter – as if the two are mutually exclusive. Practitioners have informed me that they don't have the skills to engage with the stakeholders who can affect change in a local park or school as they have been trained to build relationships with parents and young people (and not other people).

And yet what testing of Contextual Safeguarding has demonstrated is that relationships are key to increasing safety for a young person in community, school and peer contexts as well as in families. Firstly, as Ruch's presentation of relational practice suggests, part of the work to do when safeguarding young people is to support them by understanding their world. Furthermore, a fundamental challenge to full implementation of the approach has been lack of relationships between social workers and the partners required to practice in accordance with Domain 3 of the Contextual Safeguarding Framework: be it case work preventing relationships with peer groups, or perceived restrictions of a social work mandate scuppering relationships with housing departments. I have been at pains to remind practitioners that if they have the skills to speak with parents, then they also have the skills to speak with teachers, street cleaners, and store managers. These conversations may be occurring outside of the comfort zone of a family context but they are all about engagement and furthermore are the start of relationships that form around a shared desire to safeguard the welfare of children. They also hark back to relationships formed during eras of community-based social care – on this occasion building those community relationships to address contemporary challenges faced by young people and families.

The ability of a social worker to form relationships with a range of agencies/individuals will in turn inform their ability to advocate on behalf of children and families – and broker the partnerships needed to increase contextual safety. This type of work is relevant to operational models that build a 'team around the family', 'team around the school', or 'team around the professional' in a bid to safeguard a child. There seems to be no reason why the people in that team can't reach beyond healthcare practitioners, social workers, and police officers to also include residents, other parents, peers, youth workers, shopkeepers, and so on. And who is to say you couldn't have a 'team around a professional' who is supporting a peer group, or who is coordinating the plan to increase safety on a high street?

Drawing on thinking by Featherstone, et al. (2018) we have an opportunity to take this thinking one step further. They argue for an approach to relationship(s)-based practice in which we recognise the value of connection between young people, families, and the wider communities in which they are situated as opposed to solely focusing on the relationship between professionals and families. They note that:

> This is a more porous approach that encourages an understanding of the surrounding contexts and recognises the multitude of relationships (helpful and unhelpful) in children's lives … we are proposing that it is critical to move beyond the individual relationship (which is often narrowly focused on particular household members and usually gendered). Instead we want to explore the opportunities to recognise children within their communities and to work productively and collaboratively with a number of networks.
>
> (Featherstone, et al., 2018:101)

In a similar vein Hilary Cottam also drew attention to the value community networks as part of her call to 'remake relationships between us and revolutionise the welfare state'. In her book 'Radical Help' (2018) she documents a project called Loops in which various members of local communities and businesses offered young people experiences – working in hotels, theatres, and so on. Using reflective activities throughout this process fostered bonds between young people and different adults in their communities – relationships with the potential to see them through. Cottam recounted being inspired to develop the project when watching short films young people had made about what a 'good adolescence' might be like. She says:

> In every film young people connected themselves to the wider world. Yet our public services emphasise youth-only activities and so they break the natural links through which young people learn and flourish. Young people were showing us a bringing down of the walls and we needed to make that happen.
>
> (Cottam, 2018:93)

It is worth noting that the project Cottam went on to develop ran into roadblocks as fears emerged about the relationships forged between young people and wider community members – and the limited structural, parameters around them that traditional 'interventions' required. And yet in both their works Cottam and Featherstone et al. reference similar successful efforts in the US where community-driven, relationships-based interventions have proved fruitful for safeguarding the welfare of young people, their families, and residents more broadly. The idea that relationship-based social work or 'team around' frameworks must be limited to families is one grounded in the perceived parameters of child protection that need not be there. Once those parameters are broadened, the opportunities for social workers to affect change beyond, as well as within, families, by working alongside them, are plentiful.

## Similar role, broader remit

Within a Contextual Safeguarding system therefore, the social work role remains one of supporting families, coordinating plans which increase the safety and welfare of children, and ensuring that wherever possible children can remain (safely) with their families and communities. More broadly it aligns to the principles, values, and ethics of social work practice endorsed by the sector itself.

In her reflections on the social justice of social work in 2016 Jane Fenton argued that there was a large task to turn an awareness of structural inequality into a practical reality within social work – something that she sought to achieve in her book and I have set out to realise in this chapter. And yet, it would be remiss of me to suggest that when applying Contextual Safeguarding all is business as usual. The remit is broader, but the role is similar. Despite this alignment, to implement the Contextual Safeguarding framework social workers must broaden their field of vision and (re)-engage with the environments in which families raise their children and those children build independence. When it comes to extra-familial harm, this has led to the practices that are relatively novel to 21st-century social care – such as neighbourhood observations, peer-mapping, and brokering actions with town planning. By advocating to safeguard children, brokering the relationships to achieve this, and coordinating plans to bring about social change social workers act alongside families who are impacted by extra-familial abuse, rather than in judgement of them and their inability to create safety beyond their front doors. To do so (re)locates social work in the business of social justice; and conceptually broadens the parameters of child protection systems in which social workers operate.

Specific techniques have been required to realise this ambition, and demonstrate the alignment of Contextual Safeguarding with existing social worker practices. In the next chapter I will outline how approaches such as mirroring systems and co-creation have supported our position that the Contextual Safeguarding framework extends, but does not replace, existing social work practice. By detailing how these methodologies have assisted us to date, I will also highlight the risks and challenges that have come with this approach – how they have been managed so far and how they may change in the future. Recognising and understanding these tensions is critical for ensuring that the continued application and development of Contextual Safeguarding can he held within social care systems – without either compromising each other's intention.

## Notes

1 Having previously focused on two approaches – family support and child protection (Gilbert, 1997).
2 A loss of such relationships has not been unique to social workers. As noted in chapter 5, youth workers have also informed us of the impact that case management approaches have had on their partnerships (Fritz et al. 2016).

# 15 The techniques and pitfalls of change

## Mirroring, co-creation, and case studies

I'm terrible at remembering names but am adept at mirroring accents. This rarely works in my favour. While struggling to put names to faces at a group meal, staff leaving party or gathering of extended family, I find myself sliding into the lilt of an Irish accent or the twang on an American one. And I can safely say that there are few people who appreciate someone who parrots their intonation but can't recall their title. I myself have often been called Charlene, Caroline, even Kylie, before I am called Carlene – and it is a tad more than frustrating. But when on a leadership course I was once told something about imitations: that despite how embarrassing this tendency might be we often try to 'speak the same language' of those we are trying to connect with. Numerous studies have illustrated that individuals often imitate the accents, mannerisms, and facial expressions of others, often involuntarily, as a means of forming social connections (see Miller, et al., 2010).

The process of developing, scaling and embedding Contextual Safeguarding has been characterised by attempts to understand, and use, the language of child protection – attempts led by researchers who, for the most part, are using this as a second language to our philosophical, geographical, or legal disciplinary routes. Embedded in children's services departments and in conversation with a network of practice developers, the Contextual Safeguarding team have built their cultural and social capital in the field of child protection (Lloyd, Forthcoming). This has informed the design of approaches, activities, and resources being tested. It has also accelerated the pace at which others have understood, interpreted, and adopted an approach which is, in part, significantly divergent from what has come before it.

As I have instigated, and witnessed, the evolution of Contextual Safeguarding I have been struck by how straight forward some believe it to be, whereas others see it as highly complex. Some of this may be down to preferences and perspectives that individuals hold about the meaning of child protection. But it may also be because in using the language of child protection to change it, we have created an illusion that it is what we already do, but by another name. Given the change that Contextual Safeguarding requires of us all, there may come a time when we have to change, rather than simply rename, elements of child protection systems in order to create an impact that is sustained, and isn't superficial.

In this chapter I will reflect on how this tension has played out around the country. I will detail how action research methods used by the Contextual Safeguarding team have built our social and cultural capital in child protection, and how this process has cumulatively catalysed change. I will also signal the risks of this approach; how they have been mitigated to date and how they may change in the future. The process of co-creation has sat at the heart of creating meaningful transformation for the field of social work; mirroring processes/language have eased us all into this process; and case studies have served to illustrate both the need for, and benefits of, the change being created. Over time, however, the endeavour of building Contextual Safeguarding systems may require co-created methods that are less characterised by a shared language and more characterised by a shared desire for reform.

## Innovation that sticks: what we know

According to Rogers (2003), there are five key elements to successfully scaling, and rolling out, approaches that ask people to do something differently. His theory of innovation diffusion states that the proposal being made needs to: be perceived as better/advantageous to what came before it; be compatible with the existing values or practices that are used by those adopting it; have a degree of ease with which it can be adopted; be trialled alongside business as usual approaches until it can be fully embedded; and have observable results. When we first designed the Contextual Safeguarding framework, latterly set about testing it, and converting our learning into practice resources, Roger's theory was not in our mind. And yet, as we have scaled testing into further localities and I have reflected on the path trodden to get to this stage, Rogers' ideas have helped to articulate what has both enabled and at points threatened, the journey to contextualising our safeguarding system.

The Contextual Safeguarding framework was first offered at a time when social work responses to exploitation in England were under a microscope. Child sexual exploitation, and other forms of largely extra-familial harm, were being framed as abuse and child protection services were expected to respond. Contextual Safeguarding offered a language to articulate why that response was frustrated, and proposed a route to resolution: in this way it was perceived as advantageous. By designing and testing the approach within children's services departments, and alongside social workers, the research team were able to identify key levers for aligning a Contextual Safeguarding approach with existing values and practices in children's social care. The conversion of the Contextual Safeguarding framework into practical tools supported practitioners to identify straight-forward routes to implementation. The test site approach has ensured that Contextual Safeguarding systems could be designed without suspending the wider practices underway within children's services departments. Finally, from introducing safety mapping into their assessments to convening meetings around locations, those involved in testing have been able to see results. At present many of these results are case-based and anecdotal, rather than system-wide, but for the practitioner who has been able to identify a route to safeguarding a young person by undertaking safety mapping with them, or building partnerships with local businesses who are present when they are not, the difference is palpable.

When framed in this way, the rapid uptake of the language and practices of Contextual Safeguarding is somewhat unsurprising. And yet if we are to truly understand the benefits of the work to date, and the ongoing risks to mitigate, further reflection on the diffusion process is required. In particular the techniques we used to demonstrate why Contextual Safeguarding: was advantageous; was aligned to existing practices and values; could be adopted with relative ease, while wider service continued as normal, and with visible impact, have risked misapplication at times. We have had to ensure that in communicating the advantages of a Contextual Safeguarding approach it wasn't interpreted as a silver-bullet to resolve all challenges of safeguarding adolescents. There have been times when individualised, deficit-based, or process-driven elements of social work threatened to colour the application of a Contextual Safeguarding approach in our bid to align to recognisable practices in children's services. Practice tools that facilitated take-up have, at times, presented a risk of over-simplification. Enabling localities to develop the approach and capture case-studies of impact has created situations where what will likely be a decade long process of system change has appeared complete during the first stages of implementation. By reflecting on these risks, with specific references to thematic techniques that have characterised our approach to date, I use this chapter to reflect on how our approach may need to mature as we move into the next phase of testing and development. While each of the five elements of Roger's framework is evident on our journey to date, there isn't one that has been fully realised. Each aspect will require further work both within and across test sites and beyond for Contextual Safeguarding to scale and spread across England, the UK, and into international jurisdictions.

## Thematic techniques of the Contextual Safeguarding team

The Contextual Safeguarding team is primarily made up of researchers. The development of a Contextual Safeguarding Framework and testing of it however have been a collaboration between practice and research. This shared approach to knowledge creation and dissemination has applied whether we have: observed Contextual Safeguarding in action, captured that action and converted that into a resource; published that resource online for further testing and adaptation by practitioners; or reviewed case work that has latterly been converted into case studies for use in training. Three thematic techniques are evident across the collaborative research methods documented in chapters 5 and 8, and knowledge they have produced. These are using:

- *Co-creation* as a means to understanding, developing/testing, capturing and disseminating a Contextual Safeguarding approach.
- *Mirroring* terminology, practices and structures used to develop or deliver child protection systems more generally to communicate the components of a Contextual Safeguarding approach and locate it as a response to child abuse.
- *Case study development* to illustrate challenges with existing processes and the feasibility/benefits of proposed changes.

Collectively these techniques have created a common, fertile ground for the growth of Contextual Safeguarding.

### *Co-creation*

When undertaking a systematic review of co-creation studies in the field of social innovation Voorberga, et al. defined co-creation as 'the active involvement of end-users in various stages of the production process' (2014:3). For Contextual Safeguarding to take root the first set of 'end-users' was defined as the practitioners using the approach: they would ultimately use Contextual Safeguarding in their practice and also had to be the ones to nurture it. Co-creation has been imperative for achieving this level of buy-in – and not for superficial means – even though in the long-term this 'end-user' will need to be defined as the children, families and communities who the system is intended to support. Contextual Safeguarding needed to work for those affected by it – young people, parents, and practitioners. It needed to make sense of, and offer some relief to, the challenges faced when mounting a child protection response to extra-familial harm. Co-creation has provided us with many opportunities to test the usefulness of the Contextual Safeguarding Framework and update/adapt it accordingly.

In addition to ensuring usefulness and relevance, co-creation has created opportunities for co-ownership. Contextual Safeguarding has been developed within, rather than independently of but applied to, practice. This has been particularly evident across the practitioners' network, as members reflect on knowledge/resources that have been shared and identify the implications for themselves, their teams, services, areas and sectors.

An example of co-creative process was the development of the context assessment triangles (detailed in chapter 10). The first triangle was designed by a team of social workers and researchers following the testing of a peer group assessment. Notable stages in its development were a recognition by practitioners that initial assessment frameworks offered by the research team were useful for gathering information, but less so for analysing it. Then came the reflection of researchers about what the social workers had done during the testing of a peer group assessment and the key topics – guardianship, group functioning and wider environment – that they seemed to explore. After which social workers and researchers wrestled with how best to represent this approach in a way that was usable for others – and how much was already provided for in existing resources. Reflecting on the mismatch between the existing assessment framework and what the peer assessment had required resulted in the first prototype of the peer assessment triangle. The resource was then disseminated to practitioners during training events and as an online resource for our practice network, as well as additional application in test sites. The feedback we received resulted in: amendments to the initial prototype; additional guidance for how to understand the three thematic areas of assessment, and; advice about what forms of information could be used to shape the conclusions that such an assessment might draw. This bi-directional process of co-creation is an illustration of how both researcher contribution and practitioner contribution have been valued on the journey thus far and resulted in both practice and academic communities feeling a sense of ownership over the system change that we are producing.

### *Mirroring*

As our work in test sites has progressed, so has the technique of 'mirroring'. On multiple occasions we asked our practice colleagues how they might respond to abuse within families and then reflected with them on how this might apply to contexts/relationships beyond families.

Take 'thresholds' as an example (discussed in chapter 13). I recall one of the first reflective workshops in Hackney where this topic came up. We were in the throes of finalising a context assessment and a social worker asked whether an assessment would be warranted on a context such as this if Contextual Safeguarding was every day practice (rather than in test). The context was a school in which sexual harassment had been identified as a problem for multiple students; where staff were concerned (they had put themselves forward for assessment), and; where opportunities had been offered to increase protection and challenge harmful or bias attitudes amongst staff and students going forward. The threshold document had not been developed, and social workers had conducted this exercise to primarily explore what a context assessment might entail and whether it yielded a different response from multi-agency partners. There was an underlying concern about both proportionality and capacity. Were the concerns in that school such that it required social workers to conduct this level of in-depth assessment, and coordinate a multi-agency plan? And if so would their service have the capacity to regularly undertake this type of work?

My question to that social worker had been – what do you think? The assessment had thrown up some concerns about the welfare of some (but not all) young people in that school. The concerns were notable but did not suggest a risk of significant harm. The assessment had also identified guardians (school leaders and individual teachers) who wanted to improve the school's capacity to safeguard students, and who were able to engage with the support available to them. If this were a family what would they conclude?

All social workers in that meeting agreed that the school was in need of some support, but wasn't one in which young people were at risk of significant harm. And so the idea of a 'context in need' was born. The approach caught on with a pace. Social workers understood the distinction between children in need of support and children who were at risk of significant harm: mirroring that language for contexts seemed to help convey the intention behind the approach, the parameters of its reach, and its focus of safeguarding children from abuse.

The Context Assessment Triangles referenced above were one of many other examples where mirroring was used to design, frame, or communicate a Contextual Safeguarding approach. Terms such as Context Conferences (instead of child protection conferences), peer assessment triangle (instead of child and family assessment triangle), and guardianship capacity (instead of parental capacity) have all given Contextual Safeguarding a sense of familiarity. They offer an indication to practitioners of what a Contextual Safeguarding approach might entail, what it has to do with child protection, and why it should matter to them.

Mirroring is a practical reflection of what the conceptual Contextual Safeguarding framework sought to achieve: a broadening of child protection parameters/expectations. Domain 1 requires that a Contextual Safeguarding system has the capacity to reach into peer group, school, and community contexts in ways that previous child protection systems have not. Mirroring is concrete way to broaden those conceptual parameters – while still aligning the approach to Domain 2 (a safeguarding lens) of the framework.

From a systems perspective, mirroring has also been used to communicate how each part of a child protection process would also require expansion or reframing. System reviews in test sites, for example, were used to map and review a child's journey through the structures, meetings and processes to which the system functioned as Level 1 testing unfolded (Chapter 8).

When building approaches for Level 2 safeguarding systems (chapter 10), system reviews have explored how contexts (as well as children and families) would journey through this process (albeit it is not as linear the system headings of referral, assessment, planning, in previous chapters suggested). As when co-creating practice solutions, mirroring at a strategic level has aligned design ideas with Domain 2 of the Contextual Safeguarding framework and avoided the development of solely criminal justice or community safety responses to contextual harm.

### Case studies

Contextual Safeguarding emerged from case studies. In-depth analysis of how child protection systems, and the social workers within them, were responding to children like Sara, Sabrina, and Malik (chapter 2) provided the evidence base for change. This was an evidence base grounded in the reality of young people lives, the struggles of many parents and carers who were trying to keep them safe, and the wider practice environments that were without a language to articulate where risk and protection sat – and what this in turn meant for statutory services. Regardless of where one sat on the ideological spectrum of public service design, it would have been hard to argue that we had a child protection system fit for purpose. From this point onwards the generation of case studies has been a critical tool for leveraging local, national, and international interest in the Contextual Safeguarding Framework.

Firstly, whether we have used case studies to illustrate the challenges with existing practise, or to exemplify what a contextual approach might involve, case studies have translated a conceptual framework into a practical reality. There isn't just a conceptual mismatch between the parameters of child protection systems and the dynamics of extra-familial harm – there is a real life one, and cases like Sara's show not only what that means for a young person, but why that should matter for us all. Likewise, it is one thing to say we need to expand partnerships to include people that have a reach into extra-familial settings. Offering case studies of residents associations, park wardens, library staff, school leaders, and parents who have played an active role in context assessments and plans illustrates what this means in reality.

Secondly, case studies were used to facilitate a strength-based approach to system change. Contextual Safeguarding can feel like an overwhelming idea. Therefore, whenever we mapped system responses, or undertook a system review, we captured case studies which indicated elements of existing practice that were already contextual. As such Contextual Safeguarding wasn't about changing all elements of an existing approach. Instead, one could embark on creating a Contextual Safeguarding system by magnifying and mainstreaming existing workstreams so they became 'business as usual' rather than an anomaly in the system. Much of our time was spent understanding how these contextual examples came to be; identifying the conditions that supported their success; and thinking about how such conditions could be scaled over time.

Finally, it was critical that case studies were used to think about systems, rather than individuals. The risk with case studies is that they can be seen as evidence of what an individual has experienced or achieved – as opposed to reflective of the wider system in which that individual interacted. As a result we always had to identify ways to frame case studies so that they were viewed in context, whether that was: presenting examples of contextual practice within wider system-mapping activities; identifying elements of wider systems that frustrated or enabled individual practice; or dip-sampling multiple cases within specific periods of time to track patterns across cases. Ultimately, case studies ensured that Contextual Safeguarding grew out of child protection systems, could be developed within child protection systems, and spoke to the opportunities and barriers that existed within child protection systems.

**The impact and pitfalls of a shared language**

On reflection we have used co-creation, mirroring, and case studies, to facilitate the understanding, and take-up, of Contextual Safeguarding. Far from being mutually exclusive these three techniques have coalesced in ways that practitioners could create contextual approaches; understand the place of those approaches within child protection systems; and articulate how they expanded the conceptual and practical parameters of traditional responses to child abuse.

When the intricacies of this relationship align, the benefits of a shared language are evident. For example, some elements of what we have undertaken in Contextual Safeguarding require stringent ethical oversight. The idea that social workers, on behalf of the state, would be involved in the mapping and assessment of friendship groups could be alarming (and will be explored further in chapter 16). What business does the state have in young people's friendships? Is this simply increasing the state surveillance of the private lives of children? These are some of the valid questions that have been put to us since 2016. Working with practitioners to build case studies of how forms of extra-familial harm constitute abuse, and how the system is currently unable to understand or disrupt this abuse when a young person's peers are out of scope, is a critical point of putting parameters around when such an activity would or would not be appropriate. Applying the lens of threshold provides a further boundary to limiting the idea that the child protection services would seek oversight of a range of social contexts in which young people spent their time, developed, took chances, and made mistakes. If we get this right, the ambition over time may be to further decrease state oversight of community-based harm, as residents, businesses, community groups, parents, and others are equipped to safeguard children who have been exploited beyond their front doors. In the interim however, Contextual Safeguarding fills the gulf between 1:1 case work that is focused on families, and the group and network view that is required in the schools and public places where abuse can also occur.

Potential pitfalls, however, remain on the horizon. As I have accepted elsewhere in this book, many challenges exist in how individualised child protection systems (and child and family social work within this) are experienced by young people – and their parents/carers – more generally. Contextual Safeguarding is focused on a specific limitation – the lack of engagement the child protection system has with extra-familial contexts in which abuse occurs. It does not address broader limitations identified by advocates of social, ecological and systemic approaches to child protection, although it is aligned with them. As such the technique of mirroring in particular has been a risky exercise. Without much clarification – particularly regarding the values that underpin the Contextual Safeguarding framework (chapter 12) – we have left room to mirror the good, the bad, and the ugly of child protection systems into wider social contexts. If we mirror everything, for example, we could unintentionally promote punitive, pro-cedural, and de-personalised state intervention into communities that are already marginalised and experiencing multiple disadvantages. Without a clear value base mirroring could increase the numbers of children coming into the view of systems that then problematises them, rather than the situations that they face. The more Contextual Safeguarding is diffused and scaled, the greater the risk of erroneous interpretations of the approach – even though such a practice would not actually align to a Contextual Safeguarding framework in the first place.

In a similar vein, it has never been our intention to encroach on effective community development or youth work practices that already effect change in extra-familial settings. Rather we have sought to identify the circumstances in which state support and/or coordination to safeguard the welfare of children may also be required. There will be far more situations where statutory child protective services are not needed, and where investment in community organisations, parent support networks and detached youth work is the most appropriate mechanism to create safe and protective contexts for young people. I have been heartened to learn of local areas that are starting to re-invest in youth work, particularly that which is detached, in order to facilitate a Contextual Safeguarding approach. Continued monitoring will be required to ensure that contextualising child protection doesn't lead to the de-contextualising of informal or community-based support.

## Starting up versus sticking around

The techniques featured in this chapter have helped us get Contextual Safeguarding started. They won't necessarily be the ones that help it stick around. As I have stated elsewhere in this book, using a Contextual Safeguarding framework pushes the parameters of child and family social work and the systems in which it exists. Understanding what this means in practice has required individual practitioners, whole teams, and wider partnerships to understand the reason for stepping into that change, as well as visualise the difference it would make.

Mirroring has provided one way to demonstrate how Contextual Safeguarding is aligned to both the purpose and parameters of child protection and social work while also requiring something different from both. Over time, we anticipate that we will mirror less and innovate more. When first discussing context conferences with a director of children's services we both agreed that it was probably quite 'clunky'. We understood that at the time it was needed to communicate to a wider workforce and partnership why such a meeting might be called, and what it might require of them. However, we also believed that in time meetings to discuss areas where young people were at risk of significant harm would probably be called something else. As other local areas begin testing we are already seeing this play out. Some areas have set up community conferences, others are having context conferences chaired by education leads, rather than social workers, when concerns relate to a school. We anticipate a continued development of practice variations that are less wedded to mirroring and more aligned to the opportunities, partnerships, and cultures of local communities and organisations. In this respect mirroring is likely to decrease over time. Further strengthening of the Contextual Safeguarding framework, and the values that underpin it, particularly in relation to Domain 2 (chapter 12) will further facilitate this trajectory.

Comparatively we anticipate that as Contextual Safeguarding is scaled beyond formal test sites, practitioner engagement in the creation of contextual approaches will increase. As researchers, the team and I intend to continue to capture what happens, and the extent to which it helps us understand the implications of the Contextual Safeguarding framework and its feasibility. But our involvement in the creation of operational interpretations will likely decline – increasing the co-ownership of the approach.

More importantly, since 2018 we have increased our direct engagement with young people and families on the idea of Contextual Safeguarding. Prior to this, their views have incentivised the development of Contextual Safeguarding but not shaped its design. The lives of Sara, Malik, and their parents were, and remain, central to this project – but whether we are on the right track in their eyes is relatively under-explored. Initial consultation with young people and families, through to supporting their participation in the systems change process itself, is the next step for this co-creative process. As much as mirroring in likely to thin in years to come, the nature and scale of co-creation are likely to thicken.

And through both the above processes the content of case studies will shift. At the start of this journey my team and I primarily produced case studies to illustrate all that was wrong with how child protection systems responded to extra-familial abuse. During our initial years of testing we have worked alongside social workers to build cases studies that exemplified how practice and systems can begin to flex, and (re)-engage with social justice, to better accommodate extra-familial contexts. Beyond 2020 we anticipate that case studies will be created solely by practitioners, and in time between practitioners, young people and families, to demonstrate how the Contextual Safeguarding framework has been useful and what work we have yet to do.

As local systems shift to adopt a Contextual Safeguarding approach, and those who run or use those systems lead that process, the legal and policy and frameworks that govern child protection systems will be put to the test. As this and previous chapters have already indicated, even at this stage in testing fundamental questions about statutory guidelines, ethical codes and legal frameworks have begun to emerge: and it those questions to which I will dedicate the next, and penultimate chapter of this book.

# 16 The legality and ethics of Contextual Safeguarding

When I deliver speeches on Contextual Safeguarding audience members often approach me afterwards in a state of confusion. 'I don't understand why things don't work like this already' they say to me; or as one woman (whose son was being exploited at the time) reflected, 'CS doesn't stand for Contextual Safeguarding it stands for Common Sense'. For them Contextual Safeguarding is what we should have been doing all along. If we know that extra-familial harm is informed by peer, school, and neighbourhood contexts, why on earth would you not include them in a safeguarding response, and instead limit child protection practice to children and families? They have a point. I had the same question rattling in my mind when I sat with Sara and Malik's files. But over the past three years I have come to understand why change has been so slow to realise, and why practices persist which evidently do little to safeguard the welfare of children. In earlier chapters of this book I documented the road that took us to this point of bifurcation; the child protection system, never being designed for these matters, was an ill-fit for the contemporary harm it was latterly used to address. In testing Contextual Safeguarding we have developed a deeper understanding of why, despite being aware of this incongruity, the journey of embedding an alternative approach is likely to be riddled with pot holes, speed humps, re-directions, and off-roading.

As the three previous chapters illustrated, implementing Contextual Safeguarding unearths fundamental questions about child protection systems, social work practice, and the thresholds for state intervention in cases of safeguarding. It is one thing to realise the challenge of a system in which a child who has been stabbed on their way home from school won't be allocated a social worker to oversee his case because this incident wasn't perpetrated by, or attributable to, his parents. It is quite another thing to shift the goalposts of that system to include this child. To do so requires us to redefine: what social workers are tasked to address; the safeguarding duties of communities, schools, businesses, and young people's peers; and what level of street/community/school/peer harm is intolerable to the point it becomes a social work concern. On what occasions does a state have a duty to safeguard children from harm and should the state focus their attention on the parents of those children, step in to parent those children, or target the contexts that compromise both those children and their parents?

As such, those who seek to implement Contextual Safeguarding must ask questions of themselves, the services they oversee, the policies they develop, and the systems which are informed by, and inform, these practices. Do child protection systems exist to safeguard children from all forms of abuse, or to safeguard children from parents/carers who pose a risk to their welfare? When the welfare of children is compromised by factors beyond parenting, which agency of the state, if any, should coordinate/lead the response? In seeking to create safety in the range of contexts where young people have come to harm, does Contextual Safeguarding seek to socially engineer out harms that are part of society and always will be?

Such questions pertain not only to England and Wales, but, as noted in previous chapters, to many child protection systems around the globe: particularly for countries in which state bodies assess and intervene with families abstracted from the contexts which inform their lives; where child protection systems focus on fixing people, rather than places (Fenton, 2016; Gilbert, et al., 2011; Merkel-Holguin, et al., 2019). Such systems are built on the premise that families alone are the guardians of their children and that good parenting is the primary source of child safety. The role of the state therefore is to build the capacity of parents to do better, regardless of the context(s) in which they raise their child(ren) (Featherstone, et al., 2018; Gilbert, et al., 2011; Rogowoski, 2012). When improvement seems unlikely, or the pace of change is too slow, the state can intervene and assume the role of a corporate parent. This again assumes that safety lies in the parent and the risks they pose.

In regards to adolescence, this system is bolstered by wider ideas that success or failure lies in an individual's choices which, like parenting, are to be viewed independently from the contexts in which they are made. Countries that have increasingly adopted an individualised narrative around both rights and responsibilities are particularly relevant in this regard (Gilbert, et al., 2011). The state can intervene through activities which support individuals – in this case young people – to think about, and therefore make, better choices: whether that is through programmes that educate them on healthy relationships, sessions to train them into managing their anger, or projects that assign them a mentor for career advice and guidance. For the most part these time-limited interventions are sustained through the person at whom they are aimed. Neither the intervention, nor its legacy, engages with the contexts in which that individual has formed unhealthy relationships, displayed anger, or struggled to access employment. In such situations it may be unsurprising to see voluntary, charitable or community organisations at the forefront of supporting individual young people affected by exploitation and other forms of extra-familial harm, rather than child protection services. It is interesting to reflect that this was largely the situation in England in the 1990s and early 2000s – until national outcries, recognising sexual exploitation as abuse, shifted the gaze to social work practices (chapter 3).

And even in countries that appear more oriented to a 'family support' approach to child abuse (Gilbert, et al., 2011; Parton, 2014), and seek to safeguard children by meeting the wider needs of families, this is still built on the premise of the family/parent being the guardian of safety – and the role of the state being to support parents to fulfil this role. Furthermore, such systems appear to still be restricted to responding to harm instigated by, or attributable to, parenting, and appear less clear what 'family support' looks like when harms exist beyond this field. The French constitution, for example, states that the Nation 'shall provide the individual and family with the conditions necessary to their development' (1946; para10–11). Child protection services developed within this broader framework are geared around the idea that:

> the protection that parents provide their children is paramount against danger; interventions by social services can only take place when this protection is defective or missing. Interventions should try to re-establish positive parenting roles, not do away with them altogether.
>
> (Bolter & Seraphin, 2019:86)

For forms of abuse traditionally seated in the realm of child protective services such an approach appears clear. But Bolter and Seraphin (2019) have noted how this system has been challenged when faced with unaccompanied asylum-seeking children in need of protection – where the family set up defies the basic premise of the system's position.

And it is this mismatch that appears conceptually unresolved in most national systems that have been designed to offer a state response to child abuse. Hence, Rogowoski (2012) and Parton (2011) in the UK and Fong and Cardoso in the US have flagged how child sexual exploitation sits beyond the parameters of traditional child protection systems within their respective countries, despite those systems looking quite different to those operating in France. Likewise, Finland and to a lesser extent Sweden have been found to have relatively high numbers of young people living in residential children's homes (Merkel-Holguin, et al., 2019). These young people are described in child protection research as 'delinquent' or having 'behavioural issues'. Are these young people actually the same as Sara and Malik? Is this the extent of child protection responses to extra-familial harm in those countries?

The feasibility of common sense, therefore, is questionable. When it comes to Sabrina, Sara, and Malik, we are yet to agree whether: child protection systems have a role in keeping them safe; the state should effect change beyond their families to safeguard them; or if relationships beyond families that compromise their safety should be subject to state intervention – these matters are all up in the air in many international settings.

In using Contextual Safeguarding to advance child protection systems, we have challenged these fundamental assumptions about individual, family and state responsibilities. In the process quandaries have surfaced that need to be addressed before multi-country, and even cross-England, adoption of the approach can be achieved: quandaries I will begin to grapple with in this chapter. In particular I will consider: whether extra-familial harm is primarily a safeguarding and child protection or community safety and policing responsibility; the legality and ethics of including peer, community and professional, as well as family, relationships in social work assessment and safeguarding plans; and the extent to which we should attempt to change the social conditions of environments which may facilitate, but do not necessarily endorse, abusive behaviours. These three points of the discussion colour the crossroads of progression. I will not resolve them in this book, but I will detail where the debate has reached and signal where it might go next. Ultimately for Contextual Safeguarding to be common sense rather than counter culture within child protection systems, these matters require resolution.

## Common sense but counter culture: unearthing the challenges of a CS approach

What comes to your mind when you think of the term 'child protection'? Who is doing the protecting? Who are they protecting? And what are they being protected from? These questions are not reserved for those developing Contextual Safeguarding systems. They are questions that underpin the designs, doubts, and debates about the role of state services in keeping children safe around the world. We take for granted that we know the answers to these questions. Our cultures, relationships, and fields of knowledge all inform how we respond.

### *Extra-familial abuse: a concern for criminal justice or child protection agencies?*

In England the confusion is clear. When children are stabbed by their peers or groomed into selling or moving drugs, the strategy that guides local responses is designed by Community Safety Partnerships (CSPs). The role of CSPs is to:

> Work together to protect their local communities from crime and to help people feel safer. They work out how to deal with local issues like antisocial behaviour, drug or alcohol misuse and reoffending. They annually assess local crime priorities and consult partners and the local community about how to deal with them.
>
> (Home Office, 2015)

Members of Community Safety Partnerships include, police, local authorities, fire, and rescue authorities, probation service, and health agencies. Given their remit in relation to anti-social behaviour and criminality their work primarily reaches into housing estates, high streets, parks, and other public places in which such behaviours may occur.

Given their focus, one might suggest that CSPs be the principal delivery mechanism for Contextual Safeguarding in England – or even that they are already. In many respects, their work is aligned with Domain 1 of the CS Framework; they target public and community contexts in which crime occurs, with the view to supporting whole communities rather than individuals. But as noted in chapter 6, and further articulated in the above exert, the objective of CSPs is crime reduction, not child welfare. This is at odds with Domain 2 of the CS Framework which requires the primary diver of the system to be child welfare. As such, while there may be some activities undertaken by CSPs which are complimentary to the ambitions of Contextual Safeguarding, the fundamental goal of CSPs is misaligned to the objective of the CS Framework and arguably England's child protection system.

Relatedly we have been asked, not whether CSPs deliver Contextual Safeguarding, but whether the CS Framework turns social workers into housing wardens and anti-social behaviour officers. There are two points to make in this regard.

The first is that the third domain of the CS Framework requires social workers to act in *partnership* with sectors, agencies, and individuals who have a reach into extra-familial contexts – not that it becomes those individuals. As such, following assessments of public places where young people are at risk of significant harm, interventions have been delivered by housing, youth, and policing agencies to increase safety. Social workers may have coordinated or brokered some of the plans (chapter 14) but they didn't play the role of every actor who delivered on them.

The second point pertains to what is suggested about the role of community safety partnerships when the responsibility for coordinating responses to abuse rests at their door? As noted above, community safety partnerships are a collection of organisations, including local authorities, policing, and the fire service, that collaborate to address crime and anti-social behaviour. It isn't clear from this that it is the role of such partnerships to also lead the response to child abuse or to ensure child safety more broadly. When it comes to abuse within families child protection systems lead the response? When it comes to abuse outside of families is it the function of community safety partnership to safeguard those affected – and coordinate assessments and plans to achieve this end? If the answer is yes then we create a division, and potential hierarchy, in response to abuse typologies. Some forms of abuse are to be responded to by child protection agencies, and others are to be addressed by community safety or criminal justice agencies. A journey down this road takes us right back to chapters 2 and 3 of this book – one in which we might query whether extra-familial harm is abuse at all.

The risks of dividing abuse typologies are all the more concerning given that England's policy landscape already does this within the broad category of 'extra-familial harm' itself. As noted in other chapters the issue of child sexual exploitation has sat under the auspices of child protection policy and local safeguarding partnerships since 2009, if not before. Over this same time period serious youth violence, the threat of 'knife crime' and weapon-enabled violence, and even teenage relationship abuse has been overseen by national policing departments and local community safety partnerships. There appears to have been little rationale for a division that has resulted in siloed and inconsistent responses to young people who are harmed in extra-familial contexts.

In 2019 the testing of Contextual Safeguarding has surfaced, but not resolved, this discrepancy. Each test site has involved Community Safety in the approach in ways that reflects their existing partnership arrangements, the culture of those partnerships, and the resources they can bring to bear on affecting change. One thing is consistent – in every site, so far, Contextual Safeguarding has been viewed primarily as an approach for advancing how children's social care services respond to extra-familial abuse. It is they who have been most impacted by the approach, and for the most part they who are leading tests. However, in some sites the governance for testing sits jointly under Community Safety and Safeguarding partnerships. In some sites in our wider practice network, meetings to review safeguarding assessments of public places are being chaired by community safety rather than safeguarding leads. Some areas have brought all forms of extra-familial harm together under the purview of a safeguarding panels; breaking away from preceding siloed approaches that locate some forms of harm within the community safety agenda; but not all have, or intend to, move in this direction.

Whichever structures test sites and network members have used to create their CS approach, Community Safety Partnerships and the services they over-see have been central to its implementation: tests suggest it can't be delivered without them. As testing develops we will come to understand how one can see extra-familial harm as a child protection issue, while simultaneously recognising the remit of community safety agencies in safeguarding the welfare of young people. Such a resolution will need to grapple with the fact that young people's experiences of extra-familial harm don't fit neatly into the legislative remit of either child protection or community safety agencies; one, or both, may need to reform, and redefine the grounds upon which they interact, to establish Contextual Safeguarding approaches in the future.

### *Legal and moral duties: professionals, peers, and communities*

Testing of Contextual Safeguarding has raised significant legal and ethical questions about the approach; questions that require ongoing examination.

The one most attended to during initial implementation stages has been the legality and ethics of mapping young people's friendships as part of a social work assessment. We supported one test site to instruct legal advice on the matter; and in particular the grounds upon which one could attach peer maps and assessments to statutory child protection files. While the advice was useful in setting some procedural parameters around the activity and confirmed its legality in certain circumstances, the practice of actually doing the work requires ongoing ethical reflection. Speaking to practitioners on the virtual network, and in test sites, similar questions continue to come to the fore. How do you stop a map from getting 'too big', where every child's association and connection features on the document, even if it bears no relevance to the safeguarding plan being developed? How do you avoid mapping for mapping's sake and ensure that it is used as an exercise to guide decision-making and safeguarding plans? How much mapping should be shared with young people and with parents, when those maps are developed by professionals? How do we engage with the dynamic nature of young people's friendships and avoid keeping hold of maps that are outdated, and keep young people in situations (on paper) from which they have moved on (in real life)?

Underpinning all of these questions is a niggling dilemma: is it ethical, in other words okay/right//appropriate, to be doing this? In other situations, network mapping practices have been associated to an increased, unnecessary, and unethical criminalisation of young people – particularly the mapping of young people thought to be associated to 'gangs' (Williams, 2018). Without ongoing and critical debate, and further guidance about the process of peer mapping and peer assessment for the purposes of safeguarding, risks of improper use will persist.

These concerns equally apply to how social workers 'map' or 'assess' community and professional relationships that can impact the welfare of young people. Building on peer maps some sites have started to map the professionals, parents, and community members who sit around a peer group, or have reach into them. They are doing this to identify opportunities to increase safety in the networks around groups of young people – avoid duplication of efforts or worst still conflicting methods of support or advice. This approach brings to life the idea that our 'collective capacity to safeguard' comes under the microscope in a Contextual Safeguarding approach and not just the capacity of parents.

However, do states have any grounds upon which to map and assess community relationships in this way? Concerns are rightly raised about whether this increases surveillance of families and young people, and further exposes them to unethical monitoring and intervention. In the United States, fears have been expressed regarding the impact of mandatory reporting, for example, on the relationships between families and community services, such as schools: that all such services are primarily there to report families to statutory services rather than offer early help and support. Referencing these concerns Blustain & McCarthy argued that:

> It's vital to invest in communities most impacted by child welfare involvement. In these communities, schools, parks, sports and arts programs for children, mental health supports for families, affordable and safe housing, and crisis services are often inaccessible or low quality. Yet rather than target community conditions, the child welfare system targets individual families.
>
> (Blustain & McCarthy, 2019)

In our efforts to implement Contextual Safeguarding, we adopt a similar lens. Community mapping and assessment is not conducted to penalise or target individuals – it is to understand the social conditions that young people and families navigate so such conditions can be targeted for improvement. It is also important to note that these questions appear particularly pertinent in countries where child protection systems are delivered and organised from the state down, or via a statutory framework, as opposed from the bottom up – and coordinated in such a manner. Reflecting on efforts to develop collaborative approaches to child protection in more community-led settings such as Sierra Leone for example, Wessells noted that:

> this community-driven approach requires that child protection actors shift their roles from that of experts to that of facilitators who are also co-learners. When external child protection workers enter the community as experts, community understandings and practices tend to be marginalized, and communities lapse into a familiar role as beneficiaries. The facilitative approach highlighted above viewed communities fundamentally as actors, albeit imperfect, who given the appropriate space, opportunities, and encouragement for reflection motivated each other to take collective action that reduces harms to children.
>
> (Wessels, 2015:19)

In contexts more familiar in Anglo-phone countries, however, where state-organised responses dominate, questions remain about what governments can expect of these peers, community members, and their relationships with young people, in regards to child welfare? Conceptually we can, and have, stated that in order to safeguard young people in extra-familial settings we need to involve individuals and agencies who have a reach into those settings? But can this be achieved solely through good will and voluntary community engagement – or will there be occasion where such action requires statutory oversight and intervention? Where the risks to young people are significant, and the state needs to act to increase safety, what are we asking of peers, communities, and professionals?

In 2018, Netflix released a smash hit show *13 Reasons Why*. It charted the relationships and cultures of a school environment in which a young woman, Hannah, committed suicide. The first season documented her differing relationships with her peers, parents and school professionals – and the opportunities that each had to disrupt the path she ultimately took. The second season circled around a court case. The school was on trial: specifically the extent to which they were culpable for the sexual violence that had occurred between their students. Through the twists and turns of each episode the court ultimately concluded that the school were not responsible for the behaviour displayed by their students. A decision leaving Hannah's mother desperate to hold someone responsible for her daughter's death and not finding anywhere to turn.

The difficulty with the series was that it focused on legal culpability and causation. Of course there might be other school environments with all the same factors are at play and nobody takes their own life – so ultimately the environment didn't cause the act of suicide. And yet it was clearly relevant to the desperation that Hannah felt; and furthermore created a climate in which other students could harm her without consequence. It was clear that Hannah's peers and the professionals who came into contact with her shaped the culture of that school, and that this said culture informed Hannah's decisions. This was practically relevant, even if it didn't amount to legal culpability.

These are the tensions that come to fore when an area, region, or country implement a Contextual Safeguarding approach. If we hinge safeguarding on what is legally, rather than ethically or practically required, of those who interact with young people we will likely be in a perennial muddle. When I designed the CS Framework it was never my intention to create approaches which held a myriad of communities, individuals, and organisations legally liable for the contexts in which abuse occurred. How do we toe a line upon which we recognise the contribution we can all make to safeguarding young people, while not unfairly or unethically leveraging state intervention into lives of communities and non-statutory organisations?

Learning from community development offers much in the way of resolving these tensions. As first introduced in chapter 4, there is precedent for using community development techniques for resolving concerns about child abuse and broader child welfare issues (Eastham, 1990). Such work has involved families and wider residents/community members as partners in considering and resolving safeguarding concerns; building sustainable solutions through the involvement of existing community resources, and bolstering relationships between local services, families, young people, and so on. Potential limitations and risks of the approach have been noted – such as potential resource implications in social care, the complexity of trying to support families who may be isolated from or ostracized in their local community, and the risks that those who pose a risk of harm to young people may also be in those community settings (Jack & Gill, 2010). This latter point has been an ongoing question in neighbourhood assessments linked to criminal exploitation in which some local businesses have been thought to be actively involved in the abuse of children.

However, building on the positive lessons from community-driven pilots, while holding in mind the limitations, may be one way to find some much-needed balance. As it stands, many questions remain in regard to how the lens of social work can better engage with the contexts in which young people are actually abused, while also avoiding unethical state intrusion into the lives of young people and the adults who are around them. Do we require a legislative framework to guide the inclusion of non-statutory agencies and people beyond parents in the safeguarding of young people? And if the law is required to compel collective capacity to safeguard is it ethical that we do so? In some respects, we want the state to act when young people are at risk of significant harm (regardless of the context in which that harm occurs), and yet to do so meaningfully it may need to engage with contexts and individuals in ways that hasn't been required before. Proportionality will likely be a key feature of Contextual Safeguarding in action; but ongoing scrutiny and debate will be required to ensure it implementation holds fast to the values, and intention, of the Contextual Safeguarding framework.

### The risks of social engineering

By shifting the lens of states onto contexts, and their influence on individual action, are we trying to socially engineer, rather than safeguard, societies? Surely all societies feature elements of danger, risk, and disagreement? Just because there are norms in environments that are conducive with violence – it does not follow that individuals in that context will be violent? And if this is the case, are we not better to re-focus on removing individuals who have been harmful out of contexts (both protective and unprotective), rather than trying to eliminate harmful elements from all contexts in which some people are protective and others are not?

Given that the interplay between contexts and individual action appears reflexive, and non-determined, these queries are important to confront. Sat underneath them is a concern about whether states should attempt to change the social conditions of environments which may facilitate, but do not necessarily endorse or cause, abusive behaviours? If there was a causal relationship, or those who managed contexts were actively promoting or inciting harm that would be one thing. But for the most part, the case reviews that underpinned the development of the Contextual Safeguarding Framework suggest that a culmination of harmful attitudes and lack of protective resources created contexts conducive with abuse. And yet there will be many contexts which are conducive to harmful behaviours but where abuse never actually occurs. When these contexts come into the view of Contextual Safeguarding we have to consider whether seeking to increase their protective capacity is in effect an attempt at social engineering – eliminating all chances of harm as well as harm itself; and whether states have any business in doing so.

Ideally, harm at this level would not be a state concern. Should societies accept a collective, voluntary, responsibility for safeguarding the welfare of young people, and have the resources to act, then preventative/early intervention would be initiated at community rather than state level. States would only intervene in contexts where guardianship was absent or promoted harm. But we have a long way to go before communities are resourced in this way, and the tide of caseworking our way out of risk has receded. How the approach is managed in the interim period requires further consideration. To avoid all assessment of, or intervention with, contexts where there are concerns but no critical incident, also seems unethical. Why would we wait for a child to be stabbed in a park to consider what might need to happen for the park to be a safer place for children to be? Reinvestment in community development and youth work may go some way to mitigating the risks of escalating harm that goes unaddressed. However, ongoing testing of Contextual Safeguarding will also provide further indication of the parameters that are, or need to be, in place to ensure both proportionality and (wherever possible) protection.

## Ongoing rather than resolved

When extra-familial harm was initially located as a child protection issue – it was assumed that the child protection system could respond. As earlier chapters in this book illustrated, that assumption was erroneous; and resulted from an oversimplification of: what constituted a child protection system; the responsibility and remit of social workers; and the steps required to assess and intervene to protect young people harmed in schools, public places and with/by their peers. In this chapter, I have sought to avoid similar assumptions being made about the feasibility of adopting a contextual approach to safeguarding. Just because it appears 'common-sense' to assess and intervene in the contexts associated to abuse, it doesn't follow that we have the legislative framework in place to ensure that such an approach is ethical or even workable.

Prototypes and testing in England have identified the potential benefits of adopting a contextual approach – but have also highlighted where current frameworks fall short internationally. I have highlighted, in this chapter, three areas that require ongoing examination. Whether a Contextual Safeguarding approach blurs the boundaries of child protection and community safety; whether peer and community relationships are a state concern; and whether it is right or appropriate to intervene in contexts where harm is yet to have occurred.

My hope is that this book provides the motivation to resolve these queries rather than parking the approach in the 'too complicated' pile. Systems change is complicated and Contextual Safeguarding is not an intervention that can be inserted into pre-existing systems. It requires systems to adapt – and in some ways facilitates that adaption. The challenges documented in this chapter are the consequence of a system change in process. The more we implement the Contextual Safeguarding Framework, the more it will rub against pre-existing assumptions, legislative frameworks, and approaches to practice: and every time it does, fundamental questions will be asked about it, and whether the approach is possible. For example, if community development, youth work, and so on were already alive and well across local areas, the risks of drawing all extra-familial harm into the field of social work would be mitigated. We are challenged by social and political climates that are themselves at odds with a Contextual Safeguarding framework – and will require attention for the approach to become a 'business as usual' reality.

In writing this book, I intended to introduce a motivation and rationale for contextualising the way we safeguard the welfare of young people – particularly those abused in extra-familial contexts. I end this introduction by detailing fundamental questions that are critical to the future success of the Contextual Safeguarding philosophy. It is my hope that this book provides a foundation for me to work alongside social workers, activists, and scholars concerned with the welfare of young people to answer these questions – and offer a viable solution to the current challenges of safeguarding young people abused in their peer groups, schools, and neighbourhoods.

# 17 On the side of hope

## Next steps on the road to Contextual Safeguarding

My journey to Contextual Safeguarding started when I opened my first case file to review in 2011. I reached out to others for help in 2013 – both in practice locations and in my own research team – and it was in that collaboration that the Contextual Safeguarding framework was created in 2016. In the three years that followed, we have learnt much about what this framework requires of, and achieves within, child protection systems. As I have documented in this book we have learnt that to fully embed a contextual response to extra-familial harm, every nook and cranny of a child protection system – and wider safeguarding partnership – needs to be viewed through a contextual lens. The permeation of individualised narratives is such that they have resulted in practices that defy common sense – and resulted in children, whose lives are in danger, sitting beyond the parameters of the systems designed to protect them from harm. When we get lost in the detail, it is important to pull back and recognise this underlying outrage: the system as it stands/stood is not fit for purpose, and steps to contextualise it takes us some way along the path to improvement.

The notion of being 'some way' along is important for two reasons. The first is that, as this book has evidenced, Contextual Safeguarding is not, and never could be, a silver bullet for resolving all the areas in which our child protection system struggles to work for adolescents, families, or communities. And, secondly, we are some way along as we are still testing – and will be refining the approach for another three years at least.

With these caveats in mind, it remains true even at this stage that we have started to realise the ramifications of what Contextual Safeguarding means for young people, families, communities, and practitioners. We may have only added a question about a location of harm as well as child's home address to a form completed when a child is referred into children's services. We may have recorded methods used by practitioners who work with young people to map their friends well as their families during periods of assessment. But even these relatively straightforward tweaks or adaptations have led us down side-road debates about thresholds for state intervention, the role of social workers in keeping children safe, or the legality and ethics of the methods being used. Seemingly common-sense adaptations in practice have triggered complex queries and points of reflection. In, and as a result of, these moments I have reached two seemingly contradictory conclusions: that Contextual Safeguarding both rewrites what child protection is all about while simultaneously reaffirming what some think it has (or should have) always been.

## Rewriting the rules of child protection

In putting Contextual Safeguarding to the test, my goal had been to create child protection systems that would target, and where necessary, change the social rules at play in peer groups, school environments, and public spaces where young people had been abused: targeting norms and behaviours in families and individuals was insufficient to bring about safety in cases of extra-familial harm. Both our test sites and practitioners have started to achieve this in libraries, schools, parks, shopping centres and housing estates. But for this to happen, another set of rules has required a rewrite – and those were the rules (and expectations) underpinning child protection systems themselves.

To some this might read like an overstatement – particularly given that much presented in this book aligns with decades of development in the field critical and social models of social work, detailed in chapter 14. However, as many of those debates have noted, the way child protection systems in England, and in many other countries, have operated over the past 30 years, has reduced their focus to fixing people and not the situations that people are in. While Contextual Safeguarding brings some social work practice home to the IFSW statement of social work ethics, it does so with contemporary and extra-familial forms of harm in mind. The combination of a more social lens applied to extra-familial relationships, contexts, and abuses has required six forms of system change. Each of these run contrary, albeit it to varying extents, to the unwritten rules that have coloured many child protection systems in recent years.

1.  *Broadening capacity and responsibility to safeguard.*
    In a Contextual Safeguarding system, our collective capacity to protect young people is called into question – and not just the capacity of their parents. This is arguably the most fundamental shift in culture, principals, and practice that we are witnessing in test sites. We are seeing social work-ers clearly state that parents are protective but that a child remains at risk of significant harm – and then pushing wider partnerships to act who may have the capacity to create safety where parents do not. For the most part such a position runs counter to the legislative framing of child protection systems in many countries around the world – regardless of whether the system is one of a family support, child protection, or a child focused orien-tation: they are all built on the idea that the state intervenes when the action of parents/caregivers is called into question. It is of course important

to recognise that broader partnerships have mobilised in response to child abuse prior to Contextual Safeguarding – and that models of community safeguarding have been trialled in many places. Using Contextual Safeguarding we have built on these efforts and offered a language and framework that circles around 'parental capacity' – and in regards to extra-familial harm noted the range of other services whose capacity is undermined when a child is abused by peers, at school or in public places.

There are tensions with doing this, and as highlighted in the latter chapters of this book these will need to be resolved for the approach to be sustained and embedded in policy, and potentially legislation. What does this broadening mean – and how do we disentangle legal liability from social responsibility in that regard?

2.  *Working with, rather than dismantling, peer relationships.*
    The significance of peer relationships has been recognised and worked with when testing Contextual Safeguarding. This has been novel in many test sites for two reasons. Firstly, and following on from the point above, child protection systems have developed to be principally, and sometimes solely, focused on family relationships as a route to securing safety for children and young people. In many respects the need to engage with peer relationships might feel like a common-sense conclusion when we purvey the evidence base on adolescent development and extra-familial harm. But when you try to do this in a system that hasn't included them in a meaningful, consistent, and positive manner before, there are many hurdles to overcome. From defining peer relationships and working alongside young people to map and understand their friendships, through to creating the ICT and policy frameworks to hold this information and do so legally, as well as offering intervention and support to whole groups – the system has been ill-designed.

    The second issue to grapple with has been a tendency to focus on peers through a lens of deviance as opposed to protection. Research into extra-familial harm has often highlighted negative associations between peer relationships and experiences of abuse. From a practice perspective we have seen this implemented through a focus on dismantling problematic peer relationships as a route to protection. In a Contextual Safeguarding system we are asking practitioners to recognise both the positive and negative impacts that peer relationships can have on extra-familial safety – but in light of their significance to young people in the United Kingdom having an overall position that these are relationships that matter to young people and therefore must be worked with rather than against.

    Framing peer relationships both as significant and as something to be supported and nurtured has taken a lot of work in test sites – and is an ongoing challenge without national policy frameworks or thorough banks of research that evidence the best ways to integrate peer relationships into child protection practice.

3.  *Stating, and believing you can change, contextual dynamics.*

    In our first endeavours to develop and apply Contextual Safeguarding we encountered many social workers who were reluctant to record contextual issues on assessments. They argued that these matters – drug dealing in plain sight on a housing estate; poverty; high rates of school exclusion; poor relationships between adults and young people in communities; and gentrification – were entrenched. When it came to these issues there was nothing that they believed they could do to affect change. If they stated that these were factors driving the vulnerability of that young person to further harm then they would never be in a position to demonstrate the situation had improved – they would never be able to 'close the case'. As such the social work role was to build resilience for individuals living in those situations, support them to survive these challenges: fix them and not the context they were in.

    This position mirrors those critiqued by social justice and community social work commentators referenced throughout this book. For them building community networks, challenging contextual factors that undermine the welfare of children and families, and advocating for these things to change are all part of the social work role. And yet those same critiques acknowledge that in England, and in many other countries around the world, this is far from the reality of child protection systems.

    Contextual Safeguarding requires us to believe that contextual factors can be alleviated; and that this needs to happen as part of a response to abuse. Building on social justice and community social work traditions we extend this idea to contemporary forms of harm, and at present locate social workers as key to leveraging and coordinating plans around the welfare of young people – particularly those at risk of significant harm in extra-familial settings. This is important. There will be much of this work that can be achieved through informal, non-statutory arrangements – particularly in the domain of early intervention and prevention. I am not suggesting that only social workers would be central to alleviating contextual dynamics of harm. However, in cases of significant risks to the welfare (and sometimes to the lives) of young people, social workers in test sites and on our practice network have been playing a coordinating role in bringing people together to affect change in extra-familial contexts associated to abuse. They have seen abuse in context and acted to address it – moving beyond the idea that intervening with people alone is the route to protection.

4.  *Recognising an active interplay between children's plans and strategic planning.*

    One way to achieve the above approach has been to recognise and work with the interplay that exists between the success of individual plans for children and families and the strategic decisions made in a local area about service provision, planning, licencing, and so on.

Contextual approaches have evidenced thematic connections between cases, driving demand for interventions in public places, or support for peer groups. We have received reports of local areas re-investing in detached youth work provision, previously reduced or decimated, as contextual casework has evidenced a need for support that is flexible and street-based. In one assessment of a local neighbourhood, social workers invited colleagues from planning to attend the assessment review meeting. The impact that gentrification was having on young people, and the limited access they had to spaces where they felt welcomed and safe, was key to the discussion. At the same meeting, work was discussed to redesign a path that obscured line of sight and as such enabled drug dealing to take place near a number of home addresses in the same area. Practitioners on our virtual network have reported strong partnerships with licencing enforcement officers who have been brought into plans when local businesses are thought to be associated to the exploitation of young people. All of this activity supports the ability of practitioners to believe they can impact contexts beyond families; it also helps those wider agencies recognise why safeguarding, and child welfare, is also their business and responsibility.

In a Contextual Safeguarding approach, therefore, the impact that corporate and strategic decisions have on the lives of young people in a local area are recorded on social work assessments and plans. Likewise, direct work with children and families is starting to inform strategic and corporate decisions.

5.  *Building trusted relationships beyond the 'usual three'.*
    Serious case reviews and public inquiries into child abuse routinely find failings related to partnership working and the sharing of information. Different people know different things about the welfare of young people and for a myriad of reasons have not brought that information together, seen what was happening to that young person and acted sooner to keep them safe. Many efforts have been made to improve information sharing, and with that relationships, between professionals – particularly those in children's social care, the police, and health agencies.[1] In many other child protection systems, core relationships, particularly those related to information sharing, are required between social work, policing, health, and sometimes schools. While mandatory reporting has broadened this to some extent (Merkel-Holguin, et al., 2019), relationships between these core partners remain central to the delivery of child protection.

    However, building trusted relationships between these groupings alone will not leverage a Contextual Safeguarding approach. Firstly, trusted relationships are required between parents, young people, and professionals who offer them support. Secondly, and arguably most importantly, trusted relationships are required within communities and via informal connections that build guardianship of social spaces. Thirdly, a constellation of other partners including local businesses, residents associations, council services (such as waste management, licencing, and housing), schools, young people's peers, and wider community support networks, may all play a role in creating safety in extra-familial contexts. Contextual Safeguarding, therefore, requires partners in child protection to broaden – including in regards to concerns about significant harm – and not solely for the purpose of information sharing. These partners may play an active role in increasing safety in extra-familial contexts and need to see safeguarding and child protection as their responsibility too. Trust is central to this endeavour.

6.  *Holding plans on risks in contexts and not solely in people.*
    When we have tested Contextual Safeguarding approaches, school environments, public places, and friendship groups have all been the focus of plans led by child protection agencies – and not solely the young people who are at risk within them. Child protection systems have not been designed to see locations as the focus of work – albeit they may be relevant to it. And while family groups have been recognised and supported for some time, this has not extended to friendship groups.

    As research into extra-familial harm has evidenced that peer, school, and community contexts are key to creating safety – so too do they become central to the planning process. As such case management ways of delivering child protection systems require extension in Contextual Safeguarding systems in which risk can be held, managed, and reduced, on plans for contexts and not necessarily through plans that target individuals.

    Across these six areas Contextual Safeguarding extends the 'rules' of child protection; either those that have been prescribed by policy parameters of those systems or those that have emerged informally as those policy frameworks have been interpreted in practice. As such some of these norms may feel familiar to some who have practiced community social work – albeit it they are incongruent with how social work practice has evolved in many casework-based systems around the world. Others, such as the creation of plans associated to contexts and the broadening of capacity to safeguard go beyond the initial design of the child protection system in England – and are a response to that system being charged with responding to extra-familial abuse.

## Reaffirming the rules of child protection

In the process of rewriting some rules, Contextual Safeguarding also reframes or reaffirms norms of child protection systems and social work practices that exist within them.

Firstly, this is an approach that reaffirms social work as being aligned to supporting families. By recognising the contexts that surround children and families, and understanding the impact they can have on family dynamic, a Contextual Safeguarding approach values and supports families. Part of that means it is an approach that is concerned with creating the social conditions in which young people and their wider families can thrive; and where efforts are made to keep families together wherever possible (by creating safety around as well as within them).

Secondly, it recognises the duties of states to respond to the abuse of children – in all its forms. It offers a lens through which extra-familial harms can be recognised as abuse and responded to accordingly. As such it does not push the responsibility for protecting children solely onto parents and informal community structures – both of which have a role. Instead it recognises that in all settings the state has a duty of care, and that there are ways for this to be realised in regards to more contemporary forms of harm that are vexing traditional child protection models.

Finally, it reaffirms the position of structural social work, critical social work, and community social work traditions: that social work intervenes at the intersection of context and individual responsibility. The Contextual Safeguarding framework offers a concrete and practical approach for realising this ambition within child protection frameworks in England; and is working to achieve the same in Wales and Scotland from 2020 onwards.

As a result while many have said to me that Contextual Safeguarding feels like a 'seismic shift' or 'radical transformation' in how we respond to extra-familial harm – it also remains aligned to both core principles of social work and structural designs of child protection systems. In this way we have some bridges to cross to get to Contextual Safeguarding systems in different parts of the country but few unaided leaps into the unknown or wholly unfamiliar.

## On the side of hope

And so I encourage you to come to the end of this book as I do – on the side of hope. At this pit stop on the road to creating Contextual Safeguarding, we have learnt more that we can be optimistic about than matters that we feel are unresolved. Contextual Safeguarding provides a language to recognise an incongruence between the nature of extra-familial abuse and the design/intention of child protection systems. Thanks to our test sites and network members we have understood that the Contextual Safeguarding framework moves beyond a recognition of this practice challenge and towards proposing a resolution. And to get there we (the research team) have developed recommendations in partnership with the practitioners tasked with implementing them; and through this process gradually enabled the people delivering the system to also be its architects.

Maintaining a focus on these benefits of the Contextual Safeguarding approach is fundamental for sustaining the change that we have initiated. It will be easier to do this if the evidence base underpinning Contextual Safeguarding is deepened and broadened. By continuing to test and disseminate detailed technicalities of the approach, such as approaches to peer mapping and peer support, as well as context interventions, we will deepen our understanding of how the approach impacts practice. At this stage of testing, work needs to intensify to understand the legal and ethical implications of the approach – with national and international examinations of business engagement in safeguarding, the parameters of the social work role and the ethics of context intervention all broadening how the Contextual Safeguarding framework is discussed and enabled.

Through this book I have provided a baseline understanding of Contextual Safeguarding and a shared vision of what it could achieve. I hope that this foundation can be built upon with others as we seek to collectively rewrite the social, structural, and procedural rules of child protection in response to extra-familial harm – and in doing so reaffirm the social justice of social work.

## Note

1 Who, since 2019 in England, are the core statutory partners in local safeguarding children's partnerships.

# References

Allan, J., Briskman, L. & Pease, B., 2009. *Critical Social Work: Theories and Practices for a Socially Just World.* Sydney: Allen and Unwin.

Allnock, D., 2013. Child Maltreatment: How Can Friends Contribute to Safety? *Safer Communities,* 14(1), pp. 27–37.

Allnock, D., 2019. 'Snitches Get Stitches': School-Specific Barriers to Victim Disclosure and Peer Reporting of Sexual Harm Committed by Young People in School Contexts. *Child Abuse and Neglect,* 89, pp. 7–17.

Anderson, E., 1999. *Code of the Street: Decency, Violence, and the Moral Life of the Inner City.* New York: WW Norton.

Anderson, S., Kinsey, R., Loader, I. & Smith, C., 2017. *Cautionary Tales: Young People, Crime and Policing in Edinburgh.* New York: Routledge.

Ashurst, L. & McAlinden, A.-M., 2015. Young People, Peer-to-Peer Grooming and Sexual Offending: Understanding and Responding to Harmful Sexual Behaviour within a Social Media Society. *Probation Journal,* 62(4), pp. 374–388.

Bailey, R. & Brake, M., 1975. *Radical Social Work.* London: Edward Arnold.

Barter, C., 2006. Discourses of Blame: Deconstructing (Hetero)sexuality, Peer Sexual Violence and Residential Children's Homes. *Child & Family Social Work,* 11(4), pp. 347–356.

Barter, C., 2009. In the Name of Love: Partner Abuse and Violence in Teenage Relationships. *British Journal of Social Work,* 39, pp. 211–233.

Barter, C.A., Stanley, N., Wood, M., Lanau, A., Aghtaie, N., Larkins, C., & Overlien, C. 2017. Young people's online and face-to-face experiences of interpersonal violence and abuse and its subjective impact across five European countries. *Psychology of Violence,* 7 (3). pp. 375–384. ISSN 2152-0828.

BASW, 2014. *BASW Code of Ethics.* [Online] Available at: https://www.basw.co.uk/about-basw/code-ethics[Accessed 08 10 2018].

BBC, 2015. *School Sex Crime Reports in UK Top 5,500 in Three Years.* [Online] Available at: www.bbc.co.uk/news/education-34138287 [Accessed 03 12 2015].

Beckett, H. Brodie, I., Factor, F., Melrose, M., Pearce, J., Pitts, J., Shuker, L., & Warrington, C. 2013. *It's Wrong but You Get Used to It: A Qualitative Study of Gang-Associated Sexual Violence Towards, and Sexual Exploitation of, Young People in England.* London: Office of the Children's Commissioner.

Berelowitz, S., Clifton, J., Firmin, C., Gulyurtlu, S. & Edwards, G., 2013. *'If Only Someone Had Listened' Office of the Children's If Only Someone Had Listened: OCC Inquiry into Child Sexual Exploitation in Gangs and Groups Final Report.* London: Office of the Children's Commissioner.

Bevan, M., 2014. *Investigating Young People's Awareness and Understanding of the Criminal Justice System: An exploratory study,* London: The Howard League.

Bibliography Entry: HM Government, 2018. *Working Together to Safeguard Children and their Families,* London: The Stationary Office.

Blakemore, S.-J., 2018. Avoiding Social Risk in Adolescence. *Association for Psychological Science,* 27(2), pp. 116–122.

Blustain, R. & McCarthy, N., 2019. *The Harmful Effects of New York City's Over-Surveillance.* [Online] Available at: https://chronicleofsocialchange.org/child-welfare-2/the-harmful-effects-of-over-surveillance/38441 [Accessed 01 11 2019].

Bolter, F. & Seraphin, G., 2019. Child Protection in France. In: L. Merkel-Holguin, J. D. Fluke & R. D. Krugman, eds. *National Systems of Child Protection: Understanding the International Variability and Context of Developing Policy and Practice.* Basel: Springer, pp. 75–92.

Bourdieu, P., 1990. *In Other Words: Essays Towards a Reflexive Sociology.* 1 ed. Stanford: Stanford University Press.

Bourdieu, P., 2001. *Masculine Domination.* Stanford: Stanford University Press.

Brayley, H., Cockbain, E. & Laycock, G., 2011. The Value of Crime Scripting: Deconstructing Internal Child Sex Trafficking. *Policing,* 52(2), pp. 132–143.

British Transport Police, 2016. *New National Rail security campaign starts today: "See It. Say It. Sorted.".* [Online] Available at: https://www.btp.police.uk/latest_news/see_it_say_it_sorted_new_natio.aspx[Accessed 19 02 2019].

Bronfrenbrenner, U., 1979. *The Ecology of Human Development: Experiments by Nature and Design.* Cambridge, MA: Harvard University Press.

Broughton, K., 2018. *What's Happening? Tool for Parents and Carers.* [Online] Available at: https://csnetwork.org.uk/assets/images/Whats-Happening-Tool-Guidance.pdf[Accessed 12 05 2019].

Brown, S., Brady, G., Franklin, A. & Crookes, R., 2017. *The Use of Tools and Checklists to Assess Risk of Child Sexual Exploitation an Exploratory Study.* London: CSA Centre of Expertise.

Buck, G., Lawrence, A. & Raganese, E., 2017. Exploring Peer Mentoring as a Form of Innovative Practice with Young People at Risk of Child Sexual Exploitation. *British Journal of Social Work,* 47, pp. 1745–1763.

Burton, S., 2008. *A Problem-Oriented Policing Approach to Tackling Youth Crime and Anti-Social Behaviour.* London: Transport for London.

Cameron, D., 2015. *PM Unveils Tough New Measures to Tackle Child Sexual Exploitation.* [Online] Available at: www.gov.uk/government/news/pm-unveils-tough-new-measures-to-tackle-child-sexual-exploitation [Accessed 10 10 2018].

Catch 22, 2013. *The Role of the Family in Facilitating Gang Membership, Criminality and Exit.* London: Catch 22.

Clarke, R. V. & Mayhew, P., 1988. The British Gas Suicide Story and Its Criminological Implications. In: M. Tonry & N. Morris, eds. *Crime and Justice. Vol. 10.* Chicago, IL: University of Chicago Press, 79–116.

Coleman, J., 2011. *The Nature of Adolesence.* 3rd ed. Oxon: Routledge.

Coleman, J., 2014. *Why Won't My Teenage Talk to Me.* East Sussex: Routledge.

College of Policing, 2013. *Intelligence Management.* [Online] Available at: https://www.app.college.police.uk/app-content/intelligence-management/analysis/[Accessed 03 10 2019].

Community Care, 2015. *Social Workers to Face Five Years in Prison for Failing to Protect Children from Sexual Abuse, Warns Cameron.* [Online] Available at:

https://www.communitycare.co.uk/2015/03/03/social-workers-face-five-years-prison-failing-protect-children-sexual-abuse-warns-cameron/[Accessed 05. 03. 2019].

Contextual Saefguarding Network, 2019. *Context Assessment Triangles.* [Online] Available at: https://www.csnetwork.org.uk/assets/documents/Context-Assessment-Triangles.pdf[Accessed 07 10 2019].

Contextual Safeguarding Network & Redthread, 2019. *Integrating Youth Work with Contextual Safeguarding in Health Settings.* [Sound Recording] (University of Bedfordshire).

Cossar, J., Brandon, M., Bailey, S. & Belderson, P., 2013. *'It Takes a Lot to Build Trust': Recognition and Telling: Developing Earlier Routes to Help for Children and Young People.* London: Office of the Children's Commissioner.

Cottam, H., 2018. *Radical Help: How We Can Remake the Relationships Between Us and Revolutionise the Welfare State.* London: Virago Press.

Cowie, H., 2011. Understanding Why Children and Young People Engage in Bullying at School. In: D. Berridge & C. Barter, eds. *Children Behaving Badly: Peer Violence between Children and Young People.* West Sussex: John Wiley and Sons Ltd., pp. 33–47.

Cockbain, E., 2013. *The Trafficking of British Children within the UK for Sexual Exploitation: A Situational Analysis.* London: Doctoral thesis, UCL (University College London).

Cockbain, E., 2018. *Offender and Victim Networks in Human Trafficking.* 1st ed. Abingdon: Routledge.

Criminal Justice Joint Inspection, 2013. *Examining Multi-Agency Responses to Children and Young People Who Sexually Offend: A Joint Inspection of the Effectiveness of Multi-Agency Work with Children and Young People in England and Wales Who Have Committed Sexual Offences and Were Supervised in the Community.* London: HM Inspectorate of Probation.

D'Arcy, K. & Thomas, R., 2016. *Nightwatch: CSE in Plain Sight. Final Evaluation Report.* Luton: University of Bedfordshire.

Devon County Council, 2018. *Exploitation of Children Strategy 2018–2022.* Devon: Devon County Council.

Dickinson, R., 2019. *Rachel Dickinson Inaugural Presidential Address.* Manchester: ADCS.

East Riding Yorkishire Council, 2019. *Lead Professional.* [Online] Available at: https://www.eastriding.gov.uk/council/working-with-our-partners/caring-for-children/lead-professional/[Accessed 03 2019].

Eastham, D., 1990. Plan It or Suck It and See. In: G. Darvill & G. Smale, eds. *Partners in Empowerment: Networks of Innovations in Social Work.* London: National Institute of Social Work, pp. 166–179.

Eaton, J. & Holmes, D., 2017. *Working Effectively to Address Child Sexual Exploitation: Evidence Scope.* Devon: Research in Practice.

Eck, J. & Spelman, W., 1987. *Problem Solving: Problem-oriented Policing in Newport News,* Washington, DC: Police Executive Research Forum.

Ekblom, P., 1988. Preventing Post Office Robberies in London: Effects and Side Effects. *Journal of Security Administration,* 11, pp. 36–43.

El-Enany, N. & Bruce-Jone, E., 2015. *Justice, Resistance and Solidarity Race and Policing in England and Wales.* London: Runnymede.

Ellis, K., 2018. Contested Vulnerability: A Case Study of Girls in Secure Care. *Children and Youth Services Review,* 88, pp. 156–163.

Ellis, W. R. & Dietz, W., 2017. A New Framework for Addressing Adverse Childhood and Community Experiences: The Building Community Resilience Model. *Academic Pediatrics*, 17(7), pp. 86–93.

Evans, M., 2015. *'Police Treated Rotherham Sex Abuse Victims as Prostitutes', Crime Commissioner Admits.* [Online] Available at: www.telegraph.co.uk/news/uknews/crime/11583147/Police-treated-Rotherham-sex-abuse-victims-as-prostitutes-crime-commissioner-admits.html [Accessed 04 10 2018].

EVAW, 2017. *'All Day, Every Day' Legal Obligations on Schools to Prevent and Respond to Sexual Harassment and Violence against Girls.* London: EVAW.

Ewell Foster, C., Horwitz, A., Thomas, A., Opperman, K., Gipson, P; Burnside, A; Stone, D M; King, C 2017. Connectedness to Family, School, Peers, and Community in Socially Vulnerable Adolescents. *Chlid Youth Services Review*, 81, pp. 321–331.

Farrington, D., 2000. Explaining and Preventing Cirme: The Globalisation of Knowledge. *Criminology*, 38, pp. 1–24.

Featherstone, B., Gupta, A., Morris, K. & White, S., 2018. *Protecting Children: A Social Model.* 1st ed. Bristol: Policy Press.

Fenton, J., 2016. *Values in Social Work: Reconnecting with Social Justice.* London: Palgrave.

Ferguson, I., 2013. Social workers as agents of change. In: M. Gray & S. A. Webb, eds. *The New Politics of Social Work*. Basingstoke: Palgrave Macmillan.

Ferguson, G., Featherstone, B. & Morris, K., 2019. Framed to Fit? Challenging the Domestic Abuse 'Story' in Child Protection. *Critical and Radical Social Work*. Doi https://doi.org/10.1332/204986019X15668424450790.

Ferguson, I. & Woodward, R., 2009. *Radical Social Work in Practice.* Bristol: Policy Press.

Finkelhor, D., Shattuck, A., Turner, H. & Hamby, S., In Press. A Behaviourally Specific, Empirical Alternative to Bullying: Aggravated Peer Victimisation. *Journal of Adolescent Health*. doi: 10.1016/j.jadohealth.2016.05.021.

Firmin, C. et al., 2016. *Towards a Contextual Response to Peer-on-Peer Abuse: Research from MsUnderstood Local Site Work 2013–2016*, Luton: University of Bedfordshire.

Firmin, C., 2017c. *Abuse between Young People: A Contextual Account.* 1st ed. Oxon: Routledge.

Firmin, C., 2017a. Contextual Risk, Individualised Responses: An Assessment of Safeguarding Responses to Nine Cases of Peer-on-Peer Abuse. *Child Abuse Review*. 27 (1), pp. 42–57.

Firmin, C., 2017b. Contextualizing Case Reviews: A Methodology for Developing Systemic Safeguarding Practices. *Child and Family Social Work*, 23(1), pp. 45–52.

Firmin, C. & Abbott, M., 2018. A Route to Safety: Using Bus Boarding Data to Identify Roles for Transport Providers within Contextual Safeguarding Systems. *Children and Society*. doi: 10.1111/chso.12267.

Firmin, C. & Hancock, D., 2018. Profiling CSE: Building a Contextual Picture of a Local Problem. In: H. Beckett & J. Pearce, eds. *Understanding and Responding to Child Sexual Exploitation*. Oxon: Routledge, 107–120.

Firmin, C., 2019. Relocation, Relocation, Relocation: Home and School-Moves for Children Affected Extra-Familial Risks during Adolescence. *Children's Geographies*. DOI https://doi.org/10.1080/14733285.2019.1598545.

Firmin, C., Wroe, L. & Lloyd, J., 2019b. *Safeguarding and Exploitation – Complex, Contextual and Holistic Approaches: Strategic Briefing.* Dartington: Research in Practice.

Firmin, C., 2008. *Building Bridges Project*. London: ROTA.

Fong, R. & Cardoso, J. B., 2010. Child Human Trafficking Victims: Challenges for the Child Welfare System. *Evaluation and Program Planning*, 33, pp. 311–316.

Frost, L. & Hoggett, P., 2008. Human Agency and Social Suffering. *Critical Social Policy*, 28(4), pp. 438–460.

France, A. & Utting, D., 2005. The Paradigm of 'Risk and Protection-Focused Prevention' and Its Impact on Services for Children and Families. *Children and Society*, 19(2), pp. 77–90.

Fritz, D., Olatain, P. & Firmin, C., 2016. *The Role Detached Youth Work in Creating Safety for Young People in Public Spaces*. Luton: University of Bedfordshire.

Gardner, M. & Steinberg, L., 2005. Peer Influence on Risk Taking, Risk Preference, and Risky Decision Making in Adolescence and Adulthood: An Experimental Study'. *Developmental Psychology*, 41, pp. 625–635.

Geno Pro, 2016. *Introduction to the Genogram*. [Online] Available at: http://www.geno pro.com/genogram/ [Accessed 03 10 2017].

Gilbert, N., Parton, N. & Skivenes, M., 2011. *Child Protection Systems: International Trends and Orientations*. 1st ed. Oxford: Oxford University Press.

Gilligan, P., 2016. Turning It Around: What Do Young Women Say Helps them to Move On from Child Sexual Exploitation?. *Child Abuse Review*, 25(2), pp. 115–12.

Gloucestershire Safeguarding Children Board, 2018. *Child Exploitation Strategy April 2018–April 2021*. Gloucetershire: Gloucestershire Safeguarding Children Board.

Gray, D. & Manning, R., 2014. 'Oh My God, We're Not Doing Nothing': Young People's Experiences of Spatial Regulation. *British Journal of Social Psychology*, 53, pp. 640–655.

Gray, M. & Webb, S. A., 2013. Towards a New Politics of Social Work. In: M. Gray & S. A. Webb, eds. *The New Politics of Social Work*. Basingstoke: Palgrave Macmillan, 3–20.

Graybeal, C., 2001. Strengths-Based Social Work Assessment: Transforming the Dominant Paradigm. *Families in Society: the Journal of Contemporary Social Services*, 82(3), pp. 233–242.

Greenwich Safeguarding Children's Partnership, 2019. *Adolescent Strategy 2019–2023*. London: Greenwich Safeguarding Children's Partnership.

Guerette, R. T. & Bowers, K. J., 2009. Assessing the Extent of Crime Displacement and Diffusion of Benefits: A Review of Situational Crime Prevention Evaluations. *Criminology*, 47(4), pp. 1331–1368.

Gundermann, T. A. & Gest, S. D., 2018. The Peer Group: Linking Conceptualizations, Theories, and Methods. In: W. M. Bukowski, B. Laursen & K. H. Rubin, eds. *Handbook of Peer Interactions, Relationships and Groups*. New York: Guilford Press, pp. 84–106.

Hallett, S., Verbruggen, J., Buckley, K. & Robinson, A., 2019. *Keeping Safe? An Analysis of the Outcomes of Work with Sexually Exploited Young People in Wales*. Cardiff: Cardiff University.

Hanson, E., 2016. *The Relationship between Neglect and Child Sexual Exploitation: An Evidence Scope*. Totnes: Research in Practice.

Hanson, E. & Holmes, D., 2015. *The Difficult Age: Developing a More Effective Response to Risk in Adolescence*. Darlington: Research in Practice.

Harding, S., 2014. *The Street Casino: Survival in the Violent Street Gang*. Bristol: Policy Press.

Hill, N., 2019. *Serious Case Review – Chris*. London: Newham Safeguarding Children Board.

HM Government, 2014. *Consultation on Improving Safeguarding for Looked after Children: Changes to the Care Planning, Placement and Case Review (England) Regulations 2010 Government Response*. London: Stationary Office.

Holmes, D., 2018. *Transitional Safeguarding from Adolescence to Adulthood*. Dartington: Research in Practice.

HM Government, 2016. *Ending Gang Violence and Exploitation*. London: The Stationary Office.

Home Office, 2011. *Ending Gangs and Youth Violence*. London: Stationary Office.

Home Office, 2012. *Cross Government Definition of Domestic Violence - A Consultation: A Summary of Responses*. London: Home Office Crown Copyright.

Home Office, 2015. *2010 to 2015 Government Policy: Crime Prevention*. [Online] Available at: www.gov.uk/government/publications/2010-to-2015-government-policy-crime-prevention/2010-to-2015-government-policy-crime-prevention#appendix-4-community-safety-partnerships [Accessed 01 09 2019].

Home Office, 2019. *Child Exploitation Disruption Toolkit: Disruption Tactics*. [Online] Available at: https://assets.publishing.service.gov.uk/government/uploads/system/uploads/attachment_data/file/794554/6.5120_Child_exploitation_disruption_toolkit.pdf [Accessed 02 11 2019].

House of Commons, Committee, Women and Equalities, 2016. *Sexual Harassment and Sexual Violence in Schools*. London: House of Commons.

Hudeck, J., 2018. *County Lines: Scoping Report*. London: St Giles Trust.

IFSW, 2014. *Global Definition of Social Work*. [Online] Available at: https://www.ifsw.org/what-is-social-work/global-definition-of-social-work/ [Accessed 04 07 2019].

ITV News, 2018. *Headteachers Struggle to Get Support for Vulnerable and Exploited Children*. [Online] Available at: www.gettyimages.co.uk/detail/video/headteachers-struggle-to-get-support-for-vulnerable-and-news-footage/1053878896 [Accessed 31 01 2019].

Jack, G. & Gill, O., 2010. The Role of Communities in Safeguarding Children and Young People. *Child Abuse Review*, 19, pp. 82–96.

Jarrett, T. & Harker, R., 2016. *Children: Out-of-Area and Distant Placements in Residential Homes (England)*. London: House of Commons.

Jay, A., 2014. *Independent Inquiry into Child Sexual Exploitation in Rotherham (1997–2013)*. Rotherham: Rotherham LSCB.

Keenan, S., 2015. *Affirmative Consent: Are Students Really Asking?* [Online] Available at: www.nytimes.com/2015/08/02/education/edlife/affirmative-consent-are-students-really-asking.html [Accessed 30 11 2018].

Klein, A., 2012. More Police, Less Safety? In: D. Briggs, ed. *The English Riots of 2011: A Summer of Discontent*. Hampshire: Waterside Press, pp. 127–145.

Lammy, D., 2017. *The Lammy Review: An Independent Review into the Treatment of, and Outcomes for, Black, Asian and Minority Ethnic Individuals in the Criminal Justice System*. London: House of Commons.

Lawler, S., 2004. Rules of Engagement: Habitus, Power and Resistance. *Sociological Review*, 52(2), pp. 110–128.

Leeds LSCB, 2017. *LSCB Risk and Vulnerabilities Strategy 2017–2020*. Leeds: Leeds Safeguarding Children's Board.

Lefevre, M., Hickle, K. & Luckock, B., 2018. Both/and' Not 'either/or': Reconciling Rights to Protection and Participation in Working with Child Sexual Exploitation. *The British Journal of Social Work*, 49 (7), pp. 1837–1855.

Lefevre, M., Hickle, K., Luckock, B. & Ruch, G., 2017. Building Trust with Children and Young People at Risk of Child Sexual Exploitation: The Professional Challenge. *British Journal of Social Work*, 47, pp. 2456–2473.

Lewing, B., Doubell, L., Beevers, T. & Acquah, D., 2018. *Building Trusted Relationships for Vulnerable Children and Young People with Public Services*. London: Early Intervention Youth Foundation.

Lloyd, J., 2018. Abuse through Sexual Image Sharing in Schools: Response and Responsibility. *Gender and Education*. doi: https://doi.org/10.1080/09540253.2018.1513456.

Lloyd, J., Balci, M., Firmin, C. & Owens, R., 2019. *Peer Group Assessment*. Luton: University of Bedfordhsire.

Lloyd, J. & Firmin, C., 2020. No Further Action: Contextualising Social Care Decisions for Children Victimised in Extra-Familial Contexts. *Journal of Youth Justice*. doi: https://doi.org/10.1177/1473225419893789.

Lloyd, J (Forthcoming). Life in a Lanyard (Under Review).

Lloyd, S., 2019. 'She Doesn't Have to Get in the Car …': Exploring Social Workers' Understandings of Sexually Exploited Girls as Agents and Choice-Makers. *Children's Geographies*. doi: 10.1080/14733285.2019.1649360.

London Borough of Merton, 2019. *Lead Coordinator (Lead Practitioner)*. [Online] Available at: https://www.merton.gov.uk/social-care/children-young-people-and-families/safeguarding-children/mscb/professionals/well-being-model/lead-coordinator [Accessed 03 2019].

Lopez, M. L., Bouma, H., Knorth, E. J. & Grietens, H., 2019. The Dutch Child Protection System: Historical Overview and Recent Transformations. In: L. Merkel-Holguin, J. D. Fluke & R. D. Krugnman, eds. *National Systems of Child Protection: Understanding the International Variability and Context for Developing Policy and Practice*. Basel: Springer, pp. 173–192.

McElligott, T., 2018. *Barnet Vulnerable Adolescents Strategy 2018–2020*. London: Barnet Safegaurding Children's Partnership.

McVie, S., Bates, E. & Pillinger, R., 2018. *Changing Patterns of Violence in Glasgow and London: Is There Evidence of Scottish Exceptionalism?* [Online] Available at: https://blogs.lse.ac.uk/politicsandpolicy/patterns-of-violence-glasgow-london/ [Accessed 09 03 2019].

Merkel-Holguin, L., Fluke, J. & Krugman, R. D., 2019. *Naitonal Systems of Child Protection: Understanding the International Variability and Context for Developing Policy and Pratice*. 1st ed. Basel:Springer.

Miller, R. M., Sanchez, K. M. & Rosenblum, L. D., 2010. Alignment to visual speech information. *Attention, Perception, & Psychophysics*, 72(6), pp. 1614–1625.

Newton, A. D., Partridge, H. & Gill, A., 2014. Above and Below: Measuring Crime Risk in and around Underground Mass Transit Systems. *Crime Science: An Interdisciplinary Journal*, 3, pp. 1–14.

Norfolk, A., 2011. *Race Fears Deterred People From Speaking Out*. [Online] Available at: www.thetimes.co.uk/article/race-fears-deterred-people-from-speaking-out-ngxn8b5qz0m [Accessed 03 12 2018].

North Lincolnshire Children's Multi-agency Resilience and Safeguarding Board, 2018. *Child Exploitation Strategy 2018–2021*, North Lincolnshire. North Lincolnshire Children's Multi-agency Resilience and Safeguarding Board.

Nykaro, S., 2018. *Safety Mapping Exercise*. [Online] Available at: https://csnetwork.org.uk/en/toolkit/assessment/safety-mapping-tool [Accessed 01 05 2019].

Oates, K., 2019. Child Protection Systems in Australia. In: L. Merkel-Holguin, J. D. Fluke & R. D. Krugman, eds. *National Systems of Child Protection: Undertsanding the International Variability and Context for Developing Policy and Practice.* Basel: Springer, pp. 7–26.

Obama, M., 2018. *Michelle Obama: Becoming, Part 1.* [Sound Recording] (Oprah's Super Soul Conversations).

OED, 2019. *Meaning of Broker in English.* [Online] Available at: www.lexico.com/defin ition/broker [Accessed 27 06 2019].

ONS, 2019. *Crime in England and Wales: Year Ending March 2019.* [Online] Available at: https://www.ons.gov.uk/peoplepopulationandcommunity/crimeandjustice/bul letins/crimeinenglandandwales/yearendingmarch2019

Home Office, 2018. *Government Launches Trusted Relationships Fund.* [Online] Available at: www.gov.uk/government/news/government-launches-trusted-relationships-fund [Accessed 18 03 2019].

Ofsted, 2014. *From a Distance: Looked after Children Living Away from Their Home Area.* London: Ofsted.

Ofsted, 2018. *Protecting Children from Criminal Exploitation, Human Trafficking and Modern Slavery: An Addendum. November 2018 No. 180032.* London: Ofsted.

PACE, 2020. *Parents Experiences of the Children's Social Care System When a Child Is Sexually Exploited.* LeedsLeL: PACE.

Parton, N., 2014. *The Politics of Child Protection.* Basingstoke,, Palgrave.

Parton, N., 2019. Changing and Competing Conceptions of Risk and Their Implications for Public Health Approaches to Child Protection. In: B. Lonne, D. Scott, D. Higgins & T. Herrenkohl, eds. *Re-Visioning Public Health Approaches for Protecting Children.* Switzerland: Springer, pp. 49–62.

Pawlby, S., Mills, A., Taylor, A. & Quinton, D., 1997. Adolescent Friendships Mediating Childhood Adversity and Adult Outcomes. *Journal of Adolescence*, 20, pp. 633–644.

Pearce, J., 2013. A Social Model of 'Abused Consent'. In: M. Melrose & J. Pearce, eds. *Critical Perspectives on Child Sexual Exploitation and Related Trafficking.* Hampshire: Palgrave Macmillan, pp. 52–68.

Pitts, J., 2013. Drifting into Trouble: Sexual Exploitation and Gang Affiliation. In: Melrose, M & Pearce, J. *Critical Perspectives on Child Sexual Exploitation and Related Trafficking.* Basingstoke: Palgrave Macmillan, pp. 23–37.

Pivovarchuk, A., 2019. *The Me Too Movement: Changing the Rules of the Game.* [Online] Available at: www.fairobserver.com/culture/me-too-movement-history-con sequences-womens-rights-news-17621/ [Accessed 30 11 2019].

Powell, A., 2008. Amor fati? Gender Habitus and Young People's Negotiation of (Hetero)sexual Consent. *Journal of Sociology*, 44, p. 167.

Pülzl, H. & Treib, O., 2007. Implementing Public Policy. In: F. Fischer, G. J. Miller & M. S. Sidney, eds. *Handbook of Public Policy Analysis: Theory, Politics and Methods.* Boca Raton, FL: Taylor and Francis, pp. 89–108.

Reid, S., 2010. *Special Investigations: How Predatory Gangs Force Middle Class Girls into the Sex Trade.* London: Daily Mail. [Online] Available at: www.dailymail.co. uk/news/article-1301003/Special-investigation-How-predatory-gangs-force-middle-class-girls-sex-trade.html [Accessed 03 12 2018].

Rogers, E. M., 2003. *Diffusion of Innovations.* 5th ed. New York: Free Press.

Rogowoski, S., 2012. Social Work with Children and Families: Challenges and Possibilities in the Neo-Liberal World. *British Journal of Social Work*, 42, pp. 921–940.

Royal Commission Royal Commission into Institutional Responses to Child Sexual Abuse, 2017. *Royal Commission into Institutional Responses to Child Sexual Abuse: Final Report.* Sydney: Royal Commission.

Ruch, G., 2005. Relationship-Based Practice and Reflective Practice: Holistic Approaches to Contemporary Child Care Social Work. *Child and Family Social Work*, 10, pp. 111–123.

Rypi, A., Burcar, V. & Åkerström, M., 2019. Refraining from reporting crimes: accounts from young male crime victims with an immigrant background. *Nordic Social Work Research*, 9(2), pp. 131–146.

Scott , S. & Botcherby, S., 2017. *Wigan and Rochdale Child Sexual Exploitation Innovation Project Evaluation Report.* London: Department for Education.

Scott, S. & McNeish, D., 2017. *Supporting Parents of Sexually Exploited Young People an Evidence Review.* London: Centre of Expertise on Child Sexual Abuse.

Scott, S. & Skidmore, P., 2006. *Reducing the Risk: Barnardo's Support for Sexually Exploited Young People: A Two-Year Evaluation.* Barkingside: Barnardo's.

Sherman, L., 1995. Hot spots of crime and criminal careers of places. In: J. E. &. D. Weisburd, ed. *Crime and Place: Crime Prevention Studies 4.* Monsey, NY: Willow Tree Press, pp. 35–52.

Shuker, L., 2013. Constructs of Safety for Children in Care Affcted by Sexual Exploitation. In: M. Melrose & J. Pearce, eds. *Critical Perspectives on Child Sexual Exploitation and Related Trafficking.* London: Palgrave Macmillian, 125–138.

Shuker, L., 2017. *Empowering Parents: Evaluation of Parents as Partners in Safeguarding Children and Young People in Lancashire Project 2014–s2017.* Luton: University of Bedfordshire.

Smallbone, S. W., Rayment-McHugh, S. & Smith, D., 2013. *Preventing Youth Sexual Violence and Abuse in West Cairns and Aurukun: Establishing the Scope, Dimensions and Dynamics of the Problem.* Brisbane: Griffith University.

Spratt, T., Devaney, J. & Frederick, J., 2019. Adverse Childhood Experiences: Beyond Signs of Safety; Reimagining the Organisation and Practice of Social Work with Children and Families. *British Journal of Social Work*, 49(8), pp. 2042–2058.

Taylor, B. G., Stein, N. D., Mumford, E. A. & Woods, D., 2013. Shifting Boundaries: An Experimental Evaluation of a Dating Violence Prevention Program in Middle Schools. *Prevention Science*, 14(1), pp. 64–76.

Nicole Taylor *Three Girls.* 2017. [Film] Directed by Philippa Lowthorpe. London: BBC Studios.

Tameside Metropolitan Borough, 2019. *The Role of the Lead Professional.* [Online] Available at: https://www.tameside.gov.uk/CYPP/Role-of-Lead-Professional [Accessed 16 03 2019].

Tom McCarthy (Director), 2015. *Spotlight.* Participant Media and First Look Media.

Trevithick, P., 2003. Effective Relationship-Based Practice: A Theoretical Exploration. *Journal of Social Work Practice*, 17(2), pp. 163–176.

Turner, A., Belcher, L. & Pona, I., 2019. *Counting Lives: Responding to Children Who Are Criminally Exploited.* London: The Children's Society.

Ungar, M., 2002. A Deeper, More Social Ecological Social Work Practice. *Social Service Review*, 76(3), pp. 480–497.

Violence Reduction Unit, 2015. *Scottish Violence Reduction Unit 10 Year Strategic Plan.* [Online] Available at: http://actiononviolence.org/sites/default/files/10%20YEAR%20PLAN_0.PDF [Accessed 15 08 2019].

Voorberga, W. H., Bekkersa, V. J. & Tumm, L. G., 2014. A Systematic Review of Co-Creation and Co-Production: Embarking on the social innovation journey. *Public Management Review*. doi: 10.1080/14719037.2014.930505.

Warr, M., 2002. *Companions in Crime: The Social Aspects of Criminal Conduct*. Cambridge: Cambridge University Press.

Warrington, C., 2013. Partners in Care? Sexually Exploited Young People's Inclusion and Exclusion from Decision Making about Safeguarding. In: Melrose, M & Pearce, J. *Critical Perspectives on Child Sexual Exploitation and Related Trafficking*. Basingstoke: Palgrave Macmillan, pp. 110–124.

Warrington, C. & Thomas, R., 2016. *The AVA Project: Empowering Young People to Address Domestic and Sexual Violence: Final Evaluation Report*. Luton: University of Bedfordshire.

Wessells, M. G., 2015. Bottom-up approaches to strengthening child protection systems: Placing children, families, and communities at the center. *Child Abuse and Neglect*, Volume 43, pp. 8–21.

Wilkins, D., Shemmings, D. & Pascoe, C., 2019. *Child Abuse: An Evidence Base for Confident Practice*. 5th ed. London: Open University Press.

Williams, A., 2019. Family Support Services Delivered Using a Restorative Approach: A Framework for Relationship and Strengths-Based Whole-Family Practice. *Child and Family Social Work*. doi: 10.1111/cfs.12636.

Williams, P., 2018. *Being Matrixed: The (Over)policing of Gangs Suspects in London*. [Online] Available at: www.stop-watch.org/uploads/documents/Being_Matrixed.pdf [Accessed 25 09 2019].

Wood, G. & Tully, C., 2006. *The Structural Approach to Direct Practice in Social Work: A Social Constructionist Perspective*. 3rd ed. New York: Columbia University Press.

Woodward, R. & Mackay, K., 2012. Mind the Gap! Students' understanding and application of social work values. *Social Work Education: The International Journal*, 31(8), pp. 1090–1104.

Wortley, R., 1998. A Two-Stage Model of Situational Crime Prevention. *Studies on Crime and Crime Prevention*, 7, pp. 173–188.

Wortley, R. & Smallbone, S., 2006. *Situational Prevention of Child Sexual Abuse*. Monsey, NY: WIllow Tree Press.

Wroe, L., 2019. *Contextual Safeguarding and County Lines*. Luton: University of Bedfordshire.

# Index

Note: notes are indicated with *n*, figures are indicated with *f*, tables are indicated with *t*.